Makers of the New

Makers of the New

The Revolution in Literature,
1912-1939

JULIAN SYMONS

Random House   New York

First American Edition
Copyright © 1987 by Julian Symons
All rights reserved under International and Pan-American Copyright Conventions. Published in the
United States by Random House, Inc., New York. Published in Great Britain by André Deutsch Ltd.

Grateful acknowledgment is made to the following
for permission to reprint previously published material:
The Bodley Head Ltd.: Excerpt from "Twitting pan" in *Collected Poems* by E. Rickword.
Farrar, Straus and Giroux, Inc.: Excerpt from "Graduation Ode" in *Poems Written
in Early Youth* by T. S. Eliot. Copyright © 1967 by Valerie Eliot. Reprinted
by permission of Farrar, Straus and Grioux, Inc.
Open Market rights administered by Faber and Faber Limited
Dr. and Mrs. Edwin S. Fetcher, St. Paul, Minnesota: Excerpt from "Ode" in
A Poet's Life by Harriet Monroe.
Harcourt Brace Jovanovich, Inc.: Excerpt from "Chicago" in *Chicago Poems* by Carl Sandburg.
Copyright 1916 by Holt, Rinehart and Winston, Inc. Renewed 1944 by Carl Sandburg.
Excerpts from *Collected Poems 1909-1962* by T. S. Eliot. Copyright 1936 by Harcourt
Brace Jovanovich, Inc. Copyright © 1963, 1964 by T. S. Eliot. Excerpts from "The Family Reunion"
in *"The Family Reunion"* by T. S. Eliot. Copyright 1939 by T. S. Eliot. Renewed
1967 by Esme Valerie Eliot. Reprinted by permission of Harcourt Brace Jovanovich, Inc.
Liveright Publishing Corporation: Excerpts from "Harbour Dawn" and "Voyages" from *The Complete
Poems and Selected Letters and Prose of Hart Crane,* edited by Brom Weber. Copyright 1933, © 1958,
1966 by Liveright Publishing Corporation. Reprinted by permission.
Ellen Masters: Excerpt from *The Spoon River
Anthology* by Edgar Lee Masters, published by Macmillan, Inc.
New Directions Publishing Corporation: Excerpts from " To Whistler, American,"
"After Ch'u Yuan," "L'Invitation," " Sestina: Altaforte," "Mauberly," and excerpt from T. E. Hulme
from *Personae* by Ezra Pound. Copyright 1926 by Ezra Pound. Excerpt from *Selected Letters*
by Ezra Pound. Copyright 1950 by Ezra Pound. Excerpt from *The Cantos of Ezra Pound.*
Copyright 1934, 1938 by Ezra Pound.
Excerpt from "Orchard" by H.D. from *Collected Poems, 1912-1944.* Copyright © 1982 by the
Estate of Hilda Doolittle. Excerpt from *Hilda's Book* by H.D. from *End to Torment: A Memoir of
Ezra Pound.* Copyright © 1979 by the trustees of the Ezra Pound Literary Trust. Excerpt from "The
Red Wheelbarrow" by William Carlos Williams from *The Collected Poems of William Carlos Williams,*
Volume I: 1909-1939. Copyright 1938 by New Directions Publishing Corporation.
Reprinted by permission of New Directions Publishing Corporation.
W. W. Norton & Co., Inc.: Excerpt from "Wire" by Louis Zukofsky. Reprinted from
All: The Collected Short Poems of Louis Zukofsky, by permission of
W. W. Norton & Co., Inc. Copyright © 1971, 1966, 1965 by Louis Zukofsky.
Wesleyan University Press: Excerpt from "In May," from *The Complete Poems of W. H. Davies.*
Copyright © 1963 by Jonathan Cape Ltd. Reprinted by permission.
The author's thanks are due to the librarians and staff of the Berg Collection of the New York
Public Library, the Manuscript Collection of the British Library, the Department of Rare Books
at Cornell University and the Huntington Library, for making available correspondence relating
to various figures in this book.
Quotations from Wyndham Lewis, copyright the Estate of Mrs. G. A. Wyndham Lewis, by
permission of the Trustees of the Wyndham Lewis Memorial Trust (a registered charity).

Library of Congress Cataloging-in-Publication Data

Symons, Julian, 1912
Makers of the new.

Includes index.
1. English literature — 20th century — History
and criticism. 2. Modernism (Literature)
3. American literature — 20th century — History and
criticism. I. Title.
PR478.M6S96 1987 820'.9'00912 87-26412
ISBN 0-394-55397-7

Manufactured in the United States of America

2 3 4 5 6 7 8 9

First Edition

Contents

'I am informally connected with a couple of new and impecunious papers . . . the latter can pay a little, the former practically cannot pay at all, we do it for larks.'

Ezra Pound to James Joyce, December 1913

'I am writing a book *Ulysses* which however will not be finished for some years.'

James Joyce to W. B. Yeats, 1916

'I like young Eliot, he's got style,
But I ask you, is it po'try?'

Sung at *Criterion* lunches

'I see every day in a certain A.B.C. Shop at least three girls who belong to a new and unknown race. They would furnish an artist looking for an origin with a model of a new mankind.'

Wyndham Lewis, *Blast* 2, 1915

INTRODUCTION

This book is a blend of biography, literary history and criticism designed to show the course of literary modernism, as it developed in Britain and America between 1912 and 1939. It is shaped as a narrative, which tells what happened, why it happened, how it happened, and it is also an account of the principal figures involved and the ways in which they affected the movement. There are many biographical studies and personal memoirs of what Wyndham Lewis called the men of 1914, T. S. Eliot, James Joyce, Ezra Pound and himself, but none that looks at modernism through the links between these four men, without whom it would not have existed in the way that we know it. They did not form a group or cabal, and were never all four in one room at the same time, yet the links were strong and lasting. Their ideas and practice, and those of the mostly American writers who followed them, changed the nature of British and American literature in the first half of the twentieth century.

Modernism, like democracy, is a word often used but rarely defined. A book or picture is said to be modernist, or more often nowadays post- or neo-modernist, but just what does it succeed, or of what is it a revised version? It is common for essayists and reviewers to stick the word on like a label to something they are attacking or defending. 'Modernism was born at a stroke with mass commodity culture ... postmodernist art actively conspires in accepting its "ephemeral function" ... modernist art is identifiable through its ironic withdrawal, its would-be refusal of its commodity status.' These three quotations (very typical quotations) from a single review cry out for definition of what exactly is being discussed. In this book the term *modernism* is used of work whose creators were attempting consciously to change the form, language or subject matter of literature, sometimes all three. It is confined to British and American writing, and although I have referred occa-

[9]

sionally to visual art, I have done so as little as possible.

The definition may be thought unduly confining. Something equivalent to literary modernism took place in all the arts and in several countries during the first quarter of this century, and it had many variations. To deal with them adequately, however, would have been outside the scope of the book I had in mind. Even within literary modernism it would be ideally desirable to go beyond the English language, to discuss Proust, Gide and Céline in France, Brecht and Döblin in Germany, and a dozen or twenty others. Yet British and American modernism developed distinct manners and styles, and although at the beginning the leading practitioners owed much to Europe, within a very few years strongly national characteristics had become evident, particularly in America. In most accounts of modernism such characteristics are fudged or ignored. It is important to understand that the ideas and practice of the founding fathers up to 1920 were quite different from those of William Carlos Williams and his epigones. It is hardly too much to say that those who favour an Eliotian approach to poetry must consider Williams an unfortunate influence, and vice versa. The differences between European-inspired modernism and that which proclaimed a wholly American origin are great, and should be understood.

In dealing with them I have moved into criticism. Within the narrative structure, which includes brief biographies of the principal characters, I had the secondary purpose of emphasising the roles of the men of 1914, especially that of Wyndham Lewis, whose part in the modernist movement has been consistently understated or even almost ignored, especially by American writers. I hope this book may do something to set the balance right. And because the perversions and absurdities of the movement have their significance I have given space to them also. Abraham Lincoln Gillespie was, or should have been, an awful warning to writers tempted to follow the path Joyce took in *Finnegans Wake*, the Baroness Elsa and Emanuel Carnevali served notice of the dangers in thinking that verse can ever be completely free. Frivolity too may have its value. Who would have thought that *transition* ever published a guide to American slang phrases, including 'Garbo-Gilberting'? And the acuity and occasional acidity of comments by Robert McAlmon and Djuna Barnes seem to me to throw light on several period attitudes.

The opening and closing dates chosen are to some extent

arbitrary. Anglo-American literary modernism could be said to have begun in 1906 when Joyce contemplated a short story to be called 'Ulysses', or 1911 when Eliot wrote the 'The Love Song of J. Alfred Prufrock', and the year when the movement lost its sap has been placed by others as early as 1930. But 1912, when *Poetry* (Chicago) was founded, and 1939, when *Finnegans Wake* was published and the *Criterion* closed down, still seem to me reasonable dates for the beginning and end of modernism as a revolutionary literary movement.

PART ONE

The Founding Fathers

CHAPTER ONE

The Men (and a Woman) of 1912

I. EDWARD MARSH

In September 1912 Edward Marsh and his friend Rupert Brooke
talked about ways of stimulating public interest in modern poetry.
Marsh at this time was forty years old, and the archetype of a
British civil servant. He had entered the civil service straight from
Cambridge, and in 1905 had become Winston Churchill's private
secretary. 'I can see what he will expect from his P.S. and it's *simply*
frightening – all so utterly beyond my capacity,' he wrote to a
friend.[1] Fear was soon succeeded by admiring affection, and Marsh
followed his master to the Board of Trade and the Admiralty.
Efficient in his job, Marsh was a knowledgeable amateur of the arts
outside it. Within the limits of a moderate private income he bought
pictures, at first playing safe with British water-colours and drawings but in 1911 venturing into contemporary art with the purchase
of a picture of parrot tulips by Duncan Grant. Undeterred by a
friend's view that the picture was atrocious in technique and
incompetent beyond measure, Marsh, his foot dipped in, soon took
the plunge and became a collector of recent British art, buying work
by Roger Fry and Mark Gertler among others. He was even more
devoted to poetry than to painting, and in 1912 he was ready for the
kind of enterprise Brooke was proposing.

Marsh already admired both the person and the art of the man
fifteen years his junior. In 1906, Brooke's first year at Cambridge,
he had seen him playing the part of the Herald in the *Eumenides*.
Brooke wore *papier-mâché* armour, a bright red wig, a cloak of red,
blue and gold, and the effect on the impressionable bachelor was
profound. He was not alone in such admiration. Many of Brooke's
contemporaries, male and female, were bowled over by his physical
beauty, high spirits and quick intelligence. Yet he was not universally

[15]

popular. His gusting high spirits alternated with moods of depression, and an occasional fleering scepticism that might have been designed to contradict his aesthetic appearance. By 1912 Brooke had left Cambridge, published a volume of poems, and become so friendly with Marsh that he used the spare room of the civil servant's apartment near Gray's Inn Road when in London. Now, sitting on the bed in this room, the two men talked. Brooke suggested that he should write a collection of verse under several names and in several styles, a joke that when revealed was bound to shake up public taste. Marsh responded to this half-joking suggestion seriously, saying that if they both believed there were a dozen flesh-and-blood poets whose work would shake up the public similarly, 'it would be simpler to use the material which was ready to hand'.[2] It is not certain that Brooke believed the dozen poets existed, but at a luncheon in Marsh's rooms on the following day, attended by some possible contributors, Marsh deprecated Brooke's original idea. Brooke wanted only to cause a shock, Marsh to herald a poetic renaissance, and it was Marsh who prevailed.

Marsh not only prevailed; he collected the contributions, taking no more than occasional notice of suggestions from Brooke and others, and then did the masterly job of pushing the book that might be expected from a skilled civil servant. He wrote letters to reviewers and many literary friends, sent advance copies of the anthology to freelances who might possibly be able to notice it, asked the editor of *The Times Literary Supplement* for a front page review, and received an enthusiastic response sent from Italy during an editorial holiday promising 'either two cols inside before Xmas, or a front page after'.[3] He even assigned various publicity jobs to the poets themselves, asking one contributor who wrote for the *Birmingham Post* to make sure that the collection was received favourably. It is hardly surprising that, according to the same contributor, the Prime Minister's car was waiting outside Bumpus's book store to collect a copy on the day of publication.[4]

The sales justified this faith and industry. The first volume of *Georgian Poetry* (the title suggested by Marsh) was published at the end of 1912 by the Poetry Bookshop recently established by Harold Monro. In six months it ran through almost as many editions, and although the editions were small the total sale at the end of the first year must have approached ten thousand. Critical praise was almost undiluted for this first of what were to be five Georgian anthologies, the last appearing in 1922. The poets were acclaimed as bold, fresh and realistic in their use of language. Marsh's introductory note in which he claimed that this Georgian period might 'take rank in due time with the several great poetic ages of the past' was endorsed a little later by J. C. Squire when he said that in the mass of good work 'fit for the anthologies . . . I do not see any age since the Elizabethan which can compare with ours'.[5] Brooke wrote to his lover Ka Cox that Marsh had got too many rotters in, without naming any of them. He did not voice this criticism to Marsh.

Georgian Poetry 1 contained the work of seventeen writers, from the established G. K. Chesterton, Sturge Moore, Walter de la Mare and John Masefield (the most popular poet of the period, and regarded as indispensable) through those like Lascelles Abercrombie and Gordon Bottomley who had published several volumes, to young men like Brooke, D. H. Lawrence and the tramp poet W. H. Davies. The newness of the Georgian approach was particularly remarked. It is probably a tribute to Marsh's public relations skills that one of the contributors, Abercrombie, was allowed to review it in the *Manchester Guardian*. He contrasted it with Q's *Oxford Book of Victorian Verse*, and claimed that the Georgians had broken away from Victorian manner and subject. Among reviewers elsewhere, Edward Thomas saw beauty, strength and mystery, and D. H. Lawrence said the collection was 'like a big breath taken when we are waking up after a night of oppressive dreams' (the oppressive dream figures being Ibsen, Flaubert, Hardy), and asked: 'What are the Georgian poets, nearly all, but just bursting into a thick blaze of being?'[6] Edmund Gosse, chief critical magistrate of the period, praised the collection highly, although he warned against a 'violence, almost a rawness in the approach to life itself'.[7]

Such violence and rawness was represented by poems like Wilfrid Gibson's 'The Hare' which began

> My hands were hot upon a hare,
> Half-strangled, struggling in a snare

or in passages like this one from Abercrombie's 'Sale of St Thomas', celebrating an Indian king's sadistic pleasures:

> So, to better his tongue, a rope was vent
> Beneath his oxters, up he was hauled, and fire

[17]

The Founding Fathers

Let singe the soles of his feet, until his legs
Wriggled like frying eels; then the King's dogs
Were set to hunt the hirpling man. The King
Laughed greatly.

The conventional blank verse in which Abercrombie's poem, Bottomley's 'The End of the World' and Davies's 'The Child and the Mariner' were written, the thumping dullness of Gibson's long poem, should have precluded the idea that they brought anything new to poetry, as should the language and the inversion of the second line in John Drinkwater's lengthy 'The Fires of God': 'Along the ways wheredown my feet have passed'. There was much else that sounded what came to be considered the typical note of Georgian poetry, a concern with country against urban life, and an identification of the poet with that life. The note was heard in Edmund Beale Sargent's 'Cuckoo Wood' ('Cuckoo, are you calling me/Or is it a voice of wizardry?'), included by Marsh against Brooke's negative opinion, and Davies's 'In May', which began:

Yes, I will spend the livelong day
With Nature in the month of May
And sit beneath the trees, and share
My bread with birds whose homes are there.

An almost super-typical Georgian poet was Ralph Hodgson, who wore a bowler, puffed a briar pipe, and had a particular fondness for dogs. He often brought his bull pup into a restaurant, and even at a gathering of poets, dogs were his favourite topic of conversation.[8] Hodgson entered with the second volume, which included his longish 'The Bull', seen as a 'bull of blood/Newly come to lustihood', then as a fighter so powerful that there was 'Not a cow that said him nay', then a fallen chief dreaming of past glories, and at last 'an old bull forlorn' waiting for the end.

The same strain of identification with nature and the animal kingdom ran through all five anthologies, as in John Freeman's invocation (No. 4) of a Kentish river under the title of 'O Muse Divine', or the opening of the same writer's 'The Wakers':

The joyous morning ran and kissed the grass
And drew his fingers through her sleeping hair.

[18]

It was such verse that T. S. Eliot had in mind when he wrote that the Georgians' chief quality was pleasantness, either 'the insidiously didactic, or Wordsworthian (a rainbow and a cuckoo's song)' or 'the decorative, playful or solemn, minor-Keatsian, too happy happy brook', and added that 'in either variety, the Georgians caress everything they touch'.[9]

Inevitably there were other and better poems in the collections: by de la Mare, Lawrence and Harold Monro, and in the later anthologies Edmund Blunden, James Elroy Flecker, Robert Graves, Siegfried Sassoon; but the true Georgian note was that of Abercrombie in blank verse, Davies and Hodgson in country matters. The five collections were an expression of Marsh's taste. To that taste, and to Marsh's social connections, they owed the commercial success that made the last and weakest of them sell 8000 copies, and the limitations of the taste made it certain that Georgian poetry would offer nothing new in approach or language. Marsh said he liked poetry to be intelligent, musical and racy, but the last epithet indicated only his enjoyment of verse that was easy to read, amusing and cheerful. He did not care for gloomy or ornate verse – the nineties poets would have got short shrift from him – nor for cynicism, a quality that sometimes worried him in his protégé Brooke. It was Marsh who suggested the title 'The Old Vicarage, Grantchester' for the poem Brooke had originally called 'The Sentimental Exile', and he rebuked his young friend for occasional coarseness, saying that there were some things too disgusting to write about, particularly in one's own language. It is not surprising that when in the third volume Marsh included poems about the war by fighting soldiers, Graves, Sassoon and Isaac Rosenberg, he avoided the sharper and fiercer poems in Sassoon's *Counter Attack* and in Rosenberg's work. This shying away from anything gruesome, or implicitly critical of established authority, was accompanied in Marsh by enjoyment of fustian blank verse, especially in dramatic form. He was much excited by Bottomley's blank verse play *King Lear's Wife*, which he regarded as the one great literary event of 1914. He told Brooke that the poetic drama was born again in Bottomley's play, finding in it lines comparable to the best of Webster. A few weeks later Marsh saw his first Tchekov play, *Uncle Vanya*, and was greatly disappointed, calling it 'a play in which one wants to shake all the characters all the time'.[10] Neither critics nor audience shared his view of *King Lear's Wife*, which reads very much like something rejected by Savonarola Brown.

Marsh was generous and helpful towards his chosen poets. He subsidised Wilfrid Gibson by sending £1 a week to Middleton Murry, who paid Gibson the money for nominal work as sub-editor of *Rhythm*, edited by Murry with Katherine Mansfield. He tried to ease Rosenberg's life in the Army, and encouraged Graves, Sassoon, and of course Brooke. Near the end of his life he said that he bought pictures by instinct, 'but I *know* about poetry'.[11] Such knowledge, however, prompted him to reject some of the best poets who wrote in a form and manner that fitted Georgian feeling, like Edward Thomas and Charlotte Mew, and precluded acceptance of anything didactic, satirical or political. He had no regard for light verse, except as something to be written and treated as a joke, and disliked particularly poetry awkward or extravagant in expression, or difficult to understand. His literary tastes were those of an entirely conventional man, well-read and intelligent but intellectually hidebound and emotionally timid. His biographer called him, truly enough, a patron of the arts, but the patronage was given within the limits of a temperament that rejected instantly the idea of any change in the language or subject matter of poetry. The five volumes of *Georgian Poetry* are his fitting monument.

2. HARRIET MONROE

If it seems peculiarly appropriate that what was hailed as a revival of British poetry should have been sponsored by a dapper civil servant wistfully enamoured of masculine beauty, it is also proper that a similar movement in America should have had its origins in the literary aspirations of a spinster in her early fifties. Harriet Monroe was born in Chicago in 1860, the daughter of a youthfully promising but eventually unsuccessful lawyer. The family was a respected one, even though her father left no tangible estate on his death and her mother had odd habits like eating the rinds of half-a-dozen lemons every day. At her convent boarding school Harriet Monroe received the standard education for a young lady of the time, being taught to write verse as a social accomplishment like playing the piano or speaking French. She was determined to make literature her way of life, a determination enhanced by a few weeks spent in New York during her early twenties. There she met some of the local literati, Henry Harland, E. C. Stedman, Eugene Field. She told Stedman, essayist, poet, critic and Wall Street broker, of her ambition to write plays, and he approved it. People in the trade, she said in a letter home, considered such an aspiration the most natural thing in the world.

The short plays she wrote had no success, but she worked for the *Chicago Tribune* as an art critic, and in 1892 was commissioned to write an Ode for the city's World Columbian Exposition. For this she asked and surprisingly received a fee of $1000 to which, even more surprisingly, was added a further $5000 when the *New York World* jumped the gun in printing the poem, and she won a law case against the paper. The poem concerned chiefly the awakening of America, and a few lines give the flavour:

> Lo, clan on clan,
> The embattled nations gather to be one,
> Clasp hands as brothers on Columbia's shield,
> Upraise her banner to the shining sun.
> Along her sacred shore
> One heart, one song, one dream –
> Men shall be free forevermore,
> And love shall be law supreme.[12]

What she called the indomitable faith she held in her literary vocation was not really fulfilled in Chicago, which was celebrated as a meat market rather than a literary centre. In 1912 she set out to change this, and spent two months in the public library reading all the verse of the past five years published in British and American books and magazines. She then sent out a circular to some forty poets, telling them that she was starting a monthly poetry magazine, that contributions would be paid for, and that she hoped to offer yearly prizes. Unlike Marsh, who confined himself to writers living in Britain, she wrote to several poets outside her own country, including Yeats, James Stephens and Henry Newbolt, as well as to some of the Georgians already mentioned.

Although Harriet Monroe hoped there were vagabonds and artists among her ancestors she had, as her conduct over the Exposition Ode shows, a shrewd sense of the importance of money. Before sending out the circular she had obtained promises of support from a hundred Chicagoans, each of whom pledged himself to subscribe $50 a year for five years. They ranged from her relatives to lawyers, newspaper owners and editors, bank presidents and railroad stockholders. At the end of several months' work she had rather more than $5000 a year to run the magazine, along with one or two promises from men who said they could be called on if extra money was needed. She received sympathetic replies from almost all the poets, poems from some, and in October 1912 the first issue of *Poetry* (Chicago) appeared, just a few weeks before *Georgian Poetry 1*.

Although Monroe had spent eighteen months in Europe during the nineties and was a hardened traveller, she was an unsophisticated woman, who at this time knew only that she wanted to edit a poetry magazine, and to make Chicago a centre of the arts. Her editorial in the first issue must have embarrassed some of her readers by its Victorian clichés, and its implied suggestion that poetry had little to do with ordinary life. It ended:

> We hope to offer our subscribers a place of refuge, a green isle in the sea, where Beauty may plant her gardens, and Truth, austere revealer of joy and sorrow, of hidden delights and despairs, may follow her brave quest unafraid.

The idea that poetry was a kind of holiday resort for tired business men was strengthened by the sonnet, 'Poetry', which had the place of honour on the first page. It was by the American Arthur Davison Ficke, and set out to describe the nature of poetry:

> It is a little isle amid bleak seas –
> An isolate realm of garden, circled round
> By importunity of stress and sound,
> Devoid of empery to master these . . .
> It is a refuge from the stormy days,
> Breathing the peace of a remoter world.

The Georgian poets were using a clearer and less outdated literary language than this. Most of the first issue was on the same dismal level, which made two poems by Ezra Pound, 'Middle-Aged' and 'To Whistler, American', seem all the more distinctive. The poem to Whistler, which ended

> You and Abe Lincoln from that mass of dolts
> Show us there's chance at least of winning through

caused indignation among the magazine's readers, and some of its backers. Were those who backed the holiday resort of poetry with good money to be called a mass of dolts? Protests were vain, however, for even before the first issue appeared Harriet Monroe had fallen under the spell of Ezra Pound.

He was one of the poets to whom she sent the circular letter, and his reply was long, enthusiastic, and full of ideas that would involve himself. Pound had been living in London since 1908 and had published several small volumes of poems. Marsh had wanted to include his 'The Goodly Fere' in *Georgian Poetry 1*, but Pound had declined on the ground that the poem was not characteristic of his recent work, and suggested other poems Marsh found unacceptable. Now Pound told Monroe her difficult task would be to teach Americans that poetry was an art. He grandly offered to let his own poems appear exclusively in her magazine, said he could keep her in touch with whatever was most dynamic in Paris and London, and ended with a rousing call that she should speed and smooth the way towards an American Risorgimento.

Pound was at this time, and for most of his life remained, a very Europeanised American. Yet, although he had told his friend William Carlos Williams in 1909 that 'London, deah old Lundon, is the place for poesy',[13] he looked eagerly for signs of an American poetic revolution, and saw in *Poetry* (Chicago) a possible means to that end. Monroe had no such intention but, in part because of her comparative lack of sophistication, was much more receptive to a new approach to poetry than Marsh. He would at once have recognised the Ficke sonnet and much else in the magazine as fag-ends of Victorian verse, but would also have been unreceptive to the new rhythms, themes and approaches that Monroe a little uncertainly welcomed. She appointed Pound as the magazine's unpaid foreign correspondent, who would 'keep readers informed of the present interests of the art in England, France and elsewhere'.[14]

The results were immediate. The second issue contained three poems by Richard Aldington, the next five by Yeats and others from Rabindranath Tagore who, Monroe was assured by her foreign correspondent, would be the sensation of the winter in England. 'This is *the Scoop*,' Pound told her when he had secured several Tagore poems, and certainly Aldington's work, and Tagore's, was of a kind unfamiliar to most American readers. Before long Pound was

The Founding Fathers

referring to their joint policy, and saying that *Poetry* should support only poets who had a serious determination to produce master-pieces. Sending along poems by the unknown H.D. he said it was 'the sort of American stuff that I can show here and in Paris without being ridiculed'.[15] Acknowledging that, given a free hand, he would stop any periodical in a week, he added that he wanted the magazine's files to be prized and vendible in 1999.

Monroe appreciated all this energy and enthusiasm, but a woman who had performed the feat of obtaining financial backing for a verse magazine in a city jeeringly called Porkopolis ('Chicago uses the proceeds of pork for the promotion of poetry,' said a Phila-delphia paper) was not likely to be ruled by a voice from across the Atlantic. She made her own discoveries. The fourth issue contained Vachel Lindsay's 'General William Booth Enters Into Heaven', and Monroe called Lindsay perhaps the most gifted and original poet she had printed, although his jazzy rhythms are little read or regarded today. She also printed a good deal of what was then named *vers libre*, rather than free verse. Was *vers libre* poetry? Readers and writers worried about the question. The magazine's associate editor Alice Corbin Henderson wrote an article explaining that 'prose rhythms differ from poetic rhythms according to the inherent, scientific divisions of the rhythmic wave lengths'. Monroe herself explained that 'the best way of clearing our minds of error is to think of verse in terms of music', replacing 'feet' by 'bar', discarding trochees and dactyls, and classifying poetic measures instead as three-time or four-time. She then analysed a Shakespeare sonnet in terms of musical notes, quarter-notes, eighth-notes, sometimes even sixteenth-notes. Did this make things clearer? Perhaps not. How did one apply it to the 'Chicago' poems by Carl Sandburg printed in March 1914 which caused a stir? The title poem began

> Hog Butcher for the World,
> Tool Maker, Stacker of Wheat,
> Player with Railroads and the Nation's Freight Handler;
> Stormy, husky, brawling,
> City of the Big Shoulders

A rival magazine, the *Dial*, said such stuff was apparently meant to be taken as some kind of poetry, although it was in fact an impudent affront to the poetry-loving public. *Poetry* was in its first years, and has remained (it still exists as we approach 1999) a lucky dip. The editor and her increasingly influential associate printed in the first two years all kinds of poetry. A whole number was given to a blank verse play by the Illinois-born poet John G. Neihardt. Arthur Davison Ficke had an eight-page elegy on Swinburne, and Monroe showed a soft spot for what she called a conservative poet of the old school named Clark Ashton Smith. But much space was given to the poets recommended by Pound, and to American writers like Lindsay and Sandburg who also outraged conventional taste. *Poetry*'s award in its first year went to Yeats, with Lindsay as runner-up. In the following year the prize was given to Sandburg for his 'Chicago' poems. Pound often complained about the poems in the magazine, at the end of 1913 resigned his post, and although he resumed it, he had accepted by 1914 that *Poetry* (Chicago) would not be the medium through which an American Risorgimento might be achieved.

CHAPTER TWO

The Men of 1914

1. EZRA POUND

When Ezra Pound came to live in London in 1908 at the age of twenty-three it might reasonably have been said that he came to conquer literary Britain, or escape from unliterary America, or obtain a European education. Yet although his exile from his own country was self-imposed, and his dislike of the structure and standards of prosperous American life were permanent, he remained in person, style, and the form of his imagination unmistakably American. His whole literary life was an attempt to graft new forms of writing upon the cultural tree of an old world.

Ezra Loomis Pound was born in Hailey, Idaho, but the family moved to Philadelphia when he was four years old, and just outside the city three years later. His grandfather Thaddeus, who had been born in a log cabin, became a successful businessman and was elected to Congress. His father was Assistant Assayer at the US Mint. The Pounds were a solid American couple who loved their only child, loved him rather more than did most of his fellow-students at the University of Pennsylvania. Affected and conceited were words often used about Ezra Pound. Only one person in a thousand liked him, William Carlos Williams told his parents, and why? Because, although a brilliant talker and thinker, he often appeared a laughing boor. Wiliams was the one in a thousand, liking Pound's optimism, admiring his faith in himself and his self-confidence. He played tennis and lacrosse, learned to fence, got into the chess team. He wrote a sonnet a day and talked constantly about himself and what he would do with his talent. In later years Pound was often said to be a natural teacher, and even in youth his manner was pedagogic. During the years at university he did a great deal of reading, some of it unusual, much suggesting that he had an academic career in mind. He read Anglo-Saxon, the romance languages and mediaeval history, with particular concentration on the Provençal troubadours. In due course he became a Fellow of the University and spent two months in Europe doing post-graduate research into the Provençal poets and Lope de Vega. Now and always, the man who became an apostle of modernity was absorbed by the distant past.

Back home again, Pound was briefly an academic at Wabash College in Crawfordsville, Indiana, an instructor in French and Spanish. This job in what he called the sixth circle of desolation lasted only four months, when he was found to have a girl in his room. Pound's version was that she was a stranded variety actress who had rooms across the hall, and that he was sharing his meal with her. Whether or not this was true, he was summarily dismissed from the college.

This was not his first involvement with a woman. At the time of his trouble with the actress he had a tentative engagement to a girl named Mary Moore, to whom he sent as proof of his love a diamond ring given him when he was at the university by a woman concert pianist a dozen years his senior. Mary Moore may have been disconcerted by the Wabash affair. The engagement, she said later, just faded away. So had one of equal brevity but more lasting significance to Hilda Doolittle, later known as the poet H.D. She was the sister of one of Pound's fellow-students, her father taught astronomy at the university, and Pound met her first at a Hallowe'en party where he was dressed as a Tunisian prince. Hilda was tall, coltishly awkward, bony and regarded as beautiful by some but not by Williams, who thought Pound exaggerated her charms absurdly. She was, Williams said, 'a little clumsy but all to the mustard . . . A girl that's full of fun, bright, but never telling you all she knows, doesn't care if her hair is a little mussed, and wears good solid shoes.'[1]

H.D. later said that Pound forced an education on her and also educated her gastronomically, introducing her to Brie cheese. He was a bad dancer, but then one danced with him for the pleasure and interest of what he might say.[2] He called her Dryad and made for her a little hand-bound collection of his poems, which he named *Hilda's Book*. 'My lady is tall and fair to see/She swayeth as a poplar tree', ran two typically archaic lines. He read other poems to her, shouting 'The Gilliflower of Gold' and 'Two Red Roses Across the Moon' by William Morris at her across an orchard. He made her read Ibsen, Shaw, and Whistler's 'Ten O'Clock', sketching a gadfly signature on his own books in emulation of Whistler's butterfly.[3] He gave her a ring (he had not then received the one bestowed on him by the concert pianist), and in spite of Professor Doolittle's disapproval was invited to dinner. He came, not as he should have done in formal clothes, but wearing a shirt open at the neck. After dinner he read his poems, but although they may have been approved, he was not. Soon afterwards the engagement was broken, it seems by mutual consent, although the two remained on affectionate terms. Hilda went on to Bryn Mawr, and to a destiny very different from that of marriage to Ezra Pound.

Such was the young man who left America, much upset by the Wabash tragi-comedy, which he never forgot. In essence Pound remained always this young man, raw, simple, good-natured, often crass, and also as T. S. Eliot called him many years later, a dominating director with a passion to instruct. He remained also a man endlessly enthusiastic but with enthusiasms that constantly changed, a man who could say that America was very much what England would be with the two hundred most interesting people removed, yet who looked forward to the American Risorgimento, a man who called often for simplicity of speech yet spoke in his later poems with a confusion of tongues.

In June 1908 Pound paid $8 to have his first collection of poems, *A Lume Spento*, published in Venice, the edition numbering no more than a hundred copies. Three months later he came to England with the intention, as he told Williams, of having a month up the Thames somewhere and meeting Bill Yeats. He stayed for thirteen years. In London he lived in furnished rooms for a while, found them too expensive, and then settled down in a room in Church Walk, a little paved court behind St Mary Abbot's, Kensington, for which he paid eight shillings a week. Kensington was conveniently central, and the rent was low. He had some financial help from his admiring parents, and otherwise maintained himself by giving lectures at the Regent Street Polytechnic on subjects like the rise of song in Provence, mediaeval religious feeling, the Latin lyrists of the Renaissance. To *A Lume Spento* he added in the same year *A Quinzaine for This Yule*, in the next, *Personæ* and *Exultations*. The Pound who published these volumes was not yet the man who impatiently urged Harriet Monroe in the direction of the new. In these mediaeval studies, experiments and translations as he called them, there was evidence of wide reading in the Latin poets and devoted attention to the nineties, but nothing to shock Eddie Marsh, who might have thought his work old-fashioned in diction. One of the poems is sub-titled 'An Anti-Stave for Dowson', and in 1912 he was still showing nineties influence in such a poem as '*L'Invitation*' with its opening lines 'Go from me, I am one of those who spoil/And leave fair souls less fair for knowing them' (cf. Lionel Johnson's 'Go from me, I am one of those who fall'). Sometimes Browning was his master rather than Swinburne or Dowson, as in 'Sestina: Altaforte', which begins:

> Damn it all! all this our South stinks peace.
> You whoreson dog, Papiols, come! Let's to music!

Such fluent derivative verse lacks a personal note. Pound was, however, going about, meeting people and picking up ideas and attitudes that interested him. His gift for personal publicity and his desire to dominate were as evident as they had been back in Pennsylvania. Douglas Goldring, poet, novelist and reviewer, who was a frequent visitor at South Lodge, the house in Campden Hill where Ford Madox Hueffer, who had not yet changed his last name, and his mistress Violet Hunt had a literary salon, was surprised and amused by the way in which Pound organised the games of tennis played in the communal gardens opposite the house, more surprised to find the American poet at Yeats's Monday evenings handing round the cigarettes, pouring Yeats's Chianti, and laying down the law about poetry.[4] There were many who thought him a ham actor in the role of poet. He ate rose petals (or by another account tulips) at the dinner table, wore a sombrero, a coat with blue glass buttons and green trousers made from billiard cloth. A single turquoise dangled from one ear. He strove to impress, and it was felt he strove too hard. Yet there were others like Yeats and Hueffer who felt an astonished tolerant admiration of him, or who, like Goldring, found him affected but fundamentally genial and admirably free from petty jealousy. Behind the rimless pince-nez Goldring saw kind, affectionate eyes. And almost everybody agreed that, whatever might be Pound's faults and affectations, he was serious about literature. His correspondence testified to this, for it was about almost nothing else.

[29]

He never gossiped in letters, rarely mentioned his health or current events, and even his letters to Dorothy Shakespear, whom he met first in 1909 and married in 1914, are concerned much more with literary matters than with romance, although he addressed her as 'Dearest Love'. She was one of the few who found him physically beautiful.[5]

The conversion of this late Victorian to literary modernity was owed in part to Hueffer, much more to T. E. Hulme. The influence of Hueffer (or Ford, the name used hereafter) on the modern movement has been exaggerated, not least by Ford himself, but it is true that in his brief tenure on the *English Review* before it was bought by Sir Alfred Mond as a useful political outlet, Ford gave a platform to unknown and little-known writers, including Lawrence, Wyndham Lewis and Pound. The young American did more than play tennis at the South Lodge parties with 'the flaps of his polychrome shirt flying out like the petals of some flower and his red head like a flaming pistil in the middle of it'.[6] He acted as a kind of unpaid secretary to Ford, taking dictation from him, doing all kinds of odd jobs. Ford, although himself always staidly dressed, was delighted by Pound's hand-painted tie, green trousers and pink coat, his dash and style. From Ford more than anybody else Pound learned to appreciate French prose as well as Provençal poetry; through Ford he balanced his lop-sided literary education. Their relationship flourished also because Ford was amused by Pound's tendency to take charge of everything with which he was associated, although it was an exaggeration to say, as Ford did later, that in a short time 'he had taken charge of me, the review, and finally of London.'[7]

He certainly did not take charge of T. E. Hulme, the formidable philosopher and aesthetician who was more responsible than any other individual for the modern movement as conceived in Britain, the shape it took and the attitudes behind it. Hulme was born in 1883, the son of a Staffordshire country squire who was also a ceramic transfer manufacturer. A harsh early upbringing (he was often beaten for disobedience) produced a big genial argumentative intellectual roughneck, who once reduced a housemaster to tears by his combative language. At Cambridge Hulme made a mark of a kind, leaving the university sitting astride a coffin, accompanied by friends wearing deep mourning, when he was sent down for some unknown reason. Disowned by his father he went abroad for some time, then in 1908 returned to England and to London, living on a small allowance made him by an aunt, and writing without payment in the *New Age*, a weekly paper edited by A. R. Orage, chiefly from an ABC restaurant in Chancery Lane. In the *New Age* and elsewhere Hume advanced views about literature, and especially poetry, unlike anything Pound had heard before. They made a deep impression on him.

Hulme was killed in World War I and published no book in his lifetime ('I am a heavy philosopher. I shall write nothing until I am forty,' he said once), but the general tendency of his thought is clearly expressed in many articles and essays. He was opposed to humanism, believed in original sin, wanted an orderly and disciplined world. One essay begins with typical abruptness: 'It is my aim to explain in this essay why I believe in original sin, why I can't stand romanticism, and why I am a certain kind of Tory.'[8] Hulme's attitude to visual art was that the Renaissance had become a dead end and should be replaced, must be replaced, by work that was basically geometrical and opposed to naturalism and realism. He thought little of the French Post-Impressionists, but quoted approvingly Cezanne's remark that natural forms could be reduced to the cone, the cylinder and the sphere. Writing in favour of Epstein's sculpture he said it was 'the business of every honest man at the present moment to clean the world of these sloppy dregs of the Renaissance'.[9] His views in relation to poetry were equally clear:

> A reviewer writing in the *Saturday Review* last week spoke of poetry as the means by which the soul soared into higher regions, and as a means of expression by which it became merged into a higher kind of reality. Well, that is the kind of statement that I utterly detest. I want to speak of verse in a plain way as I would of pigs.[10]

The purpose of poetry, Hulme said, was not to express feelings but to evoke an image. In reading verse the mind should constantly be arrested by pictures, and these pictures had their own reality. 'Stupid little poems about flowers and spring' were nothing more than imitations of the past, with 'no *new* emotion in them'.[11] Poetry did not *mean* something, it *was* something. 'Everything for art is a thing in itself, cf the café at Clapham as a thing in itself.'[12]

Hulme advanced such ideas, and variations on them, tirelessly at what was called a club, although it was simply a group of the philosopher's friends and admirers. They met first, in 1909, at the Eiffel Tower restaurant in Percy Street, later at the rooms in Frith Street where Hulme lived with his mistress, the well-to-do Ethel Kibblewhite. Pound went to some of the Eiffel Tower meetings, and there read 'Sestina: Altaforte' in ringing tones that surprised the listeners. Among the more regular attendants were Yeats's friend the actress Florence Farr, and a young poet fluent in several languages named Frank Stewart Flint. Hulme's attitude towards Pound was patronising, perhaps even contemptuous, and he avoided conversation with the American as much as possible. When asked how much longer he would tolerate Pound, he said he knew exactly when he would have to kick him downstairs, although in fact this never happened.

Among those who came to the Frith Street evenings were artists as well as writers. They included Epstein, who made a fine bust of Hulme, Spencer Gore, Edward Wadsworth, C. R. W. Nevinson, Walter Sickert. Among the writers were, surprisingly, several of the Georgians. Marsh and Brooke were to be seen there, and so was Wyndham Lewis, who later called Hulme a talkative jolly giant and a great laugher. One of the things Hulme talked most about was women and his conquests among them. He impressed his listeners by detailed accounts of sexual adventures with shop girls and others, on one occasion pulling out his watch and saying that he had a pressing engagement in five minutes, then returning with the information that the steel staircase of the emergency exit at Piccadilly tube station was the most uncomfortable place in which he had ever copulated. There were those, like Richard Aldington, who were repelled by Hulme's coarse joviality. Rebuked by a constable while urinating in Soho Square he silenced the man by asking, 'Do you realise you are addressing a member of the middle class?', and in the same square ended an argument with Wyndham Lewis by hanging him upside down on the railings, a story that sounds intrinsically improbable but is authenticated by Lewis himself.[13]

The contempt Hulme felt for all romanticism (he rejected chess as a romantic game, preferring the Japanese Go), and his certainty that after a romantic century a classical revival was on the way, explains in part why he thought little of Pound's poetry. The fact that Pound had published in 1910 a prose book based on his

The Men of 1914

Polytechnic lectures called *The Spirit of Romance* can hardly have raised his stature in Hulme's eyes. Pound's clothes, his literary antics, his striking of attitudes, were all romantic gestures of a kind alien to Hulme. Pound also had a reputation as a womaniser. It is not certain that this was justified, even though he told Williams that England was 'the land for the male with the phallus erectus,[14]' but it is possible that Hulme saw Pound as a sexual rival, as he certainly regarded Lewis as an intellectual one.

It is easy to see reasons for Hulme's rejection of Pound, harder to understand why Pound, who was, as he later said, still drunk with Celticism and Dowson's 'Cynara', should have been so thoroughly bowled over by Hulme's theories about painting and poetry. In 1912 he appended to his volume *Ripostes* 'the complete poetical works of T. E. Hulme', which consisted of five poems, the longest no more than five lines. A straight-faced note said that in publishing his complete works so early, Hulme had 'set an enviable example to many of his contemporaries who have had less to say'. Hulme went along with the joke, but Pound's further comment that the poems were printed partly in remembrance of past evenings 'dull enough at the time, but rather pleasant to look back upon' has a suggestion of friendship not justified by the two men's relationship. Five was not the complete tally of Hulme's verses, but he barely reached double figures.

Hulme enlisted enthusiastically for service in the war, was wounded, and died in 1917, with the manuscript of his book on Epstein lost, his work on expression and style unwritten like his projected anti-humanist and anti-romantic pamphlets, leaving only the collections of brilliant bits later gathered up as *Speculations* and *Further Speculations*.

Pound's failure to understand Hulme's distaste for him sprang partly from obliviousness to the effect he made, but also from lack of interest in personal relationships. The tireless efforts he made in the next decade to promote the work of other writers were done out of respect for their talents, not because they were close personal friends. If he had noticed Hulme's dislike, it would not have affected him, and Hulme's certainty about what poetry and visual art should be, his insistence that the new visual art should be geometric and the new poetry created in terms of pictures, impressed a man conscious of deep dissatisfaction with the poetry and prose being written in self-satisfied Georgian Britain and intellectually somnolent America, but with little idea of what might replace it. Hulme did not provide Pound with answers so much as clues. Many of Hulme's aesthetic and philosophical attitudes must have been uncongenial to the Americans – his identification of romantics as 'all those who do not believe in the Fall of Man[15],' his desire to speak of verse as plainly as of pigs, his admiration for the Frenchman Sorel because he was absolutist in ethics. Pound had no intention of abandoning his own romanticism or love of the past, but he found in Hulme's insistence on the power of the image, and his rejection of regular metre as cramping, jangling, meaningless and out of place in modern poetry, a way of blending old and new. The poetic movement called Imagism sprang from the adaptation of some of Hulme's ideas.

2. IMAGISM, WHAT WAS IT?

In England Pound did not forget American friends. Williams, who was in the process of making a division in his life between medicine and literature, visited England in 1910 and saw something of Pound. He was surprised by the smallness of his friend's room, impressed by his routine of making filter coffee by placing a teaspoonful on a cloth over his cup and dripping water slowly through it. (Pound was already, or soon after became, an excellent cook.) Williams heard Yeats read 'Cynara' in a darkened room, visited a family in Buckinghamshire and went for a walk which, he later said, had been England to him ever since. His description of ivied church wall, daisy- and primrose-covered lawn, a bird rising at his feet in a field, would have pleased the Georgian poets.[16] Williams was writing poems and publishing them at his own expense. Pound, when asked for comments, wrote freely and sometimes harshly, saying in 1909 that although Williams's collection was poetic, it was neither original nor individual. However, by 1912, when Pound invented Imagism, William Carlos Williams was writing poems that his friend liked much better.

In a literal sense it is wrong to say that Pound invented Imagism or even that he coined the word, since he called it Imagisme. It was Hulme who had proclaimed the vital importance of the image, and

[34]

his handful of poems were the first written in accordance with that idea. This one was typical:

> Above the quiet dock in midnight,
> Tangled in the tall mast's corded height,
> Hangs the moon. What seemed so far away
> Is but a child's balloon, forgotten after play.

Hulme was a model, although not exactly *the* model, for Imagist poets, which is what Pound told Aldington and H.D. they were, after he had read their poems in a Kensington teashop. Hilda Doolittle, like Williams, had come to London, and had written poems which she signed H.D. At a party she met handsome Richard Aldington. He also was writing poems while trying to make a living as a literary freelance, and Pound, after looking at the poems, said that the twenty-year-old Aldington needed no help from him. His reaction to H.D.'s poems as expressed to Monroe has already been mentioned. She signed them 'H.D., Imagiste'.

What was an Imagiste? F. S. Flint, who accepted the label, said they were poets determined to write in accordance with the best tradition as found in the best writers, 'Sappho, Catullus, Villon', and were determined not to tolerate anything less good. Their few rules, Flint said, were direct treatment of any subject, the use only of words that contributed to the presentation, and composition 'in sequence of the musical phrase, not of the metronome'. He later elaborated on this, dating the origins of Imagisme back to the dinners arranged by Hulme in 1909, and pointing out that when Pound printed Hulme's five poems at the end of *Ripostes* he had called the Imagistes 'the descendants of the forgotten school of 1909[17].' Pound's 'A Few Don'ts by an Imagiste' which accompanied an article by Flint in *Poetry* explained that 'an "Image" is that which presents an intellectual and emotional complex in an instant of time', and claimed that such an instantaneous presentation marked the greatest works of art. Hulme's doctrine is characteristically brisker and clearer: a poem was made from images, the images should be constantly visualised and not just literary phrases, and regular metre was to be avoided. Upon such pedestals Pound built the anthology he edited, called *Des Imagistes*, which was published early in 1914 by Harold Monro's Poetry Bookshop. A little earlier Marsh wrote to Brooke that he had been told of a movement by the

'Pound-Flint-Hulme school' to produce an anthology. These, he said, were writers who resented being left out of the Georgian anthology, but he thought nothing would come of it.[18] He was wrong in this, but right in thinking that in Britain the collection would cause only the faintest ripple of interest. In America it received more attention.

Of the eleven contributors to *Des Imagistes* only four are to be found in most collections of modern verse: H.D., Williams, James Joyce and Pound himself. Most of the others hardly survive as poetic names, although Amy Lowell and Richard Aldington were once highly regarded. The principal contributors were Aldington, H.D. and Pound, and the instantly noticeable thing about their poems is the influence on them of Greek or Chinese models. Aldington later said of H.D. that he had never known anybody with so vivid an aesthetic appreciation, and the two encouraged each other in producing work much indebted to the Greek Anthology. Pound had recently developed what was to be a permanent interest in Chinese literature. Eliot later called him the inventor of Chinese poetry for our time, a phrase which seems more and more ambiguous the longer one looks at it. Many of the poems based on Chinese models written by Pound at this time are pretty, stylish and delicate, including 'After Ch'u Yuan', 'Ts'ai Chi'h' and 'Fan-Piece, For Her Imperial Lord', but although their approach is unusual, the language is not particularly original. 'I will walk in the glade,/I will come out from the new thicket/and accost the procession of maidens', the end of 'After Ch'u Yuan', is written in a language no less literary than that rejected by both Pound and the Georgians as outdated, its obsolescence concealed by the fact of its translation or adaptation from the Chinese original. And the language used by H.D. and Aldington was not much nearer to what Pound was asking of Harriet Monroe when he said she should print only poetry written in words that could naturally be spoken. H.D.'s 'Priapus' (later called 'Orchard') begins:

> I saw the first pear
> As it fell, .
> The honey-seeking, golden-banded,
> The yellow swarm
> Was not more fleet than I,
> (Spare us from loveliness!)

And I fell prostrate,
Crying.
Thou has flayed us with thy blossoms;
Spare us the beauty
Of fruit-trees!

A line like 'Thou has flayed us with thy blossoms' is not only comic in itself (the equivalent of being whipped with feathers), but extremely literary in its language.

How much did the poems in this collection fulfil the doctrine laid down by Hulme and elaborated by Flint and Pound? The first rule, 'direct treatment of the "thing", whether subjective or objective' proved literally impossible to follow in any poem of more than half-a-dozen lines. If followed faithfully, it must have excluded all metaphor, and any expression of personal feeling such as the wish to be spared the beauty of fruit-trees. Since the 'thing' in H.D.'s poem was the pear-tree, personal feelings could not be a direct treatment of it, individual to the tree, but emotions that might be aroused equally by a sunset or a profile. Flint's attempt in 'The Swan' to reproduce what might be called the essence of swanness faltered after description of the swan's tarnished copper neck and beak and its slow floating towards deep black water, in the direction of the irrelevantly personal:

Into the dark of the arch the swan floats
and the black depth of my sorrow
bears a white rose of flame.

Even Hulme's four lines, which find the moon first appearing tangled in a mast, then described by metaphor, cannot truly be called direct.

It proved similarly impracticable to use only words that contributed to the 'presentation' of a single image: the rejection of descriptive language suggested by such a rule would have been hopelessly limiting, and was not seriously attempted. James Joyce's 'I Hear An Army' had no relationship at all to Imagiste precepts, but with that poem put aside, the only 'rule' observed by the other contributors was the one saying they should compose in sequence of the musical phrase, not in sequence of a metronome. In other words, none except Joyce wrote poems in a metre with recognisable and regular stresses, and some expressed their rejection of regularity

[37]

by abandoning the use of capital letters when starting another line. They felt that such capitals were an arbitrary interference with natural rhythm.

About most of this there was nothing new, for both Monro and Monroe had been worrying about 'free verse' a year or two earlier. The need to justify such writing disturbed editors for another decade or more, but Pound's anthology posed the problem more sharply than it had been presented previously. Most of the work printed in *Poetry* (Chicago) used regular stresses and rhymes, and all the Georgians adhered to capital letters at the beginning of lines. Only in these respects was *Des Imagistes* a portent. In everything else the movement was a false start, or a dead end. It is likely that Pound would soon have realised this, since in these years he was continually searching for a language and a style. Probably Imagisme would have been only a stopping place on his journey towards the terminus finally reached in his Cantos. His interest in the Chinese ideogram as a means of instant compressed expression is related to his search for something similar in the individual image. But the decision whether, or how, to continue the movement was taken out of his hands by another of the women who affected the development of modernism. Imagisme was stolen from him, and turned into Imagism, by Amy Lowell.

This was done through the power of money. Where Pound scraped a living by teaching, lecturing and journalism, Amy Lowell, cousin of James Russell Lowell, was a member of the best Boston society. She was born in 1874, the last child (the first, her brother Percival, was nineteen years her senior) of Augustus Lowell, who was both a prosperous businessman and a Vice President of the American Academy of Arts and Sciences. Amy was a spoiled, clever child, and also an unusually large and awkward one. Af fifteen she noted in her diary that she was 'a great rough masculine, strong thing', and a little later remarked gloomily, 'really, you know, I am appaulingly fat'.[19] When she was a debutante sixty dinners were given for her, and there were proposals of marriage which she rejected. She banted, became ill, took to smoking light manila cigars after trying cigarettes and pipes, and eventually accepted her great rough strong masculinity. In 1909 her brother Lawrence became President of Harvard, and Amy lacked neither money nor influence. Sevenels, her house at Brookline outside Boston, had a Monet over the reception room mantel, cornices and mouldings done after Adam designs, a library panelled with oak brought over from England and with two fireplaces framed in swags of fruit and flowers carved after Grinling Gibbons. In 1912 she published a volume of undistinguished Keatsian verse, but in the following year after reading some poems by H.D. she exclaimed: 'Why, I, too, am an Imagiste.'[20]

From this time her verse changed. Without abandoning the love of colour or the sensuous feeling for shapes and aspects of the visible world which had particularly attracted her in Keats, she began to experiment with varying lengths of line, loose varying rhythms and highly-coloured prose poetry. In 1913 she came to England, stayed at the Berkeley, invited Pound to dinner. First impressions were favourable on both sides. She found his conversation delightful, he remarked that she was pleasingly intelligent and said he would like to print a poem of hers in the anthology he was preparing. She happily accepted.

A year later, however, she crossed the Atlantic again, stayed again at the Berkeley, accompanied by maid, companion, and maroon touring car with chauffeur, and this time things were different. Pound always viewed her as a source of finance rather than a poet, but his attempt to get her to provide him with $5000 a year for the *Mercure de France*, which she would own and he edit, was unsuccessful. She had already conveyed her displeasure at the fact that she had been represented in *Des Imagistes* by a single poem and now, summoning the contributors to the drawing room of her suite, she suggested that all the poets should be equally represented in terms of space. She had obtained the agreement of Aldington and H.D. and now the others consented too, with the exception of Pound. She offered the lure of what she called a publisher of reputable standing (although the Poetry Bookshop was perfectly reputable, and had sold *Georgian Poetry* in large numbers), and said that if necessary she would pay for the book's publication in America. Pound had no editorial rights in the anthology except moral ones, and since he was not supported by the other contributors had no choice but to bow out. Thereafter the Imagist movement belonged to her. Pound took an awkward, clownish revenge when she gave an Imagist dinner, at which several speeches were made. He went out, returned with a bathtub, and said that it was the symbol of the Nagiste or bathtub school of poetry of which Lowell's 'In a Garden', with its last line: 'Night, and the water, and you in your whiteness, bathing', was the first poem. The attempt to make her look absurd fell flat, as Lowell said that Ezra must have his little joke. She could afford to be gracious.

The second anthology, *Some Imagist Poets* (it was at this point that the 'e' was officially dropped) was edited by Amy Lowell, and so were the third and fourth, the last appearing in 1917. She felt proprietorially about all the poets, perhaps particularly about John Gould Fletcher who had been born in Arkansas, then sent to a New England school followed by Harvard, and had been in London since 1909. In 1913 Fletcher had published five books of verse in a single month, all at his own expense and all unnoticed. He was not unnaturally delighted when Lowell told him he was a genius, and with her encouragement rapidly produced several poetic symphonies, called Blue, Green, Gold and White, and then began to write what both he and Lowell agreed to call polyphonic prose. Fletcher, when invited to Sevenels, was quite overwhelmed by the splendour in which Amy Lowell lived.

Aldington and H.D. had married in October 1913, after a trip to Italy where Pound, whose attitude towards H.D. remained possessive, joined them. He was a witness at their registry office wedding in Kensington. The marriage was not a success, chiefly no doubt because H.D. was basically lesbian, even though in 1919 she had a child by the composer Cecil Gray. By that time she had parted from Aldington although they remained on friendly terms, but in this summer of 1914 Amy Lowell thought them a perfectly charming young couple. Richard, long-haired and hatless, seemed to her like a boy on holiday. Both husband and wife liked her, Aldington going so far as to say that it would have been hard to resist her vivacious intelligence. He wrote later that he saw nothing wrong with her idea of 'publishing quietly and modestly as a group of friends with similar tendencies'.[21]

The three volumes of *Some Imagist Poets* contained only five contributors apart from Lowell: Aldington, H.D., Fletcher, Flint and Lawrence. She made no attempt to extend the movement, nor further to define it. When the third volume appeared she wrote finis to the whole thing in a magisterial manner. 'These three little books are the germ, the nucleus, of the school,' she said, and its further development 'must be sought in the published work of the individual members of the group'.[22] That was the end of the Imagist movement. By the time *An Imagist Anthology* appeared in 1930, with a nostalgic introduction by Ford, the different approaches and purposes of the contributors were apparent. Some had altogether abandoned Hulme's doctrine, like Aldington who had always disliked Hulme and denied any debt to him. In 1924 Aldington wrote to Herbert Read, who had made some criticisms of his long poem 'A Fool i' the Forest' as loose in structure, that five years ago he might have said Amen to the criticism, but now 'you call "loose" what I call ease, fluidity, clarity . . . I abandon, cast off, utterly deny the virtue of "extreme compression and essential significance of every word". I say that is the narrow path that leadeth to sterility.'[23] By 1930 Flint had ceased to publish poetry, Fletcher outlived the vogue for his attempts to equate poetry with music and colour, Lawrence long forgotten any influence Lowell had had on him, and of them all only H.D. still perhaps adhered to the doctrine of the Image.

If the three Imagist volumes Lowell edited offered nothing new, they enabled her to consolidate her position as a fairly benevolent literary dictator, who demanded and generally received respect. In her days of power and influence, from 1917 until her sudden death in 1924, she wrote all night and slept until three in the afternoon, after which she dictated the bulk of her correspondence to one or other of her secretaries. She took to smoking a hookah. She complained to Harriet Monroe of a failure to mention her in *Poetry* editorials and called the omission a studied insult, and after an unfriendly review of one of her volumes of poems had appeared, suggested to her publisher that since he advertised in the paper he should be able to force them into a less hostile attitude to one of their authors.[24] She died a famous woman, but by 1930 was already an almost forgotten poet. Some of Pound's comments on her show a touch of malice, as when he called her the only hippopoetess in their zoo. Before he lost control of Imagisme, however, he was already concerned with another literary movement: Vorticism.

3. WYNDHAM LEWIS

In 1914 Percy Wyndham Lewis had published nothing more than a few stories, but had become known as a visual artist of a revolutionary kind. His gigantic 'Kermesse', a picture nine feet square which showed strongly the influence of Cubism, was praised by fellow-artists and critics as varied as Sickert, Augustus John and Roger Fry. But in October 1913 Lewis had quarrelled bitterly with Fry about a commission which Lewis said should have been given to him, but had instead been intercepted by Fry and passed by him to the Omega Workshops which he ran as a co-operative venture. The round-robin letter issued by Lewis with the support of three others linked to the Omega Workshops said that the venture merely pretended to be avant-garde:

> The Idol is still Prettiness, with its mid-Victorian languish of the neck, and its skin is 'greenery-yallery', despite the Post-What-Not fashionableness of its draperies. This family of Strayed and Dissenting Aesthetes, however, were compelled to call in as much modern talent as they could find, to do the rough and masculine work without which they knew their efforts would not rise above the level of a pleasant tea-party, or command more attention.[25]

The attack was made directly on Fry, who was accused of underhand and dishonest dealing, but the quarrel was really with the Bloomsbury version of Post-Impressionism and Cubism that often confused art with decoration. In March 1914 Lewis, with the financial support of Kate Lechmere, who was first Lewis's and then Hulme's mistress, founded the Rebel Art Centre, in opposition to Bloomsbury and all its works.

Lewis was thirty-one, not by any means a youthful rebel. As man and artist he was a late developer. He was born in Nova Scotia in 1882, on a yacht bought four years earlier by his father, Charles Edward Lewis. 'The old Rip' as his son called him was a lively but idle character fond of hunting and sailing, who was financially supported throughout his life by his prosperous family. When Percy was eleven, his father ran off with a housemaid. Thereafter the boy was in the care of his mother, who was provided with an income by other members of the family. In addition she received occasional gifts from them, and from her husband.

Anne Stuart Lewis was in her early thirties when she was deserted, and the rest of her life was given to the care of her son. Soon after the parting she told her husband that she lived only for

Percy, and 'could not mar his youth so greatly as to have it ever said this his parents were divorced'.[26] She came to England, lived in a number of London suburbs, and added to her uncertain income by starting a dressmaking business. Percy had an undistinguished career at Rugby (paid for by his father), marked only by a gift for painting. He went on to the Slade, which he entered in 1898 and left in 1901, disliked by most of the teachers but greatly admired by fellow-students.

Lewis later said he learned little at the Slade, which he called 'a training of a type so uncraftsmanlike that it surprises me it remained uncriticised'.[27] He spent most of the next seven years wandering about Europe, some of them in Paris and Munich, learning about art and living a bohemian and impoverished life. He became friendly with Augustus John, sired the first of several illegitimate children, and contracted for the first time one of the venereal infections that damaged his health in later years. To maintain this life he depended almost entirely on his mother. With almost every letter she sent him money, sometimes as little as five shillings, rarely more than £2. She accompanied the money with injunctions to economy because times were hard, business poor, cash short. Their relationship was frank and easy, she combining the roles of mother, impartial adviser and indulgent friend. He told her about his love affairs, the people he met, the paintings he looked at, his erratic bowel movements. In October 1905 when the question arose of marriage to his German mistress Ida, Mrs Lewis went to St Pancras Town Hall on his behalf, but 'found I could not give notice of your marriage, *you* must do that . . . Why not have been married in Elberfeld? . . . If you bring the fraulein's sister over here and I am expected to entertain her I do not know what I can do.'[28] Lewis did not come back, although she sent money for his passage, and did not get married. Three years later Ida had his child, and a few months afterwards he separated from her for good. Mrs Lewis was indulgent. She liked Ida, she said, but 'I always thought that the association was unwise, even in the beginning, for you both[29].'

At twenty-seven, when he returned to live in England, Lewis was emotionally still a self-indulgent boy, who refused to consider the need to make a living, was physically attracted by women but intellectually contemptuous of them, liked the easy life of the rich but scorned their concern with money. In other respects, however, he was now formidably equipped to challenge the conventions of his time. He had read a great deal, had formulated a philosophy vague in detail but deliberately tuned to the noise, clatter and movement of the internal combustion engine and all it implied, and was an adult and original visual artist. The end of the would-be potboiler he wrote at this time, a book that found no publisher until 1977, saw the heroine asking her lover, 'the king of aviation, the idol of the people', to 'take me for a fly':

> And soon they were flying for all they were worth over Paris, and to the amazement and delight of the Parisian population, alighted in the open space usually given over to diabolo at the observatory side of the [Luxembourg] gardens, facing the clock of the palace.[30]

Along with a passion for the modern in the form of new shapes and new machinery, Lewis's thinking embraced what might be considered its contrary: an insistence on the importance of what was hieratic, hard and sharply defined, in both graphic and literary work. He looked, now and in the future, for an art whose energy was controlled and confined, photographically still but denying the delicate soft tones a photograph can offer. In literature he aspired to an art that should, like that of Dickens, show character through intense, exaggerated, sometimes caricatural observation of individuals, their shapes, clothing and surroundings. His mouthpiece Tarr, in the novel he was working on at this time, said that art is 'life with all the humbug taken out of it . . . Art is identical with the idea of permanence . . . but life is the idea of the person . . . *Death* is the thing that differentiates art and life.'[31]

Such were the ideas of the figure, tall, thin and swarthy, long-haired and with black coat buttoned to the chin, seen by Ford, then editor of the *English Review*, when according to Ford's story Lewis climbed the stairs to the editor's apartment, found him in the bath, announced his own genius, read the manuscript of his story 'The Pole', and left when Ford had agreed to publish it. It was this figure who in 1909 met Pound for the first time in the Vienna café in New Oxford Street. Pound recalled the occasion in one of the Cantos written during his incarceration in Pisa, and in his passion for the foreign changed Vienna to Wiener. The meeting had come about through Laurence Binyon:

[44]

So it is to Mr Binyon that I owe, initially
Mr Lewis, Mr P. Wyndham Lewis. His bull-dog, me,
   as it were against old Sturge M's bulldog, Mr T. Sturge
Moore's bulldog.[32]

The bulldogs got along badly at first. Lewis described his attitude to Pound as one of complete passivity tinctured with surliness,[33] but Pound was not the man to be deterred by a little surliness. He recognised in Lewis's stories, and in the harsh extraordinary painting and drawings which tended increasingly to abstraction, something new in art and writing. He was delighted to support the Rebel Art Centre, and to be in at the birth of a new art movement. It was Pound who named this movement Vorticism.

The name was a British reply, response to, or contradiction of Italian Futurism. The spokesman of Futurism, although far from its most interesting artist, was F. T. Marinetti, who had lectured on the movement in England in 1910, and now in the spring of 1914 came again to London. Marinetti claimed the English rebels for Futurism, but with the exception of the youthful C.R.W. Nevinson they angrily rejected any such adherence, and led by Lewis broke up a Marinetti poetry reading at which the poet was accompanied by Nevinson beating a drum. Lewis had with him Hulme, the painter Edward Wadsworth and the sculptor Gaudier-Brzeska among others. In June 1914 the large (12 by 14 inches) puce-coloured magazine *Blast* appeared, the first and in appearance most remarkable of the magazines Lewis edited.

Blast, which was announced as a quarterly although in fact the only other issue appeared a year later, contained not one but two general manifestos. Eleven signatures were appended to them, among which those of Aldington, Gaudier-Brzeska, Pound, Wadsworth, William Roberts and Lewis are remembered today. The chief manifesto has the unmistakable stamp of Lewis's style, blending dogmatic and visionary statements. At a preliminary tea party a list of things and people to be Blessed and Blasted was drawn up. Lewis and Pound presided, and exchanged meaningful glances as institutions and individuals were named. England was Blasted for its climate, France for its 'sentimental Gallic gush' and 'Parisian Parochialism', the 'Britannic Aesthete' was called the 'sneak and swot of the schoolroom', Humour the 'quack English drug'. A page of general Blasts included the Post Office, John Galsworthy, the Clan Meynell and the Clan Strachey. But then England was also Blessed, along with the Hairdresser ('Hourly he ploughs heads for sixpence'), English Humour ('the great barbarous weapon of the genius among races'), France, and a page of names known and unknown, including Kate Lechmere who had provided some financial backing for the magazine, Frank Rutter and P. G. Konody (art critics on Lewis's side in the Fry battle), castor oil, the Pope, and the racing crook Robert Sievier. All this was shown in sans serif type, with some letters six inches high. It was difficult to find a printer who would carry out such outrageous typesetting, but Douglas Goldring, editor of a short-lived magazine called *The Tramp*, which had printed work by Lewis, found a jobbing printer in north London prepared to do just what he was told. The typography of *Blast* much impressed other European *avant-garde* artists, particularly those in Tsarist Russia.

The Blasts and Blessings were publicity devices. Inevitably they attracted attention, at the expense of the reproductions of work by Lewis, Roberts, Epstein, Gaudier-Brzeska and others, the story by Rebecca West, the first instalment of a Ford novel, Pound's poems, Lewis's play *The Enemy of the Stars* and his vigorous comments on Futurism, Picasso and other aspects of recent art. At the insistence of John Lane, who published the magazine, three lines in a poem by Pound were blacked out. They said that 'With minds still hovering about their testicles' some French and English poets complained 'In delicate and exhausted metres/That the twitching of three abdominal muscles/Is incapable of producing a lasting Nirvana'. Lewis said the transparency of the black bars laid across the lines helped the sales. In fact, however, these were disappointing, in spite of a preliminary party and a celebratory dinner at the Dieudonné restaurant in Ryder Street attended by a sceptical Amy Lowell, who disapproved of the Blasts and was then in the process of weaning the Imagistes away from Pound.

Was *Blast* a success? It obtained a good deal of notice, for Lewis especially and some of the writers and artists too, but much of this was in the form of ridicule. Lewis was asked to lunch at 10 Downing Street and had some conversation about art with Asquith, then Prime Minister, who saw in the Vortex a political portent. He also met and became friendly with Asquith's confidante Venetia Stanley, who invited him to the opera even though she felt sure that Lewis and his associates would hold up their hands in horror at the idea of listening to Mozart.[34] But *Blast* did not make money, and led to a quarrel with Lechmere about the complicated financial arrangement she had with Lewis. She complained that he was never at the Rebel Art Centre, made no attempt to pay the rent, and reminded him that she had paid £100 towards the production of *Blast*. Lewis replied that she had pictures to cover the money, and their relations became stormy. 'After your behaviour and language of this morning I think it is better that matters should be wound up as soon as possible,' she wrote to him in July 1914, and four months after its opening the Rebel Art Centre closed. Many years later she remembered the occasion more gently, as the time when 'you flapped your new check lined coat at me beating your wings like an old raven and remarking how unobservant women were'.[35]

Blast also made Lewis known in 'society', but although he was a guest at many dinner parties this was chiefly for his curiosity value as a wild man, and few who invited him bought his pictures. He had almost complete supremacy over the small group of artists who followed him. One of them, Frederick Etchells, said at the time of the Fry quarrel that he gave Lewis full power to vote for him, and later wrote reproachfully when accused of betraying a Lewisian confidence, that 'leaving cunts on one side, you're the only person in London I really care to see or talk to'.[36] Another, William Roberts, recalled Lewis's alertness, assurance and provocative swagger, and David Bomberg remembered an evening when Lewis appeared unexpectedly at his East End flat and they had a whole night of conversation at the end of which Bomberg recognised a man 'honouring the same pledge to which I was staking my life'.[37] The two women Vorticists, Jessica Dismorr and Helen Saunders, were both in love with him.

In 1914, just before the war began, Wyndham Lewis had made a reputation as a painter, although hardly as a writer. His chief problem at this time seemed to him lack of money, but in general he had reason for optimism about the future. He did not think much of Pound as a poet but was impressed by the American's energy, and the fact that he contributed to so many periodicals. In 1913, as the result of a meeting with Rebecca West, Pound had taken charge of the literary side of a feminist magazine called the *New Freewoman*.

[47]

To capture the literary pages of a magazine, even one of an eccentric feminist kind, was something Lewis could respect. Pound on his side paid attention, it was said, to the opinions of only two people: Yeats, whom he called the eagle, and Lewis. From the time of *Blast* onwards, Pound and Lewis were firm allies.

4. JAMES JOYCE

In 1913 James Joyce was living in Trieste, as he had been for the past eight years, scraping along by teaching English and giving occasional lectures. In the previous year he had almost been put out of his flat, along with his wife and two children, because of failure to pay the rent. Joyce, on a visit to Ireland when the threat was made, was prepared to be put out on the street *in absentia* (although of course his wife Nora and the children George and Lucia were present), but his brother Stanislaus found the family another and smaller flat and moved their furniture into it. Stanislaus had come out to Trieste some years earlier, at his brother's suggestion. There was a vacancy for an English teacher at the Scuola Berlitz, James said, and Trieste was better than Dublin. Stanislaus was twenty at the time, two and a half years younger than James and temperamentally his opposite, cautious, shrewd and sceptical while James was improvident, volatile and optimistic. Joyce's sister Eileen recalled an occasion when James had been paid for a lesson. There was no other money in the house and he went out to buy food, but returned instead with a hand-painted silk scarf for Nora. Stanislaus pointed out to his brother that, even though 1910 and 1911 had been difficult years, they had made £200 each by teaching, which should have been enough to live on.

Stanislaus, as the diary he kept in his teens showed, was highly intelligent and had literary-critical gifts, but his life was spent in subservience to his brother's genius. James had, he told his diary, 'a wolf-like intellect . . . lean and ravenous, tearing the heart out of his subject'.[38] He told the diary that Jim was often drunk, did not talk decently of women, but had more literary talent than anybody else in Ireland except Yeats. James Joyce listened to his brother, at times quarrelled with him, but paid no lasting attention to what he said. During the Trieste years James had planned at different times to make money by becoming a commission agent for the sale of Irish tweeds in the city, by a career as a professional tenor, and by attempting to win a £250 prize in a puzzle contest. (His entry was a day late.) The most serious of these schemes arose out of a remark made by one of his sisters that there was no cinema in Dublin. Joyce found some Italian businessmen who were running cinemas successfully in Trieste and Bucharest and were prepared to start them in Dublin and give Joyce ten per cent of the profits for his role in originating the scheme and acting as their agent. In that capacity he visited Dublin in 1909, all expenses paid. A site was found, his partners saw and approved it, benches and two hundred Windsor chairs were bought and the Volta cinema opened. It was run by the owner of a bicycle shop in Trieste and, perhaps because of an emphasis on Italian films, quickly failed.[39] Two years later Joyce made what was by his standards a determined attempt to obtain a teaching position in an Italian school, a post that would have given him a regular income. He had to pass examinations set by the Italian government, and did so triumphantly, several with maximum marks. Complications arose, however, because Joyce's Dublin degree did not conform with the requirements of the Italian bureaucracy, and he gave up the idea.

In February 1913 he celebrated his thirty-first birthday. He would have seemed to an outsider who knew something of his background and early promise a perfect example of a talented Irishman who would never amount to anything more than a good singer, a great talker and a companionable drinker. If the outsider had had a sharp tongue he might have added that Jimmy Joyce was always calling himself a writer, and it was a pity that he could never get anything published.

It was true that Joyce's literary career so far had been marked by extreme bad luck. From early childhood he had shown a talent for literature. Sent away from home at the age of six to board at the Jesuit College of Clongowes he memorised passages of Milton, Byron and Newman. When he was nine, encouraged by talk at home about the betrayal of Parnell, he wrote a poem about the leader's fall. He left Clongowes soon afterwards because of family financial problems, and went free of fees to a Jesuit day school, Belvedere College. One of his weekly essays written there has survived, and although it is full of rhetorical flourishes, the range of vocabulary used by the young boy is remarkable. In his mid-teens he was reading Ibsen, and at eighteen he wrote an article about the dramatist that appeared in the *Fortnightly Review*, earned him twelve guineas, and brought a complimentary note from the master sent via the famous critic William Archer. Very soon he was sending Archer his first long literary work, an Ibsenish play called *A Brilliant Career*, and receiving a long considered letter commending his talent but saying that the piece was 'utterly impossible' for the commercial stage.[40] His very ninetyish poems went to Yeats, who wrote a friendly and interested letter about them. George Moore, however, who saw the poems a little later, returned them with the single word: 'Symons'.

Moore was right. Arthur Symons's *The Symbolist Movement in Modern Literature*, published in 1899, had great influence on many writers of Joyce's generation, Pound, Eliot and Conrad Aiken among them. When one reads the book today it seems not much more than a useful introduction to writers who have been written about at greater length and more informatively by later critics – Verlaine, Rimbaud, Mallarmé, Laforgue and others. But at the end of the nineteenth century and in the following decade, what Symons said was a revelation. Here were writers not bound by the everyday and humdrum in either technique or subject, who used unfamiliar styles and rhythms, avoided dull realism and approached poetry instead through the indirection of symbols. In America the book had its effect on writers already oriented towards European models, but in Britain it created a split between those like the Georgians who found Symons's ideas and his advocacy of a group of Frenchmen vaguely unhealthy (would Verlaine or Rimbaud have gone around accompanied by pipe and bulldog like Hodgson?), and those who saw something that could be adapted to their own purposes. Joyce found less in the book than Eliot or Aiken. He was not interested in broken rhythms or ironic juxtapositions, but in his poems blended a little French symbolism with the romanticism of early Yeats and the nostalgic impressionism of Symons's own nineties work, to produce poems that were mostly an imitation of what others were doing better. Symons had mixed feelings about Joyce when they met around this time, but was later staunchly friendly in helping to get Joyce's collection *Chamber Music* published, and writing the first review of it when the volume appeared in 1907.

This first book could not be said to have fulfilled the promise of Joyce's youth, nor to have suggested the emergence of any but a minor talent. Joyce himself had twinges of regret before it appeared, telling Stanislaus these were poems for lovers and he was no love poet, hence they were insincere and indeed fakes. Stanislaus persuaded him against abandoning publication, and he was right in the sense that the poems represent part of Joyce's nature in their wistful nostalgia, their delicate Irish romanticism. *Chamber Music*, predictably, caused no stir, in part because the nineties were over and out of fashion. Reviews were few, and in the first year only 127 copies were sold. Joyce's unhappy relationships with publishers had begun when Grant Richards, to whom he sent the poems, lost the manuscript and then offered to publish the second copy sent to him only if Joyce contributed money towards the book. Undeterred by this, at the end of 1905 Joyce sent to Richards a collection of short stories called *Dubliners*.

Joyce felt more assurance about his short stories than about his poetry, and one cannot doubt that he was right. In a technical sense the fifteen stories in the book as finally published owe something to an early reading of Ibsen, and 'The Dead', perhaps the finest of them, is at times slightly Dickensian. Yet in the context of the time the sympathetic realism of the stories, together with the fine background evocation of Dublin and its people, made them markedly unusual and original. In a way Joyce's choice of Richards was a good one, for he was young, enterprising, and eager to publish new writers. He was, however, also careless, extravagant, and prone to costly experiments like producing fiction in paper covers. He had, as Bernard Shaw told him, an expensive taste for literature.

Richards accepted the book, and passed on to the printer additional stories sent by Joyce without reading them. When, however, the printer objected to setting some passages, Richards told the author that alterations must be made. There ensued a long exchange of letters in which Joyce, having learned what the printer refused to set, pointed out that similar passages had been approved. Richards then objected to them also. He was unmoved when Joyce told him that English literature was the laughing stock of Europe, and finally refused to publish the book. Joyce threatened legal action, but desisted when told by a lawyer that he was unlikely to win the case. *Dubliners* was then rejected by three other publishers. It was accepted in 1909 by the Dublin firm of Maunsel, but one of the partners soon had doubts about it and demanded indemnification against possible prosecution. Three years after Maunsel's acceptance the printed sheets were destroyed, either by fire or by pulping.

Publication was finally achieved in June 1914, eight years after Joyce had signed the first contract. Stanislaus had been promised the dedication of the book but in the event did not get it, something which increased his feeling of being slighted by his brother. The eventual publisher, surprisingly enough, was Richards, who had had a change of heart about the book. When the publisher wrote his autobiography, however, Joyce remained unmentioned.

What was it that Richards, Maunsel, and no doubt the other publishers who rejected the book, found unacceptable? Again in the context of the time, a minority of the stories used objectionable words and phrases. 'Bloody', used in four different stories, would not then have caused the book to be banned except perhaps in Ireland, but Richards did not like it. The printer objected to a man 'having' a girl, and to a woman changing the position of her legs. The Dublin publisher was concerned by vulgar expressions used in 'Ivy Day in the Committee Room', and worried about a Vigilance Committee which was on the lookout for writings of an immoral tendency. And an old friend of Joyce thought 'An Encounter', in which two boys meet a homosexual who talks to them about boys being whipped, and either urinates or masturbates (the story leaves it undefined) on leaving them, was the most outspoken story he had ever read.[41] Such a theme was certainly daring, as was that of 'Two Gallants', in which a young man boasts to a friend about sexual conquests ('There's nothing to touch a good slavey') and takes money from one of them, and of 'Grace', which begins with a drunk falling down the stairs of a pub lavatory so that his clothes are 'smeared with the filth and ooze of the floor on which he had lain'.

In 1913 Richards had not yet re-emerged as publisher. A play called *Exiles*, still uncompleted, seemed likely to have no fortunate fate. *A Portrait of the Artist as a Young Man*, which had been developed from an early draft called *Stephen Hero*, was still unfinished, although Joyce had been working on it for years. At one point he threw the manuscript into the fire, from which it was rescued by his sister. But in 1913 it must have seemed hardly worth completing the book. After all, who would publish it? Joyce was naturally optimistic, yet it must have seemed to him sometimes that the promise of his youth, when he had won the admiration of all his Irish friends and a great future had been predicted for him, would remain forever unfulfilled. His total published work was one small collection of poems.

In December of this gloomy year Joyce received a letter from Ezra Pound, a name he is unlikely to have known. Pound said he was informally connected with two papers, the *Egoist* and the *Cerebralist* (which expired after a single issue), and also collected material for two American papers, the *Smart Set* and *Poetry*. Yeats had mentioned Joyce's name, and Pound would be pleased to read anything he cared to send, although 'I . . . don't in the least know that I can be of any use to you – or you to me'. He briskly added that Joyce should mark a minimum price on anything he sent, as well as the figure he would like to receive.[42]

This must have sounded encouragingly businesslike. Before Joyce could reply another letter arrived, saying that Yeats had shown Pound the poem 'I Hear an Army', and Pound would like to use it in his anthology *Des Imagistes*. In this second letter Pound said money was not the primary object of himself or his friends. 'We do it for larks and to have a place for marketing modern stuff.'[43]

The relationship thus casually established was within a few years to change Joyce's fortunes and his life.

5. T.S. ELIOT

In 1909 Conrad Aiken was standing outside the door of the *Harvard Lampoon* when 'a singularly attractive, tall and rather dapper young man with a somewhat Lamian smile' came reeling out and embraced him. A friend said that the embrace 'if Tom remembers it to-morrow, will cause him to suffer agonies of shyness'.[44] This was the first meeting between Aiken and T. S. Eliot, the start of a friendship between two poets which lasted throughout their lives, yet was never altogether easy. In later days, when both were established writers, Eliot was sometimes to say that he wished he could help Aiken, although he made little practical attempt to do so, and Aiken to complain that Eliot kept him at arm's length and, while full of protestations of friendliness, never went further than to say that they must have dinner one night next month, or the year after next.[45] Any alienation, although that is too strong a word, was on Eliot's side. Perhaps he did not care to be reminded of their close literary association at Harvard, perhaps he thought little of Aiken's poetry, or it may be that as Aiken suggested he was conscious of a debt to some of his friend's work and did not wish to acknowledge it.[46]

It is possible also that Eliot, who had an intellectual desire for order, was aware of his friend's emotional instability, and found it uncongenial. The course of Aiken's life and poetry was determined by the tragedy of his childhood, when at the age of eleven he heard revolver shots in the next room and went in to find that his father had shot his wife and then himself. Aiken's writing was frequently an attempt to explain to himself, often in psychoanalytical terms, this event and its effect on him. He did so most clearly not in poems, but in the remarkable, neglected novel *Great Circle*. In social life, however, Aiken was not melancholy but a lively talker and charming companion, susceptible to women and a steady drinker. At Harvard he was poetically under Masefield's influence but would have agreed with Eliot in finding the American literary scene between the beginning of the century and 1914 a complete blank. Eliot said later that he could not recall the name of a single American poet writing in the period that he had read, and that there was no poet in England or America who would have been of use to a beginner in 1908.[47]

What then did the beginners read? In the Union Library Arthur Symons and the Symbolist poets were encountered and rifled, and Eliot later acknowledged his great debt to Symons. It was through him that the young man heard of Laforgue and Rimbaud, began to read Verlaine and eventually came to Corbière. That current of French poetry stemming from Baudelaire, Eliot said, had affected all the English poetry of the time that mattered. Aiken perhaps would not have agreed entirely, in part because he was never so proficient in French as Eliot and so took from the Symbolists only a general sense of the possibilities in a more flexible use of rhyme and line-lengths than was in favour at the time.[48]

Eliot, born in 1888, was a year older than his friend. He was brought up in St Louis, the last among the six surviving children of a successful businessman. Thomas Stearns Eliot was physically the runt of the litter, born with a double hernia which necessitated the wearing of a truss. His eldest sister Ada was nineteen years his senior, his only brother Henry nine years his elder. He grew up, as such children often do, highly intelligent and spoiled by the rest of the family. His sister and brother in later life talked more about their father than their mother, but Tom was devoted to his mother and by most accounts much less close to his father with whom he shared, however, a liking for practical jokes. He also admired Ada, the most intellectual of the family, and later said that she was the Mycroft to his Sherlock Holmes.

The young Eliot, like the young Joyce, was precocious. At the age of eleven he brought out eight issues of a magazine called *The Fireside*, edited and written by T. S. Eliot, the T. S. Eliot Company, St Louis.[49] At fourteen he was overwhelmed by Fitzgerald's *Rubaiyat*, and when he went to Harvard in 1906 after a year at Boston's famous Milton Academy he was already formidably well-read. His reading, like that of many American students, was wide rather than concentrated, ranging at Harvard from German grammar through Greek and French literature to ancient and modern philosophy. Unlike most students, however, he worked with intensity. Barred by his physical disability from sports, and still physically frail, he became a scholar. It was as an impartially interested scholar that he studied Sanskrit and oriental religion, attended the Sorbonne in 1911 and listened to Bergson's lectures. By 1913 he seemed to have settled down to a life spent in Harvard's philosophy department, while contemplating a thesis on the ideas of F. H. Bradley, whose insistence on the existence of an Absolute and distrust of any kind of relativism had a strong appeal to a young man looking for certainties. His interest in Bradley's ideas was perhaps also a reaction against the Unitarianism in which he had been brought up. Eliot's grandfather had been a Unitarian minister, and Bradley's absolutism must have seemed refreshing set against the finicky distinctions of Unitarian doctrine. In 1914 he took up the option of a travelling scholarship offered him by Harvard, planning to complete the thesis on Bradley at Merton College, Oxford.[50] In August of that year he came to England, after some time spent in Germany, Belgium and Italy. He felt as great a distaste as Pound for cultural America but was by no means fleeing his native country, and did not intend to make England his permanent home.

Eliot said in later life that he had been a priggish child, and it would be fair to add that he grew up into a priggish young man. The

letters he wrote to Aiken as he moved through Europe are touched
by a distinct condescension towards the Continent. He found an air
of putridity in Bruges and other old towns, thought much of Italy
stank in the same way, and regarded the summer spent in Germany
as a period of exile, although he liked German food. The effect of
Blast on him was made apparent in a series of Blasts and Blessings
at the top of one letter.[51] He sent Aiken poems with which he
expressed dissatisfaction. What would be a good basis for poetry? A
commonplace happiness, he suggested, although it might also be
stimulating to have several women fall in love with him.[52] When
he got to Merton he found Oxford pleasant but intellectually
unexciting.

Eliot was in outward appearance suave and calm, in manner and
dress conventional. In company he was shy, unaggressive, inclined
to silence. Some thought him handsome, others like Bertrand
Russell found him lacking in vigour. This stiff, slightly stuffy figure
was a perfectly 'real' Eliot, and he could present such an appearance
to strangers until the end of his life. There was, however, an equally
'real' Eliot who enjoyed practical jokes and verbal tricks, was sharply
critical of the literary skills and sensibilities of his contemporaries,
took much pleasure in music hall turns, and found an outlet for the
sexual repression of conventional Mr Eliot in writing obscene verses
about King Bolo and His Great Black Queen. The King Bolo
verses, written to Aiken and other friends, are in the manner of the
famous 'Good Ship Venus', but lack the fantastic pornographic wit
of lines like those about the cabin boy named Dipper who 'stuffed
his arse with broken glass and circumcised the skipper', although
they sometimes deal with similar material. They amused Eliot,
however, and he continued to send them to friends for several years.
In writing to Aiken he Blessed and Blasted characters from the Bolo
saga.

It was conventional Mr Eliot who wrote the competent, intelligent, but rarely very original poems which appeared in the *Harvard
Advocate*. When he graduated from Milton Academy in 1905 he
recited a poem still showing Fitzgeraldian influence, in which he
reflected that the yearly student classes were

> A bubble on the surface of the stream,
> A drop of dew upon the morning grass . . .

One of the more interesting of these early poems is 'Spleen', which in some phrases prefigures 'Prufrock' and also suggests Eliot's feeling for Bradleyan philosophy when it pictures Life, punctiliously suited, hat and gloves in hand, waiting 'on the doorstep of the Absolute'. 'The Death of Saint Narcissus', suppressed in proof, contains several lines later used almost without alteration in *The Waste Land*.[53] 'The Love Song of J. Alfred Prufrock' was written in 1911 and, like 'Spleen', was markedly different from the work produced before Eliot had read the French Symbolists. He did not attempt to publish it, but Aiken made a copy of the poem, presumably with the poet's consent, and showed it to Harold Monro. The owner of the Poetry Bookshop said he thought the poem 'absolutely insane', a remark indicating the gap that yawned between Georgian standards and what was soon to be called modernism.

In 1914 T. S. Eliot was entirely unknown as a literary figure. He too was to establish a reputation in the following five years, with considerable help from Ezra Pound.

CHAPTER THREE

The Nature of Modernism

I. THE BACKGROUND

It seems right at this point to deal with some reasonable questions. Why did writers and visual artists feel that drastic changes had to be made in approaching art and literature? Why should poets have wanted to change and loosen the rhythm of their work and painters have become so much concerned with speed and machinery? What was the *need* for free verse?

Such questions are misconceived insofar as they consider the arts of painting, poetry and fiction as a kind of seamless carpet with an unchanging pattern. The carpet was never seamless, and the pattern changed continually. In Britain it shifted in art dramatically from Reynolds to Constable, in drama from Elizabethan blank verse to Restoration comedy. If the process of change was less dramatic in America it was because traditions there were based on British models so wholly accepted that only a talent as original as Whitman's could break away from them decisively. The belief that the basis of poetry in the English language was to be found in the lyrics of Palgrave's *Golden Treasury* may seem absurd today but was widespread in 1914. It was, indeed, taken for granted by most of the contributors to *Georgian Poetry*.

If we go on to ask why such changes took place, the answers cannot be plotted like a graph on a chart or tested like a scientific theory, even though they clearly involve social, economic and technical developments. An example particularly relevant to this book will make the point: the change from standard eighteenth-century diction in poetry to the language used in *Lyrical Ballads*. In demonstrating the need for change, Wordsworth used for comparison a sonnet by Gray in which the sun was called 'reddening Phoebus', birds joined in 'amorous descant', and fields put on 'their green attire'. Wordsworth proposed to replace such language by poetry written in 'a selection of language really used by men':

> Poetry sheds no tears 'such as Angels weep', but natural and human tears; she can boast of no celestial ichor that distinguishes her vital juices from that of prose; the same human blood circulates through the veins of them both.

But the changes effected by the Lake poets were not only a matter of language. They had their roots also in two revolutions, the French, which at the time roused Wordsworth's enthusiasm, and the Industrial which he abhorred. Against the vision of humanity degraded by industrial toil Wordsworth and Coleridge opposed an ideal image of Man and Nature, and their romantic successors Keats and Shelley enlarged this into the idea that man was unique and almost divine. The change was both philosophical and social. To the Augustans man was a unit in society, and they would have thought it impious to suppose anything else. For Shelley, however, man aspired to divinity, and not only man but all human creation. When he wrote that a skylark was not a bird but a blithe spirit, he meant what he said. It was an observation that Pope or Dryden would have found absurd or incomprehensible.

Technical development may involve cultural change, but throughout the nineteenth century the vast social changes brought by the Industrial Revolution were not matched by comparable shifts in literature. The novel developed and flowered because it necessarily reflects the life of a time, and by the end of the century many novelists in Britain and America were treating their subjects in ways that mirrored contemporary manners, morals and social habits. Poetry, however, still derived its impulses and language from the Romantic movement, with results that became feebler in each decade. The British poets of the second half of the nineteenth century all look minor when put beside Wordsworth, Byron, Coleridge and the early Tennyson, although some may well have been as talented. Browning, Hardy, Hopkins, Meredith, Clough, all found themselves struggling against the inert language in which the characteristic poetry of the time was written. They tried to move out of the sluggish main stream through eccentricities of language, often with remarkable results. But by the end of the century even so great a poet as Yeats was, in his earlier incarnations, dwelling in the Celtic

The Founding Fathers

twilight of a language that had lost power and savour because it no longer bore a relation to contemporary ways of thought and feeling.

In part, then, the rebellion of the men of 1914 was against an outmoded diction, like Wordsworth's against the Augustans. But poets, painters and novelists rebelled also against an art quite unlinked to modern life. Perhaps the world is always in a state of chassis, as is suggested in *Juno and the Paycock*, but at some times this is more evident than at others, and it seemed wonderfully or painfully clear to those who thought of themselves as belonging to the twentieth and not the nineteenth century. Tennyson had felt it his duty to approve the mechanical marvels of science in 'Locksley Hall' but he did so uneasily, and no other important Victorian poet concerned himself with the spread of the railway network or the development of electricity. When the late Victorian John Davidson wrote a long poem about the Crystal Palace he said that nothing could make its glass and iron beautiful, and looked forward to a time when men would 'abhor you, and destroy you and repent!'[1] The Georgian poets, naturally enough, averted their eyes and thoughts from machinery. There were Victorian painters who exploited the pictorial dramatic possibilities of the railway, but they used it only as an accessory to human drama, tearful hellos and farewells. They would have seen no point in the blessing of 'ports, restless machines' in *Blast*, nor in its emphasis on the virtues of

> Scooped out basins
> heavy insect dredgers
> monotonous cranes
> stations
> lighthouses, blazing through the frosty starlight
>   cutting the storm like a cake
> beaks of infant boats, side by side,
> heavy chaos of wharves,
> steep walls of factories
> womanly town

Nor would they have approved the blessing of England as 'Industrial island machine, pyramidal workshop'.[2]

The Futurist movement had begun in 1909, when Marinetti issued the 'Foundation Manifesto of Futurism', and it died or faded away during World War I. Its announced intentions were to depict and celebrate in art the speed, constant movement and volatility of modern life, and to make a similar celebration in words through declamatory readings accompanied by noise machines and megaphones. In particular Futurism exalted youth and action. The initial Manifesto praised 'aggressive action, the mortal leap, the punch and the slap'. The beauty of speed was expressed in the motorcar: 'a roaring car that seems to ride on grapeshot is more beautiful than the Victory of Samothrace.' War was glorified, museums, libraries and academies were objects to be destroyed, along with moralism and feminism. In a rousing burst of infantile nihilism the Manifesto urged Futurists to 'set fire to the library shelves ... flood the museums! ... Take up your pickaxes, your axes and hammers and wreck, wreck the venerable cities, pitilessly!'[3]

In the next four years there followed a battery of manifestos from Italian painters, musicians, photographers and sculptors, including in 1913 the Futurist Manifesto of Lust ('Art and war are the great manifestations of sensuality: lust is their flower').[4] A year earlier a Futurist Exhibition in London caused much indignation. Sir Philip Burne-Jones said that the paintings were altogether outside the pale of art, the *Morning Post* refused to print a review of the show, and cartoonists had a field day.[5] Marinetti, who knew exactly how to exploit and scandalise the press, was delighted. London, he said, was a Futurist city, full of coloured flashing advertisement lights, garish posters, brightly coloured motor buses, above all full of *movement*. When he came over in 1914, just before the appearance of *Blast*, Marinetti performed at the Coliseum, offering among other things 'A Meeting of Motor-Cars and Aeroplanes' done with the help of twenty-three noise organs operated by a fellow-Futurist.

In artistic terms Marinetti was a clown, and Futurist contributions to literature were never more than jokes or trivialities. In art, however, some of the painters who adhered to the view of the Technical Manifesto that what appeared on canvas should no longer be 'a fixed *moment* in universal dynamism' but 'the *dynamic sensation* itself'[6] produced work that still looks remarkable. Such Futurist paintings sought to exemplify the idea that everything in the universe intermingled in a great mêlée of splintered bodies, buses, furniture, houses, literally everything blended in one great whirling pudding. ('Our bodies penetrate the sofas upon which we sit, the sofas penetrate our bodies.') Paintings like Balla's 'Dynamics of a Dog on

[61]

a Leash' and 'Little Girl Running on a Balcony', Bragaglia's 'Young Man Rocking', Boccioni's 'Burst of Laughter', Severini's 'Party in Montmartre' show the splintering, the speed, the simultaneity, demanded by the Technical Manifesto, although perhaps it might also be said that they were trying to reproduce photographic experiments in paint.

The vitality Futurism engendered was brief: the emphasis on motion had its obvious limitations, and even if World War I had not over-fulfilled the demand for destructive action, the movement could not have lasted long. The limitations are implied in the Futurist aesthetic. If you are committed to showing the flux of movement in every painting and sculpture, it is inevitable that you must soon repeat yourself.

The Futurists did not flinch from fulfilling the implications of their manifestos. Balla, Carra, Marinetti, Luigi Russolo and the architect Antonio Sant'Elia, all enlisted in the Volunteer Cyclists (plenty of movement in a bicycle wheel) as soon as Italy entered the war. Marinetti and Russolo were badly wounded, Sant'Elia killed in action, and the movement's most lucid theorist Boccioni died after a fall from a horse. The last sound of Futurism came from Balla in 1918 when he praised 'the Futurist Universe' in terms of gleaming electric irons, the architectural qualities of typewriters, dancing shoes, multi-coloured parasols, all of them superior to 'the grimy little pictures' found on studio walls.[7] Within a few years the surviving Futurists, in particular Severini and Carra, had changed altogether their approach to painting.

The originality of the best artists in the movement can be seen by comparing their work with that of its only English adherent, C. R. W. Nevinson, whose paintings at the time were never more than cleverly derivative, particularly of Severini and Boccioni. The most remarkable Futurist talent was that of Sant'Elia, who was twenty-eight when killed in action. His designs for La Città Nuova, for power stations and blocks of flats, have a visionary originality and power. The Pompidou Beaubourg centre must owe something to Sant'Elia's design for a block on three street levels, with external lifts 'swarming up the façades like serpents of glass and iron'.

The total rejection of humanist and liberal views is what marks off Futurism from such purely technical developments as Cubism. The other Futurists did not have Marinetti's desire for the total destruction of existing civilisation, nor the basic contempt for art which made him a precursor of Dada rather than an appropriate leader for a movement most of whose adherents believed with Boccioni that 'motion and light destroy the materiality of bodies', and that this could be shown in painting. Yet although the other Futurists did not emulate their leader's bloodthirsty rhetoric, they had a similar hatred of everything traditionally accepted as art, calling for a destruction in sculpture of 'the traditional "sublime" ' and demanding that painters should 'destroy the cult of the past, the obsession with the ancients, pedantry and academic formalism' (Painting Manifesto, 1910). The philosophy behind Futurism's 'dynamic movement' emphasised the importance of continual change, the value of impermanence. There was no doubt a contradiction in placing little or no value on individual lives yet praising things like aeroplanes, steamers, railway stations and bridges which implied the existence of people, and even their mastery of the machines. Futurists, it might be said, were prepared to admit the role of human beings in the world, provided they understood their essential subordination to machines in a universe of 'dynamic sensation' and *didn't last too long.*

How did Vorticism differ from Futurism? Near the end of his life Lewis said that 'Vorticism . . . was what I, personally, did, and said, at a certain period.'[8] This begs rather than answers the question. There is a view, which seems to me too solemn, that when Pound thought of the name he had in mind the spiral patterns that nineteenth-century astronomers found in star systems.[9] It was, surely, chosen rather to represent the still point of maximum energy in the midst of conflicting forces, as there is said to be stillness at the heart of a whirlpool. Pound compared the vortex also to any kind of geyser, from jetting sperm which would repopulate Britain with active and vigorous animals, to the violence of a storm at sea, and said it would 'sweep out the past century as surely as Attila swept across Europe'.[10]

That was a phrase Marinetti might have used, and *Blast*'s encomiums on cranes, dredgers and factories were similar to the Futurist enthusiasm for trains, railway stations and bridges. There is no doubt that Lewis and Pound were impressed by what Lewis called the vivacity and high spirits of the Futurists, and by the multiple manifestos. The movements shared a rejection of much

[63]

past art, and in particular nineteenth-century painting, yet their philosophies were far from identical, and Vorticist painting and drawing differed as much from Futurism as both did from Cubism. *Blast* neither glorified war nor applauded the idea of the glorious canvases drifting helplessly, and Lewis specifically deplored the 'war-talk' which he said Marinetti had picked up from Nietzsche.

It might be asked why H. G. Wells was not regarded as a prophet by adherents to the tenets of these art movements. He had envisaged many mechanical marvels and horrors, invented an invisible man, anticipated the tank and a war of the worlds in which invading Martians arrived in space cylinders and destroyed their enemies by heat rays. But Wells's basic message was optimistic, and he viewed the marvels he invented with a schoolboy's enthusiasm, as tools which mankind could use well or badly. To such a view Lewis was totally antipathetic – as Wells wrote to him some years later, 'You have a mind alien to mine.'[11] For Lewis the interest of machines was that they were non-human, something separate from 'Life'. From such a point of view Wells's attitude to machinery was romanticism of an uninteresting kind. 'In a Vorticist Universe we don't get excited at what we have invented.' And Futurism also, in its desire for movement and action, was in the service of Life – Life not seen, as Lewis thought it should be, as 'good dinner, sleep and copulation' and nothing more, but as an abode of emotion, 'a hospital for the weak and incompetent':

> 'Life' is a retreat of the defeated.
> It is very salubrious – The cooking is good –
> Amusements are provided.[12]

The Vorticist not only made a distinction between Art and Life, he believed that Life was Art's positive enemy. Comically but with a touch of seriousness, or seriously with a touch of comedy, Lewis proclaimed that

> The Vorticist does not suck up to Life.
> He lets Life know its place in a Vorticist Universe!

The art that proceeded from these conclusions differed from Futurist art in being deliberately static. In a typical Futurist painting things are whirling about in a form generally circular. A characteristic Vorticist painting is composed of sharply angled lines and blocks of colour, the colours for the most part hard and harsh, bitter yellows, savage blacks, grating blues, deliberately avoiding any possible accusation of 'good taste'. Figures are to be seen dancing, laughing or quarrelling, often with a suggestion of violence, the violence always controlled. Such remarks apply particularly to Lewis's work up to 1914, but they are relevant also to paintings like Roberts's 'Dancers' of the same period, and work by Wadsworth and Etchells. The last two in particular abandoned, under the influence of Vorticism, the delicate, conventional naturalistic work they were producing as late as 1912. It is not likely that the other Vorticists accepted wholly Lewis's ideas about the opposition between Life and Art, or believed in the definition Lewis put into the mouth of his spokesman Tarr in the novel with that title: '*Deadness* is the first condition of art . . . The second is absence of *soul*, in the sentimental human sense. The lines and masses of the statue are its soul . . . It has no inside. This is another condition of art; *to have no inside*, nothing you cannot see.'[13] But one may be influenced by a theory without fully understanding it, and the best of the Vorticists were rowelled into producing very personal and original work.

Futurism, Vorticism and modernist literature are linked by the ideas of Hulme, for whom a belief in the possibilities open to mankind seemed merely a perversion of religion, so that he regarded romantic poets and artists alike as flying away into 'the circumambient gas'. He would have agreed heartily that a statue could have no soul, and to those who said that modern art was not beautiful he responded that 'If a work is intended to satisfy a desire and mental need different from your own, it will necessarily appear to you to be grotesque and meaningless.'[14] The social implications of such views were greatly attractive to Lewis and Eliot. The position Hulme adumbrated but never exactly defined was opposed to any idea that social improvement could be reached through better living conditions or by forcing education on those who did not know the alphabet, was hostile to feminism, and was contemptuous of the hypocrisies that were an inevitable part of late nineteenth- and early twentieth-century liberalism. Lewis accepted and later expanded on Hulme's thought about the break-up of Renaissance humanism, and on his praise of Sorel as 'a revolutionary who is anti-democratic, an absolutist in ethics, rejecting all rationalism and relativism'.[15] Eliot in 1916 was giving lectures on French literature which discussed romanticism and its opposite, the romantic being conceived as an adherent of Rousseau, his classical opposite as a believer in Original Sin. A few years later Eliot acknowledged his debt to Hulme, calling him 'classical, reactionary and revolutionary . . . the antipodes of the eclectic, tolerant and democratic mind of the last century'. Hulme's ideas, Eliot said, 'should be the twentieth-century mind, if the twentieth century is to have a mind of its own'.[16] Classical, reactionary *and revolutionary*: neither Eliot nor Lewis saw any contradiction in a technically revolutionary art opposed to revolutionary change in society. This was a basic feature of much modernist art and literature.

It is doubtful if Pound at this time held any views that could properly be described as political, although even in youth he expressed contempt for what he called the mob. Vorticism provided a better picture of the new than Imagism and had as its leader a figure Pound admired. But his most permanent occupation was the attempt to free his own poetry from the tangle of past literature in which his early work had been embedded. Typically, he attempted to do this through immersion in other and still earlier poets. Once it had been Swinburne and Browning and Dowson, then the Provençal ballad makers, Anglo-Saxon verse, then again Chinese poetry. His Chinese versions or translations in *Cathay* were praised, and nobody else was doing anything like them, but Pound must have worried about whether they were really new.

It is fair enough, and natural enough, to laugh at Pound's posing and pedantry, his shrill voice and the play he made with stick and pince-nez. His anti-Semitism was even then noticeable (a poem in *Blast* exhorted readers to be 'done with Jews and Jobbery' and to 'SPIT upon those who fawn on the JEWS for their money'), and so was his frequent pretence to more influence than he possessed. Yet his sensibility to what was fresh and interesting in literature at this time was unique, even though he tended to regard the writers whose cause he took up as his personal property, and to fall out with them if they seemed to fail in continual novelty. He was an early advocate of the unknown Robert Frost, and reviewed Frost's first collection *A Boy's Will* not only in England, but in *Poetry* as well. Pound, however, saw Frost as a simple home-grown American who might be moulded into a modern poet. He may have annoyed Frost by urging him to write free verse, and certainly did so by sending a poem of Frost's to the *Smart Set* without the writer's permission, but the basic differences between them arose from the speedy realisation by both men that Frost was not, in Pound's terms, modern. The fact that Pound was a decade the junior of the two no doubt added to Frost's feeling that he was being patronised, a feeling vented in a poem in which he accused Pound of being concerned only with his power to 'Thrust anything upon the world/Were it never so humble'. Pound remained genial, as he usually did in personal matters, but thereafter excluded Frost from the pantheon of modernity.

Pound was also able to appreciate at least some of D. H. Lawrence's merits, telling Monroe that they were lucky to get him for *Poetry*, and saying that Lawrence had been before him in understanding the proper treatment of modern subjects. But Lawrence's emphasis on the importance of 'Life' for a writer, and his lack of interest in the ideas behind literary movements (he was the only poet to appear in both Georgian and Imagist collections, although neither a Georgian nor an Imagist) meant that the two soon found they had little in common. At first meeting Lawrence thought Pound was a bit of a genius, and the admiration seems to have been reciprocated. Soon, however, Pound was calling Lawrence a detestable person, and Lawrence was mercilessly mimicking Pound's shrill voice and his affectations. Pound's dislike did not lead him to deny Lawrence's talent, and he admired the Englishman's readiness to treat tabooed subjects in fiction. Otherwise he regarded both Lawrence and Frost as writers whose conventional use of language put them outside the modern movement.

2. LANGUAGE AND SUBJECT

A look at the books most mentioned and most praised in 1914 shows how writers, poets particularly, were working in a tradition almost wholly drained of worth. In March and April Henry James contributed to *The Times Literary Supplement* two long articles on 'the younger generation' of novelists. The six writers he chose to represent the hope and future of English letters were Arnold Bennett, Gilbert Cannan, Joseph Conrad, Compton Mackenzie,

The Founding Fathers

Hugh Walpole and H. G. Wells, with a friendly side glance at Edith Wharton. Of these, Conrad was in his early sixties, and Bennett and Wells over fifty, so that this was hardly a younger generation. More important, however, was the fact that all of them, with the possible exception of Cannan, accepted the standards and manners of Victorian or Edwardian society. The prose style they used was that of the Victorian novel, and they saw no reason to diverge from it (as Meredith, and Wilde in his single novel, had variously diverged). Alone among them Wells was regarded as a social rebel, but in fiction he had hardly earned this reputation. The novels by Wells that questioned accepted social *mores*, like *Ann Veronica* and *Marriage*, did so with the earnestness of the Fabian reformer Wells was, rather than with any particular imaginative originality. Of the younger writers Mackenzie and Walpole were set in the Edwardian age, and showed no awareness that any new themes, attitudes or styles called for attention.

In the same year *The Times Literary Supplement*, a useful guide to current opinion then as now, praised warmly Wells's *The Wife of Sir Isaac Harman*, and gave qualified approval to Cannan's *Old Mole*, but was not enthusiastic about the second volume of Mackenzie's *Sinister Street*, Bennett's *The Price of Love* or Walpole's *The Duchess of Wrexe*. Joyce's *Dubliners* received a fairly short and tepid review. The periodical's real enthusiasm was reserved for novels by William de Morgan and Gerald O'Donovan, whose *Waiting*, a novel about 'the Irish Question', was said to contain a scene 'not unworthy of Swift'. In America the most popular novels of the year were written by Eleanor H. Porter, the American novelist Winston Churchill, W. J. Locke, Booth Tarkington, and Frances Hodgson Burnett. The American novel was thought to be in a poor way, and the *Bookman* published an article asking 'Where Is the Man?', the Man being the true American novelist. Dreiser was dismissed as vastly overrated, and the writer came up with the names of Jack London, Upton Sinclair and Henry Sydnor Harrison, the last recommended as a writer 'altogether free from the taint of vulgarity'. An article by W. L. George, trying to discover 'the young giant who will one day make the sacred footprints on the sands of time' most recently trodden in George's view by Bennett, Wells and Galsworthy, did not mention a single American name.

The poetry most highly praised in *The Times Literary Supplement* during the year was a new volume by Masefield, said to show 'a loveliness always transfigured by the inward assurance of a beauty within', and the *Collected Poems* of Margaret L. Woods, which received a lead review headed 'A Woman's Genius', and evoked comparisons with Gray and Browning. Frost's second volume *North of Boston* was put last among five books, the others all by poets long forgotten. *New Numbers*, a collection of Georgians including Brooke and Abercrombie, was called a brave, bold venture. An article in the American *Bookman* certified poetry healthy in Britain but not in the United States, and another piece by William Aspenwall Bradley said that the writers renewing the inspiration of English poetry were those like Masefield and Abercrombie, 'least inclined to question the old metrical conventions'. *Des Imagistes* was briefly and tartly reviewed.

Not an exhilarating year, 1914, as seen in such official records. The giants named were all figures established for years or even decades, and those mentioned as possible successors were possessed of only modest talents. In poetry, indeed, nothing at all in the way of a youthful giant was visible. It was not necessary to believe with Pound that Ford and Yeats were the only writers of worth in London, and that Bennett, Galsworthy and their followers were 'unspeakable canaille',[17] to see that the structure of the House of Letters in Britain was shaky, ready for destruction. (In America the House had not been built.) The chosen weapon for the twentieth-century revolution was, as it had been for Wordsworth and Coleridge, language. The Edwardians and Georgians accepted that there was a particular language in which poetry should be written, and that some subjects should not be treated in prose fiction. Modernist writers questioned both these assumptions.

Almost a century earlier Carlyle, writing to his friend John Sterling in justification of his own allusive, colloquial, and as many of his contemporaries thought barbarous and almost unintelligible style, said:

> If one has thoughts not hitherto uttered in English books, I see nothing for it but you must use words *not* found there, must *make* words . . . With whole ragged battalions of Scott's novel Scotch, with Irish, German, French, and even newspaper Cockney . . . storming in on us, and the whole structure of our Johnsonian English breaking up from its foundations, revolution *there* is visible as everywhere else.[18]

The Founding Fathers

Similar thoughts were in the minds of Joyce, Lewis and Eliot. In Joyce's case they were to result in an explosion of language, the compound words and neologisms sparkling like roman candles, whirring like catherine wheels, the puns startling as firecrackers. Joyce *made* words, in Carlyle's phrase, in part for the sheer pleasure of it, but also because his desire to convey aspects of human feeling and experience never before put down in print demanded new forms of expression. Lewis invented no words, but his use of language, already glimpsed in his contributions to *Blast* and fully apparent when *Tarr* appeared in print, used words and phrases as though they were metal blocks to be set against each other, the effect jarring and disturbing, so that even passages of dialogue gave the impression of powerful forces struggling for supremacy. A first encounter with the work of Joyce after *Dubliners* and Lewis after *Blast* was likely to make those accustomed to reading Galsworthy, Wells and Bennett, even James and Conrad, cry out that this was not fiction as they knew it, nor as it should be written.

An even greater shock awaited those who read Eliot's poems. Again the chief barrier was that of language, for many readers and writers were sure that this was not the language of poetry. Casual and apparently random lines, conversations, odd juxtapositions, drops into triviality, lines about the stale smell of beer and steaks in passageways, were utterly unacceptable to established critics and poets, the more so because such phrases were apparently not to be regarded as light verse, but advanced with serious intentions. Arthur Waugh spoke for many when he said that Eliot's and Pound's poetry, as found in the *Catholic Anthology 1914–1915* edited by Pound, represented literary licence reduced to absurdity. If 'the unmetrical, incoherent banalities of these literary "Cubists" were to triumph, the State of Poetry would be threatened with anarchy'. Waugh thought this unlikely. 'From such a catastrophe the humour, commonsense, and artistic judgment of the best of the new "Georgians" will assuredly save their generation.'[19] Eliot was represented in the collection by 'The Love Song of J. Alfred Prufrock'.

The fact that their writing was unlikely to be popular was accepted by the men of 1914. They were the first writers not just to exemplify the split in literary culture between 'Highbrow' and 'Lowbrow' that had begun in 1850 with the publication of the pre-Raphaelite *The Germ*, the first 'little' magazine, but also consciously to accept that division. They may have wished for a wide readership, but knew they were not likely to get it. They were not writing for money, as do most novelists and journalists, and among them perhaps only Pound positively expected to make a living by his pen. In 1912 he told his prospective father-in-law that his income from writing was £400 a year,[20] on which it would have been possible for a couple to live with reasonable comfort, but this was probably doubling the actual amount. In the year from November 1914 to October 1915 his earnings were only £42 10s, so that he was in effect supported by his wife's annuity of £150 a year. Pound sometimes complained of poverty but was still ready to write articles without payment.

Of the others Joyce, as has been said, was scratching a living in Trieste, helped by Stanislaus, hampered by his own spendthrift nature. Lewis at this time regarded writing as an adjunct to painting in a monetary sense. *Tarr* remained unfinished in 1914. His mother now often asked for support. In a letter of 1912 she said that he should come back from Belgium, 'get yourself tested on Sunday and see your publisher as *early* as you can Monday – I want that money awfully'. The testing possibly related to a venereal infection. In another letter she told him, 'money *frightfully* scarce – try to get me £10 by Friday.'[21] Perhaps Lewis helped her, although like Joyce when he had money he spent it. Of the four only Eliot took an extra-literary job that brought in a regular income. In 1915 he married Vivien Haigh-Wood, and when she became ill shortly after the marriage, and doctors' fees had to be paid, Eliot took a post as schoolmaster at Highgate Junior School. He disliked teaching, resigned at the end of 1916, and after a brief attempt to make a living as a freelance reviewer, obtained a position in Lloyds Bank on the recommendation of his wife's family. That, however, lay in the future. Throughout 1914 and until his marriage Eliot remained free of financial responsibilities, reading philosophy at Merton in a slightly desultory way, writing poems, and doing a lot of reading outside of what was required for his philosophical thesis.

These were, to use Lewis's later phrase for Auden and his friends, the new men in the landscape, although their presence went almost unnoticed. Through the enterprise of Ezra Pound it was now to be made apparent.

[71]

CHAPTER FOUR

The *Egoist* and the *Little Review*

I. THE FIRST ANGEL: HARRIET SHAW WEAVER

For some time Pound had longed to be the directing power of a literary magazine, print the work of writers he admired, act as their impresario, make sure they read the right books, met the right people, had enough to eat. His connection with *Poetry* was maintained, but he was fretful about Monroe's conservatism and caution. What he wanted was an angel who would start a new magazine or buy an old one, and leave Pound to run it. The unsuccessful manoeuvrings with Amy Lowell were designed to this purpose. When they ended Lowell told Monroe that Pound's work lacked the quality of soul, and that she feared a tuberculous condition might have affected his brain.

In the summer of 1913 Pound met at one of Violet Hunt's parties the youthful Rebecca West. She was handling the literary side of a monthly called the *New Freewoman*, was impressed by Pound's energy and flow of ideas, and thought he would be a lively literary editor. Pound was soon writing to Dora Marsden, owner of the paper, suggesting that he should fill a page a number, giving his own work free but paying other contributors, the money for such payments to come from an unnamed patron. Dora Marsden was nervous – it was her paper, but Pound made it clear that he wanted sole charge of the literary section. All he asked for was a single page. 'I don't want to be "boss", but if I am to make the page efficient, I must follow my own scheme.'[1] She eventually agreed, and within a month or two the single page had become five, in which Pound printed work by Ford, Aldington, Flint and Williams. A little later he said the magazine's title should be changed. How, Marsden asked Harriet Shaw Weaver, who kept the records and paid the bills, could Mr Pound be kept under control?

[72]

The Egoist *and the* Little Review

These were two unusual women. (Rebecca West had become ill and retired from the paper.) Dora Marsden, at this time thirty-one, had been a teacher, and a member of the Women's Militant Suffrage Society who had been to prison for the cause. She quarrelled with the Suffrage Society, joined the Women's Freedom League, and when forced to resign from that started her own paper. But by 1914 her interest had moved away from practical issues like women's suffrage into linguistic philosophy. She was at work on a vast book which would make clear the precise relationship of mind to matter, the imaginary to the real, the nature of language and conceptual activity, and for good measure would offer also a theory of knowledge and a definition of the soul. The *New Freewoman*, which had begun as a suffragette journal in opposition to the Pankhursts, was now a vehicle for the definition of Marsden's ever more abstract philosophy. Discussions at Eustace Miles's vegetarian restaurant on 'Celibacy, Prostitution and the Abolition of Domestic Drudgery' were replaced by others on 'Language and the Origination of the Concept'.

Her friends were agreed that Dora Marsden was a genius, but she was a poor organiser and careless in money matters. When she found that Harriet Shaw Weaver, an enthusiastic supporter of the periodical, was prepared to act as treasurer of the New Freewoman Company and handle the accounts, she was delighted. Harriet, who thought Dora had the face of a Florentine angel, was at first no more than a worshipful helper, but within a short time the assistant had become the controller of the paper that in January 1914 turned into the *Egoist*, 'An Individualist Review', published twice a month. For six months the editor was named as 'Dora Marsden, BA', but in June she was replaced by Weaver. It was by no means a deposition, for Marsden resigned the editorship so that she could work on her book full time, and long extracts from it appeared in the paper.

Harriet Shaw Weaver once gave James Joyce a brief account of her background in a letter, telling him she came from 'an overgrown village, Frodsham, on a flat stretch of land at the foot of a range of hills halfway between Chester and Warrington. My father was the doctor of the district and I lived there till I was fifteen . . . I am afraid I am hopelessly English, unadulterated Saxon. My mother came from Lancashire – her father a cotton mill owner in the Manchester district . . . I have, by the way, cousins in Belfast, who are violent

[73]

The Founding Fathers

Orangemen!'[2] Her background was not only unadulterated Saxon but evangelical Christian. The Weavers were loving parents but brought up their children strictly. (Harriet was the sixth, born in 1876.) Family prayers were read twice daily, reading was strictly supervised. Dr Weaver, a lover of poetry, recited passages to his children frequently and expected that they would be learned. Harriet was educated at home, by her father and a governess interested in history and current affairs. In 1892 the family moved from Frodsham to Hampstead, and when Harriet's education ended she taught an infants class at the local Sunday school for six years. For another ten she did voluntary social work, at first in connection with the Invalid Children's Aid Association, then with other groups who sought to relieve the condition of the poor and help them find work. These activities led her first to question, then to reject the faith of her parents, and led also to an interest in women's suffrage. Such a progress seems logical enough, but there is no obvious reason why it should have led to a concern with modern literature.[3]

Photographs of Harriet Shaw Weaver taken when she was in her late twenties and early thirties show a neat, pretty, unremarkable face. She was calm and reserved, a listener rather than a talker, little interested in social life. Behind her modesty and reserve, however, was an independent mind and determined spirit. She loved her parents and rarely argued with them, but remembered to the end of her life an incident in her late teens when *Adam Bede* was taken away from her as an unsuitable book by an equally unsuitable writer, and the vicar was called in to rebuke her for such reading. When her mother died in 1909, she became financially independent. Neither now nor at a later time did she contemplate marriage or any sexual involvement, but her life and interests widened. She took a three-room service flat in Marylebone, put up £200 to take shares in the *New Freewoman* and then another £100 into the *Egoist*.

These were to be the first of many benefactions. The *Egoist* was in financial straits from its inception. The printing order was a thousand copies, but the sales peak was no more than four hundred, and there was no money for contributors. In an attempt to raise the wind Pound, with Marsden's approval, approached Lowell and asked if she would like to edit the paper. Assuming an authority he did not possess, Pound said two of the contributors must be fired and the feminism dropped, but with that done she could run the

[74]

paper from Boston, putting Ford, Pound and 'anybody you've a mind to pay for' on the staff. Lowell rejected this, like Pound's other suggestions, although she was prepared to be the paper's American correspondent and to see her poems printed in it. When the Lowell hope faded Weaver, a little disappointed in Pound, took over the editorship, at first reluctantly and on a temporary basis. The assistant editors were Aldington and, for a few months, Leonard Compton-Rickett, who had been invited to join the paper by Marsden in the hope that he would put up some money. When he failed to come up to scratch he was dropped. Pound's direct editorial connection ceased, but he still regarded himself as empowered to look for and accept contributions.

The periodical begun thus haphazardly was one of the strangest publications of the twentieth century, and so far as the modern movement was concerned perhaps the most influential. It was almost throughout its life two papers, one concerned with Marsden's ideas and philosophy, the other devoted to printing modernist poets and prose writers. Weaver remained editor during the six years of the paper's existence and poured money into it yearly as the circulation steadily declined. From 1917 onwards it never exceeded two hundred, and at the end was down to a hundred and fifty. The paper's influence, however, bore no relation to its sales. In those years it was a place where any work new in form or subject could be sure of a welcome.

The *Egoist*'s first achievement was owed entirely to Pound. Joyce had been sufficiently encouraged by Pound's letters to send him the first chapter of *A Portrait of the Artist as a Young Man*, along with a manuscript of *Dubliners*. Pound was enthusiastic, and his enthusiasm was quickly translated into action. Joyce had sent also an account of his tribulations at the hands of his publishers, Richards and Maunsel (this was before Richards reopened negotiations for the publication of *Dubliners*), and under the heading 'A Curious History' this appeared in the second issue. The third contained the first instalment of *A Portrait*. Weaver's crusading spirit had been moved by the account of the way Joyce's work had been censored, and henceforth she was his ardent supporter. That the novel should have been accepted for serial publication on the strength of the opening chapter shows the casual way in which the *Egoist* operated and the urgent need for contributions to fill the literary pages.

Pound followed up the arrangement about *A Portrait* with a review of *Dubliners* on its publication. He had told Joyce with assumed modesty that he was not supposed to know anything about prose (implying that he knew everything about poetry), but this did not stop him from saying that Joyce's stories marked the return of style into English prose, and soon he was invoking the names of Stendhal and Flaubert for comparison with *A Portrait*. As the instalments came in, sent from Trieste to Pound in London, Weaver too felt she was printing a work of genius.

A Portrait was autobiographical, like all Joyce's work. His subject was Dublin and his own youth and early manhood in the city he had left in 1904, when he had eloped to Paris with Nora Barnacle, without money and even without boots as he had told a friend in the course of pleading for a pair, along with 'any coat and vest you have to spare[4].' Joyce had deliberately cut himself off from Ireland, not only by leaving it but by doing so in the company of an ill-educated baker's daughter to whom he was not married. He returned in 1909 to arrange for the purchase of the cinema, and again in 1912, but these were no more than visits without a permanent stay in mind. He had exiled himself, it seems in retrospect, so that by doing so he could write more easily about his country and his youth. Again and again he invoked them, his spendthrift hard-drinking father, his uncles and aunts and family friends, school teachers and boys he had known, drinking acquaintances, those he had liked and quarrelled and argued with like Oliver St John Gogarty. (Stanislaus was displeased because he had been an important character in *Stephen Hero* but was eliminated from *A Portrait*.) Along with the people went the sights, sounds and smells of the Dublin he remembered with photographic accuracy and in extraordinary detail. He said on the 1909 visit that he loathed Ireland and the Irish and it was not good for him to be there, but still the Ireland of his youth absorbed him totally. He never broke free of the country or its people, any more than he broke free from the Jesuit training of his youth, even though he told Nora in 1904 that his mind rejected both Christianity and the existing social order, so that for a while he supported Sinn Fein and regarded himself as a socialist.

A Portrait is an account of Stephen Dedalus's youth, his loss of faith, the struggle in him between sexual instinct and religious teaching. The book was bound to distress and anger a number of the people portrayed in it. There were hints of homosexuality, references to sexual pleasure and religion as incompatible. They do not seem shocking now, but in 1914 some of the attitudes expressed and some of the language used were certain to cause trouble. However, the printers raised no objection to the first instalments. The troubles that lay ahead were to rouse all Weaver's dislike of literary censorship, a feeling no doubt connected with the limitation of her own reading in youth. Joyce's story had the further attraction for her that it was about a young man who lost his faith, as she had lost hers.

For the rest of the literary end of the paper she relied in the first year or two on Aldington's taste and Pound's push. The Imagists bulked large, H.D., Fletcher, Flint, Lowell, and that courtesy Imagist Lawrence among them. There was a long poem by Williams, and Frost's 'The Housekeeper' took up two of the paper's twenty large (12 × 8 inch) pages. Weaver liked Aldington, and he wrote many articles, including a front-page lead reviewing *Des Imagistes*, in which he said how much the theory of Imagism owed to Flint. When *Blast* appeared, Aldington hailed it as 'The most amazing, energised, stimulating production I have ever seen. Death to the *English Review*! Death to the *Times*!'[5] He also wrote a parody of Pound's celebrated two-line poem 'In a Station of the Metro'.

Pound was not idle. He had turned into an art critic and said that a modern must prefer Lewis to Poussin. He also took a further step in liberating himself from his own poetic past, and even from his recent adherence to Imagisme, by proclaiming: 'Regarding this pother about the Greeks: some few of us are at last liberated from the idea that "THE BEAUTIFUL" is the caressable, the physically attractive.'[6] This might have been seen as a hit at Aldington or H.D., but also involved was the replacement of the Image by the Vortex in Pound's scale of values. Most of the poets he introduced were American, something that did not go unnoticed – for instance by Douglas Goldring, in a couplet comparing Georgians and moderns:

> Here's J. C. Squire and here the laurell'd Shanks;
> There's Ezra's circle of performing Yanks.

The war which began in August 1914 seemed likely to cut off or much affect communications with the United States and German-occupied Europe. Pound advised suspension of the *Egoist* for the duration, but Weaver instead sent out an appeal to potential subscribers and made an arrangement to have Joyce's text sent to her via Italy and Switzerland, although publication of the novel had to be suspended from September 1914 until the end of the year. It began again in January 1915, by which time the financial position demanded economies. Six months' sales and subscriptions had brought in £37 (at a publication price of sixpence) against expenses of £337. The number of pages was cut to sixteen, the paper became monthly instead of fortnightly, the printing order was reduced to 750, editorial salaries were also reduced – and Harriet Weaver put in more money.

The resumption of *A Portrait* led to trouble with the printers. They objected to a passage in which Stephen, walking on the seashore and looking at school friends, felt 'a swordlike pain to see the signs of adolescence that made repellent their pitiable naked-ness', to the description of a girl's full thighs and the 'white fingers of her drawers . . . like featherings of soft white down'. They not only objected to these passages but also excised them. In August a new printer refused to accept the words *fart* and *ballocks*. They were unknown to Weaver, but when (as one assumes) she discovered their meanings she was not deterred. One word was deleted, the other replaced by asterisks. She wrote apologetically to Joyce:

> It was because of Messrs Partridge & Coopers' stupid censoring of your novel that we left them – that is, they had objected once or twice to things in other parts of the paper, but their behaviour over your novel was the crowning offence . . . I'm very sorry to say that Messrs Ballantyne are now acting in the same way. They refuse to print certain passages in the August instalment.[7]

Joyce complained a little, but not much: he was too pleased to be printed. And he did not complain at all about the printers' failure to respect his only typographical innovation, the replacement of inverted commas round dialogue by a dash before any spoken passage, even though he thought the latter smoother and less artificial. In the opening instalment his wishes were observed, but by July 1914 inverted commas had been reinstated, and were used until the serialisation ended in September 1915.

In June of that year, when Italy entered the war, Joyce was forced to leave Trieste. He rejected Pound's suggestion that he should come to England and instead moved to Zurich, where he was even

worse off than in Trieste. Pound, who had been telling all those
ready to listen of Joyce's genius (he had been overwhelmed by the
ending of *A Portrait*, which he compared to Hardy and James) now
busied himself with obtaining a grant for the Irishman from the
Royal Literary Fund, which had been helping indigent writers for
many years. He spurred Yeats into action, and Yeats, long convinced
of Joyce's talent and now believing that the novel was 'a very great
book',[8] approached Edmund Gosse. It is unlikely that Gosse had
read anything by Joyce, and he was disturbed by the fact that neither
Joyce nor Yeats professed loyalty to the Allied cause. Yeats soothed
him by saying, not quite accurately, that he thought Joyce had only
literary and philosophic sympathies, not political ones. Gosse wrote
to the secretary of the Fund, of which he was himself an official,
Yeats and Pound supported the application, Joyce gave an account
of his poverty, and he was awarded £75 payable over nine months.[9]
This may sound a small sum (Lawrence had received £50 from the
Fund in 1914), but was a godsend to Joyce, both in practical terms
and as an official acknowledgement of his literary existence.

Better still, of course, would be publication of his novel in book
form, which Weaver was now contemplating. She did so after a
period of uncharacteristic gloom about the *Egoist*. She was still
devoted to Dora Marsden, who continued to provide long articles
struggling with philosophy, but confided to Dora her doubts about
whether it was worth going on with the paper. The reply she
received blended good sense with Marsden's particular kind of
silliness. The paper, Marsden said, was slowly fizzling out, the
heaviness of Egoism was not being lightened by 'the equally
unleavened heaviness of Imagism', they were not just risking but
chasing failure, and the only possibilities were indefinite suspension
or handing over the paper to Aldington in the hope that, through his
friendship with Lowell, he might secure her financial support. So far
common sense. But with a sudden *volte-face* Marsden then reached
the conclusion that she could save the paper herself. She would
return to London from Southport where she lived with her mother,
find new writers 'of a different brand from Imagists', and discover a
replacement for Aldington. Before she could put any of this into
practice, however, the first Zeppelin raid on London alarmed her.
She abandoned any idea of coming to the capital and urged her
friend to take refuge in the country.[10] Weaver, unalarmed by raids,

ignored the suggestion and forgot about abandoning the paper. She wrote a front-page article herself for the first time, and made plans for enlargement, so that the *Egoist* should be not only a magazine but a publishing house.

2. THE HIGHLY MECHANISED TYPING VOLCANO

By now Weaver was corresponding frequently with Joyce, although the sense of propriety that had for a long time led her to avoid the use of a Christian name in writing or speaking to Dora Marsden kept the letters formal. When Joyce, cast down by English rejections of his novel by Richards, Martin Secker and Duckworth, contemplated publication in Paris, she replied that at the moment this might be difficult. (It was November 1915, and the German Army was still menacingly near the French capital.) Perhaps the *Egoist* could publish the book, although she modestly added that what she called a proper book publisher would be much more satisfactory. Joyce, who had no idea that the paper's staff was simply Weaver and Aldington, said he would be glad if she could lay the proposal before her staff and the company. Weaver told Marsden, who was nervous about this publishing venture, that Joyce had a friend who would indemnify the paper against loss (she herself being in fact the 'friend'), and informed Joyce that economies had improved the financial position, and they would pay him £50 for the serial rights. A few weeks later she heard from Pound of Joyce's hard times in Zurich and wrote to tell him of the debt she and the paper owed him for 'your wonderful book'.[11]

The difficulty of publishing Joyce was increased by the ban on Lawrence's *The Rainbow*. This was Lawrence's fourth novel, the eagerly awaited successor to *Sons and Lovers*, which critics had thought strange but remarkable, original, even masterly. It should be emphasised that Lawrence was not, except in his treatment of taboo subjects, a modernist. He made no attempt to go outside the language or form of the novel of the period, and when he was called 'difficult' it was because the attitude from which he wrote was unclear, or not easy to sympathise with. He had worked harder on *The Rainbow* than on any previous novel. He wrote four complete versions of the book, changed the title twice, and late in the day decided to split what would have been a very long book into two, *The Rainbow* and what eventually became *Women in Love*. Lawrence said in 1917, in one of those comments that must make even his most ardent admirers wince, that it was 'a kind of working up to the dark sensual or Dionysiac or Aphrodisiac ecstasy, which does actually burst the world, burst the world-consciousness in every individual'.[12] A good deal of the book exemplifies such an attitude, but the widespread condemnation of it startled both Lawrence and his reader and adviser Edward Garnett. Robert Lynd called the novel a monotonous wilderness of phallicism and said that if Lawrence had written the *Iliad* he would have made Paris and Helen a pair of furious animals, Clement Shorter that it was 'an orgie [*sic*] of sexiness', and James Douglas that it expressed the unspeakable and hinted at the unutterable, referring no doubt to the suggestion of a lesbian relationship between Ursula and a teacher. Douglas had no doubt that 'a book of this kind has no right to exist', and soon it did not exist. The legal machinery was set in motion, the prosecution said that the book was a mass of obscenity in thought, idea and action, the publishers made no defence and said they regretted its publication, and an order for destruction was made and carried out. Protests were ineffective.[13]

The emotional climate of wartime was not favourable to the publication of anything that might be thought blasphemous or obscene, and by March 1916 seven printers had refused to handle *A Portrait* as it stood. Weaver wrote to Joyce that she was becoming fairly hopeless. In another couple of months the seven refusals had increased to a dozen.[14] Pound made the ingenious suggestion that blank spaces should be left for the offending passages, which could then be filled in by typewriter. Joyce was prepared to agree to this but Weaver, no doubt rightly, flinched from it. Pound wrote endless letters urging the book's publication in his role as what he himself called a highly mechanised typing volcano, and at last they produced a result. The New York publisher Ben Huebsch agreed to print the book as it stood, and although he offered a royalty of only ten per cent compared to the *Egoist*'s handsome twenty-five per cent, Joyce accepted it – at the time he would have accepted anything. Weaver kept him in touch with everything that happened and passed on Pound's suggestion that Edward Marsh might write an introduction. She herself, she said, would prefer reviews by Marsh and others like

Wells and George Moore, and thought it would be a good idea to have an article about Joyce's work written by Pound. This was done, and Pound was active also in obtaining reviews elsewhere as soon as the book appeared. In the *Nation* Wells praised its 'quintessential and unfailing reality', although he thought Joyce had a cloacal obsession.

The novel appeared in America in December 1916, and two months later Weaver published the English edition. There was no prosecution but sales were slow because, as she revealed to Joyce, 'we are at a disadvantage in having no agents or travellers, in fact no business staff at all'.[15] However, the 750 copies she had imported in sheets sold out during the summer. She planned a second edition before the first was sold out, and found a printer prepared to go ahead without deletions, so that the second edition of a thousand copies appeared in March 1918. In the meantime she arranged through a solicitor for Joyce to be sent on behalf of 'an admirer of your writing, who desires to remain anonymous', £50 a quarter for the following twelve months. She continued the gift for another year and in 1919, again anonymously, settled on Joyce the income from £5000 of five per cent War Loan, amounting to £250 a year. For some time he had no idea of the donor's identity.

Pound was in constant touch with Joyce, sending news and gossip. He told the sometimes depressed English teacher in Zurich that he should not worry about the poor sales of *Dubliners*, and passed on Yeats's good words about *A Portrait*. Activity on Joyce's behalf was only one among his many literary activities. In September 1914 Pound and his recent wife Dorothy were visited by Eliot, whose name had been mentioned to Pound by Aiken. Eliot either left poems with his fellow-American or sent some to him after their meeting. Among them was 'Prufrock', which Pound sent at once to Harriet Monroe with the strongest possible endorsement. Eliot, he told her, was somebody who had trained and modernised himself entirely on his own, unlike most of the young. 'It is such a comfort to meet a man and not to have to tell him to wash his face, wipe his feet, and remember the date on the calendar.'[16] The editor of *Poetry*, however, was by no means sure that she either admired or understood the poem, and deliberated on it for months. Pound, already annoyed by her delay in printing other work he had sent her, expostulated, argued, cajoled, and sent her a letter in May 1915 which began 'My gawdd! This *is* a ROTTEN number of *Poetry*.'[17] In the following month she took the plunge and printed 'Prufrock'. The most violent reaction to it was that of Louis Untermeyer, who called the poem 'the muse in a psychopathic ward drinking the stale dregs of revolt'.

At about the same time Pound introduced Eliot to Lewis, who found him 'a sleek, tall, attractive transatlantic apparition', a Prufrock to whom the mermaids would undoubtedly have sung, 'a very attractive young Prufrock indeed, blushfully *tacquineur*'.[18] The meeting took place in what Lewis called Pound's triangular room in Church Walk, described by many visitors, but perhaps most clearly and closely by John Gould Fletcher. There was, he said, a white enamelled bedstead at the right beside the door, a long oak table used as a desk, on which stood a typewriter and a pile of manuscripts, a wardrobe, washstand, another small square table, and two or three chairs. In the fireplace could often be seen scraps of torn-up manuscripts and letters.[19] Others recalled the small bath kept under the bed and filled with cans of hot water from the kitchen boiler, and the squeaky cane chairs. There were books everywhere, old leather trunks bulging with them, at one time a sofa which they supported. Here Pound received dozens of visitors including Aldington and H.D., Flint, Ford, Lawrence. It is not likely that Eliot said much at this first meeting with Lewis, who was more impressed by the American's poems than he later admitted. 'Preludes' and 'Rhapsody on a Windy Night' appeared in the second issue of *Blast*, and Lewis called this very respectable intelligent verse. He rejected two King Bolo poems called 'Bullshit' and 'The Ballad of Big Louise' on the ground of a 'naif determination to have no words ending in -Uck, -Unt and -Ugger'.[20] Eliot told Aiken that he thought little of Pound's poetry but was grateful to him for his help and enthusiasm. He changed his mind about the poetry within a year or two.

Eliot, then, was added to Joyce and Lewis among the writers for whom the mechanised typing volcano worked. Lewis had been much occupied before the war and in its first years with love affairs. The better the social position of the women involved, the worse he treated them, or so it appears from his letters. Mary Borden Turner, heiress and novelist, with an apartment in Park Lane and a large rented house in Berwickshire, called him a great artist but a faulty human being, although she said in another letter that 'you make anyone else seem flat – just as your pictures make other pictures look dull'.[21] She bought pictures and commissioned him to decorate her Park Lane dining room. Lewis complained that she was not primitive enough, which surprised her, and in the end they quarrelled over money. If she had plans, as Lewis told Pound, to take a large studio near Park Lane, house his pictures there, and provide 'a stage for Theatrical Performances, Lectures, etc',[22] this came to nothing. It is possible that she helped to pay for *Blast 2*, which was very much the mixture as before, with Lewis providing the bulk of the prose and Pound some poems and notes. An ironic poem by Pound, written with Brooke in mind and published after his death although written before it, caused some indignation. But the times were not propitious for Blasting, and this second and final issue attracted less attention than the first.

For much of this period Lewis was hard up. Pound suggested that the *Egoist* might publish his now completed *Tarr* as a successor to Joyce's book, and arranged for Lewis to meet Weaver. He read the first few pages of the novel to her 'and then left off, as I was sure she would not like it, and we were in an empty room under depressing conditions'.[23] It seems clear that neither cared much for the other, but finding enough interesting material for the paper was a continual problem for Harriet Weaver. She told Lewis that she had read Part I of his novel and did not like it, but was still prepared to use it as a serial. 'May I make a quite frank criticism of it? Well, then, on my part I should class it as of the same family as Mr Bernard Shaw's plays – "diabolically clever", yes, & very interesting, but *not* a genuine work of art. The characters appear to be mechanical automatons, wound up in order to spout forth opinions, instead of breathing with life.'[24] She offered £50 for the serial rights, which Lewis immediately accepted. He returned a genial reply to her remarks, saying he agreed with them himself, which seems unlikely, and making no demur to the cuts necessary for serial publication. In March 1916, perhaps as a means of escape from financial and sexual entanglements (by now he had three illegitimate children) rather than from enthusiasm for war service, he volunteered as a gunner in the Royal Artillery. In the following month *Tarr* began to appear as a serial. In the April and May issues the novel occupied almost half the paper.

[84]

Pound's letters of the period show him often dissatisfied, in part no doubt because of an uncomfortable awareness that unlike Eliot he had not yet modernised himself 'on his own'. The dissatisfaction found expression in an increased determination to find a periodical in which he could control what appeared in the literary pages. He had almost given up hope of influencing *Poetry* as he would have wished, and Aldington's choice of poetry for the *Egoist* was still based on an Imagism over which hovered the enormous shadow of Amy Lowell. Some of her poems were printed in 1916, and Flint, Fletcher, H.D. (who had joined Aldington as Assistant Editor) and Aldington himself were the other poets most often printed. Perhaps Pound felt himself being edged out. He renewed a curious suggestion made earlier, that he should be leased space in the paper at an agreed rate. Weaver consulted Marsden, who pointed out that Pound was really asking to edit half or more of the *Egoist*. And was he suggesting that Aldington should be sacked? Not at all, Pound said, there would be room for Aldington in his scheme. But the idea was rejected, and after the summer of 1916 he gave up hope of using the magazine as a Poundian platform.

Yet he continued to exercise influence. When Aldington was called up, Pound persuaded Weaver to take on Eliot as Assistant Editor. She had previously asked of Eliot, 'What is his line?', but since then had met and liked him. It was in March 1917 that Eliot took up his job with Lloyds Bank, and from June onwards his name appeared on the *Egoist*'s masthead. He was paid £9 a quarter, of which, unknown to him, Pound contributed more than half, although not from his own pocket. It came from John Quinn.

3. THE SECOND ANGEL: JOHN QUINN

The involvement of John Quinn with the modernist movement is perhaps the strangest of Pound's successes as propagandist. Quinn was born in 1870, eldest among the eight children of a prosperous baker in Ohio. His biographer calls him peculiarly American, a prime example of the successful and strongly practical man of affairs who longs to have a connection with artistic creation. Quinn was, however, even more peculiarly or particularly Irish-American. His father came from County Limerick, his mother from County Cork, and Quinn was from early manhood greatly drawn to Irish art and artists, and in a lesser way to Irish causes. He was generous, enthusiastic, irascible, a passionately patriotic American who had little time for any recent immigrants and none at all for Jews. The irascibility quickly boiled over into anger. A friend called him a bully good Irishman.

Quinn's business career flourished from the start. He became an attorney in his late twenties, moved to New York, was drawn into Tammany, and before long was a very successful lawyer handling financial agreements and contracts for banks and corporations. He was also, from his youth, interested in art and literature and spent a large part of his increasing income on them. At first his adult artistic interests were directed towards Ireland. He started buying Jack Yeats's pictures in 1902, commissioned portraits of such Irish literary men as AE and Douglas Hyde, acted as literary agent in America for W. B. Yeats and AE, and sold two stories by Yeats to *McClure's Magazine*. In 1912 Quinn discovered Post-Impressionism, and in that year bought pictures by Cézanne, van Gogh and Gauguin. Thereafter he made what was, for a private man without inherited wealth, an astonishing collection of French and other modern art. Matisse, Derain, Rousseau, Picasso, Juan Gris, are only a few of the artists he collected, in addition to those already named. He did not confine himself to mainland Europe. In 1908 he began to buy Augustus John's work, and in ten years spent $50,000 on John paintings and drawings. He supported literature as well as graphic art. Chief among his literary gods was Conrad. He corresponded with the novelist, bought some of his manuscripts, and in 1915 arranged with Doubleday to publish a complete edition of Conrad's works. Quinn found it difficult to embark on any project without trying to take charge of it, and in the matter of the Conrad American edition as on other occasions this led to trouble. He assumed direction of the enterprise, advising both publisher and author about such matters as typography and binding, and eventually fell out with both.

In 1915 this erratic benefactor of the arts wrote to Pound, to rebut an article in the *New Age* in which Pound had remarked scornfully on American collectors who bought autograph manuscripts and collected fake Rembrandts and van Dycks but left a modern sculptor like Epstein to starve. Quinn listed his collection of modern artists, including 'three or four fine Picassos ... perhaps the largest collection of paintings by Augustus John in the world', some Americans – and half-a-dozen Epsteins. More than that, he told Pound, he had written every word and line of a new tariff specifically designed to exclude the importation of fakes into the United States, and claimed with justice to be the most lively collector of contemporary art 'for a man with moderate means'. He ended by asking where he could get hold of Gaudier-Brzeska's work, praised in the article.[25]

Quinn had met Pound some years earlier in the company of J. B. Yeats, and liked him. He had even, in a way, liked the article, or at least had admired a man who 'hit straight from the shoulder'. Pound saw in Quinn the man he had been looking for, somebody with a feeling for the modern and with sufficient money to act as a patron for Pound's chosen artists and writers. In fact Quinn's tastes in painting were far from identical with Pound's, but he was a man who loved enthusiasm, and for a while was happy to accept Pound's advocacy of some recent British artists. He joined Augustus John as Quinn's London adviser, and soon Quinn was accepting Pound as a guide rather than John, who said that Epstein's 'Rock Drill' was the most hideous thing he had seen. Within weeks of Pound's first letter Quinn had sent £30 to help Lewis, of whose work he was ignorant, and on learning of Gaudier-Brzeska's death at the front he told Pound to buy anything by Gaudier he could find. Getting hold of Gaudier's work proved difficult because of the high prices asked by Sophie Brzeska but Pound did his best, and Quinn, in a flush of excitement, guaranteed financial backing for a Vorticist exhibition in New York.

This took place early in 1917, and was an unmitigated failure. Quinn's New York friends thought little of the paintings, the show was 'tabooed by the whole damn crew of critics',[26] and hardly a picture or drawing was sold – except to Quinn, who bought twenty-four paintings and drawings by Lewis, and a few works by other Vorticists. Lewis said his support had been a privilege and a tonic, but after the exhibition's failure Quinn's opinion of modern British art gradually declined. He corresponded with Lewis, now a soldier in France, who summed up the relics he would leave behind if he did not survive. There would be 'five or six books to be got out of my stuff', including *Tarr*, *Our Wild Body*, and 'a book of theory called *Kill John Bull With Art*; *The Enemy of the Stars* + poems, sonnets, etc; The Bull Gun (papers, one or two of which I have written, dealing with present life.)' He added that his preparations for extinction were precautionary, not pessimistic. 'But should the eclipse occur, these books I have mentioned, with two or three sturdy blasts from my tried friends, should bring a rich little crowd staring round; and I think there is something in them, the books, *bien entendu*, that should make them a permanent public property.'[27]

The latter may have been designed – Lewis was rarely undesigning – to shift Quinn's interest in the direction of his writing. If so it was unnecessary, for the lawyer was already using his considerable energies in the cause of getting Pound's friends, and Pound himself, published in America. Pound had interested him also in the idea of supporting a literary magazine. It was Quinn's backing that had enabled Pound to make the suggestion about renting pages of the *Egoist*, as it was Quinn's money that went to Eliot. He had been prepared to support Pound in obtaining control of the weekly *Academy*, or in starting a paper of his own. These ideas came to nothing, but the approaches to American publishers had better results.

Quinn's first success was in persuading the recently established Alfred Knopf to publish Pound's *Lustra*, to which the poet added 'Three Cantos of a Poem of Some Length', the first appearance of his Cantos in book form. Quinn loved editing the work of creative artists and made many corrections approved by Pound, although they irritated Knopf. The lawyer paid $25 so that the large capital initial letters originally used should be reduced to standard size. No sooner was the agreement for Pound's own book made than he was urging *Tarr* and Eliot's poems on this American angel. Quinn duly approached Knopf, who agreed to publish Lewis's novel. Eliot's first collection of poems, *Prufrock and Other Observations*, had been published by the Egoist Press in summer 1917, in an edition of 500 copies. Pound, unknown to Eliot, had managed to borrow the money to pay most of the printing costs. Quinn sent a copy of the book to Knopf with a strong recommendation, but although Knopf said he had read the poems with immense enjoyment, he thought there were not enough of them. In the end he published a larger volume in 1920.

Quinn admired all the writers in Pound's stable, but his greatest

feeling was for Joyce. He had nothing to do with the publication of
A Portrait, but when Huebsch (reluctantly acknowledged by Quinn
as 'the good Jew') sent a note saying he thought the book was a work
of genius, Quinn read it, and agreed. The Irish background was
intensely moving and interesting to him, and although it is unlikely
that he made any personal identification with Stephen Dedalus, the
problem of growing up in Ireland and emancipating oneself from the
Catholic Church was one with which he could sympathise. No Irish
writing since Synge had interested him so personally,[28] and he
immediately set out to help Joyce. He bought twenty-five or thirty
copies of the book and sent them to friends, wrote an article in
Vanity Fair, and began to buy Joyce manuscripts, a course he
preferred to making gifts. In typically Quinnish style he concerned
himself with the eye trouble that first affected Joyce seriously in
1917, when he suffered an attack of glaucoma in the street that left
him unable to move for twenty minutes. Glaucoma clouds the vision,
and if untreated can lead to blindness. From across the Atlantic
Quinn sent a long letter of advice, along with a gift of £20, and told
Pound he would do his best for Joyce. When the gifts from an
anonymous admirer arrived it was natural that both Pound and Joyce
should mistakenly assume that the benefactor was Quinn, and not
Harriet Weaver.

By the end of 1917 Pound had arranged the publication of novels
by Joyce and Lewis on both sides of the Atlantic and of Eliot's
poems in Britain, and had been chiefly responsible for the sale of
many pictures by Lewis. Weaver and Quinn provided the money,
and in Quinn's case the influence, to oil the wheels of publication,
but the achievement otherwise was Pound's alone. In a sense these
years were the finest of his life, years in which he recognised work
that was truly modern and original, and worked selflessly to see it
published. Yet it was this propaganda work, even more than his
pontifical airs, that some other writers found objectionable. Aiken
thought him inclined to be tyrannical, resembling the Old Man of
the Sea,[29] and Fletcher was infuriated by Pound's tendency to
lecture strangers for hours about his theories of verse.[30] Flint, after
being told by Pound that at risk of being disagreeable he must say
Flint's account of the history of Imagism was bullshit, replied that
'you are indeed a disagreeable person, as you say, it is one of the
regrets of all those who have ever known you.'[31] Joseph Conrad told

Quinn that the critics in Britain 'consider him [Pound] harmless; but as he has, I believe, a very great opinion of himself I don't suppose he worries his head about the critics very much'.[32] Yeats looked upon Pound with a benevolent but puzzled eye, and Ford also was benevolent as he was to all the enterprising young. Pound stayed with Ford and Violet Hunt at their country cottage that had once belonged to Milton, and as he wrote to his mother, played chess and discussed style with his host.

Iris Barry, who had had the misfortune to be born Freda Crump, produced the most vivid portrait of Pound in these years. She had rectified the disadvantage of her name by the time she came to London to seek, not her fortune but literary bohemian company. She had been corresponding with Pound after the appearance of some of her poems in Harold Monro's *Poetry and Drama*. He met her on a bench in Hyde Park, and later took her for a walk on Wimbledon Common. She found his voice, style, and subject matter all extraordinary:

> His is almost a wholly original accent, the base of American mingled with a dozen assorted 'English society' and Cockney accents inserted in mockery, French, Spanish and Greek exclamations, strange cries and catcalls, the whole very oddly inflected, with dramatic pauses and *diminuendos* . . . I knew as little as a dog he might have been taking for a walk of even the sort of thing he was talking about; and, in addition, was too agitated to grasp much.[33]

She was enchanted by the variety of his activities as well as their nature. His worktable was full of manuscripts which he read, criticised, blue-pencilled, discussed 'in explosive letters many pages long'. He began signing his letters with a seal in the Chinese manner, and 'turned from cooking dinner (one of the things he does to perfection) wrapped in a flowing and worn dressing-gown, to the harpsichord Dolmetsch made for him'.[34] He took over her literary education, and prescribed for her a very Poundian course of reading. Greek was the thing, he said, full of wonderful rhythms, but perhaps she couldn't read it in the original. English translations were hopeless, she had better read Greek in English prose. A bewildering variety of do's and don'ts followed. Catullus, Propertius, Horace and Ovid were recommended, Virgil called a second-rater. British and American poets remained unmentioned.[35] And her own poems? Too many of her lines were in the old pentameter, and 'a lot of lines with no variety won't do'. Iris Barry may have been stunned by the reading list, but she liked Ezra Pound. It is easy to believe her when she says that at this time no one was ever busier or gayer. She met Dorothy Pound, who had 'a clear and lovely profile' and 'carried herself delicately with the air of a young Victorian lady out skating',[36] although she was already emotionally detached from her husband in the way that made Pound say he had fallen in love with a beautiful picture that never came alive.

Although Iris Barry admired Pound, she fell in love with Lewis, lived with him for some four years, and had two children by him. Lewis refused to acknowledge or provide for the children, and behaved very badly to her. Most of her surviving letters to him in this period are requests for pathetically small amounts of money, often only a few shillings. They alternate with notes saying things like 'my letter is dull because I fear the ironical lift of your eyebrows when you read it'.[37]

Pound, then, had achieved much of what he set out to do, although those are not the terms in which he would have thought of it. He was still, however, looking for a place where, as he put it, 'I and T. S. Eliot can appear once a month (or once an "issue") and where Joyce can appear when he likes, and where Wyndham Lewis can appear if he comes back from the war.'[38] In the *Little Review*, at last, he found it.

4. THE *Little Review*

'I don't think that many people ever escape RESPONSIBILITY,' Margaret Anderson wrote to a friend in 1969, in old age.[39] She set out from youth to be one of them. She escaped from family life in Columbus, Indiana, by writing to an 'agony aunt' working for *Good Housekeeping* in Chicago, who offered to take the young girl 'under her wing'. Whether Margaret Anderson had yet discovered her own lesbian orientation is uncertain, but in Chicago she began a career concerned less with literature than with bohemian life. The connection of modernism with such very unliterary women as Weaver and Anderson is a curious one. Anderson said later that her prime purpose in starting a literary review was to fill it with the best conversation the world had to offer.[40]

With this in mind, and with encouragement from some of Chicago's literati, the *Little Review* appeared. 'Life is a glorious performance,' said her introductory announcement. 'And close to Life . . . is this eager, panting Art who shows us the wonder of the way as we rush along.' She wrote to John Galsworthy asking for an encouraging message, and printed his reply in the first number, along with an ecstatic review of his work which she wrote herself. Galsworthy too spoke of Life and gave it a capital letter. 'It seems you are setting out to watch the street of Life from a high balcony,' he said, and went on to express the hope that she would sleep out in the fresh air under the stars, rather than in 'the hothouse air of temples, clubs and coteries'.

This first number was published early in 1914. Anderson later admitted that it betrayed nothing but her adolescence, and much the same could be said about the contents of the magazine in its next three years. Anderson was attractive, and talked about what she hoped to do with an enthusiasm that induced cynical publishers to buy advertising space, but she had no literary or social ideas beyond a vague anarchism that made her write articles in passionate support of Emma Goldman. Perhaps it was this romantic anarchism that led a clergyman to write asking that she stop sending the magazine to his daughter, who had had 'the folly of undiscriminating youth to fall in the diabolical snare by joining the ungodly family of your subscribers'.[41] He surely cannot have been upset by the articles attacking and defending *vers libre*, or the poems by writers most of whom also appeared in *Poetry*. Maxwell Bodenheim, who thought that rhymed verse 'mutilates and cramps poetry', contributed a piece that might have been a parody of Pound, 'After Feeling Deux Arabesques by Debussy':

> I stuffed my ears with faded stars
> From the little universe of music pent in me,
> For your fiendish ripple must be heard but once.

Bodenheim came to see Anderson. He had a bad stutter, but was of proper bohemian appearance, smoking a long white pipe decorated with a knot of baby blue ribbon. Rupert Brooke called when visiting Chicago, shy as a girl and, Anderson thought, with a girl's beauty. He promised poems but never sent them. Harriet Monroe appeared with Amy Lowell, 'who was so huge that she entered the door with difficulty'. Anderson heard about the row with Pound, and of Lowell's determination to advertise herself so much that Pound would regret not going in with her. She now offered to give Anderson $150 a month, asking only that she should direct the poetry department. 'You can count on me never to dictate.'[42] Lowell was not pleased when Anderson rejected the offer.

It is not clear how the magazine existed through these early years, even though no payment was made for contributions. The poet Eunice Tietjens gave a diamond ring to be sold, Frank Lloyd Wright a present of a hundred dollars. Somehow the magazine survived. 'Chicago was thrilling ... Life is just one ecstasy after another.'[43] The most important of these ecstasies appeared in February 1916, bearing the name of Jane Heap.

Jane Heap's photograph shows a super-typical lesbian of the period, mannish, short-haired, wearing a bow-tie. Opinions of her vary, but few are favourable. Quinn told Pound that Margaret Anderson was 'a damned attractive young woman, one of the handsomest I have ever seen, very high-spirited, very courageous', but dismissed her companion as a typical Washington Squareite, by which he meant a layabout.[44] William Carlos Williams, who found Anderson a beauty in the grand style, thought Heap looked like a heavy-set Eskimo. Anderson, however, said Heap was the finest talker she had ever heard, and we have seen the high value she placed on conversation. 'Things become known to me,' Jane Heap said, and 'Chaliapin's school of gestures might be classed under secondary feminine traits,' and 'Elizabeth and Essex are one of the great cases of alter-ego.' These and similar remarks seemed to Anderson profound. Heap was soon joint editor of the magazine, and all-too-frequent contributor of reviews and notes signed jane heap or j.h., marked by the secondhand would-be profundity quoted above. After j.h. had arrived her fellow-editor wrote a penitent, emotional editorial:

> I am afraid to write anything. I am ashamed. I have been realizing the ridiculous tragedy of the *Little Review*. It has been published for over two years without realizing its ideal.[45]

j.h.'s influence can be seen in the following issue, which offered twelve blank pages and only sixteen pages of text, mostly advertisements and reviews. The editorial said: 'The *Little Review* hopes to become a magazine of Art. The September issue is offered as a Want Ad.'[46]

The Want Ad was answered by Pound. Within two or three months he was Foreign Editor, and the magazine had been transformed. From May 1917, when a Pound editorial was carried on the first page, for perhaps two or three years, the best work published was of astonishing quality. The innocent and sometimes ludicrous enthusiasm of Anderson, the desperate pseudo-sophistication of j.h., were still represented, but for the most part the editors printed what Pound sent to them. In June there was a new sub-head saying that this was a magazine 'Making No Compromise With The Public Taste', replaced a few months later by 'The Magazine That Is Read By Those Who Write The Others'. In July there were four poems by Eliot, in October Lewis's story 'Cantleman's Spring Mate'. In March 1918 the first extract from *Ulysses* appeared, in September a wonderful issue included Yeats's 'In Memory of Robert Gregory', four more Eliot poems and a story by Sherwood Anderson, as well as another instalment of *Ulysses*. This halcyon year ended with Djuna Barnes's 'A Night Among The Horses'. It is no wonder that Anderson said the magazine had at last arrived at the place from which she had wanted it to start.

It did not reach that place without some ructions. Pound made it plain that he thought little of some of the most favoured contributors. He dismissed Bodenheim as lacking originality, and thought H.D., Williams and Aldington had made little progress since contributing to his *Des Imagistes* anthology. Lowell was excoriated, although if she offered cash and appeared in a part of the magazine over which Pound had no control, 'THEN would I be right glad to see her milked of her money, mashed into moonshine, at mercy of monitors'.[47] A bewildering variety of reading was, as usual, advocated, and the merits of Iris Barry and John Rodker advanced. Anderson survived all this, along with complaints about the 'BLOODY goddamndamnblasted bitchbornsonofaputridseahorseof a foetid and stinkerous printer', and even enjoyed it. Readers, or some of them, complained bitterly about the change of tone. There was also trouble with the censor, first about Lewis's story, then over *Ulysses*.

'Cantleman's Spring Mate', Lewis's story, reflects his early distaste for Army life, and his fury at the fact that copulation leads to birth. Cantleman dislikes his fellow soldiers, feels himself at one with nature in the sense that he has the same feeling as birds, pigs, and the horses that 'considered the mares appetising masses of quivering shiny flesh'. He meets a village girl, copulates with her, and ignores the letter he receives in the trenches telling him she is pregnant. When the issue was confiscated, the defence in the court case that followed was conducted by Quinn, although neither Anderson nor Heap liked him or believed his support to be whole-hearted. It was true that Quinn strongly disapproved of both revolutionary politics and sexual licence and may have agreed with Judge Augustus N. Hand's view that in the story 'the young girl and the relations of the man with her are described with a degree of detail that does not appear necessary to teach the desired lesson, whatever it may be'. Probably the sentence that gave most offence was: 'That night he spat out, in gushes of thick delicious rage, all the lust that had gathered in his body.' The case was lost, and that issue destroyed.

The magazine's greatest achievement was undoubtedly the printing in part of *Ulysses*, about which Anderson said when she read the second section beginning 'Ineluctable modality of the visible' that this was something they would print if it was the last effort of their lives. It was an achievement shared with Weaver, who corresponded direct with Joyce, while Anderson and Heap were allowed to do so only through Pound.

Before moving on to the battle of *Ulysses* something more should be said about Weaver and the *Egoist*'s progress. The circulation moved slowly downwards – from a circulation of two hundred any descent is likely to be slow. Yet in this last phase Eliot put his stamp on the magazine as Aldington would not have done, or perhaps wished to do. There was much more emphasis on contemporary poetry, and the reviewing tone became sharper and more scholarly. In January 1918 four pages were given to a celebration of Henry James, with contributions by Pound and Arthur Waley in addition to Eliot's own front-page article. This compelled Dora Marsden's exclusion from the paper, although she returned in full force with seven pages on 'The Power of the Will' in the following issue. Pound's chief allegiance was now to the *Little Review* but he continued to write in the *Egoist*, producing a curious series on 'Elizabethan Classicists' which ranged from an attack on Milton to offhand remarks about Greek and Latin poets, such as the question whether in comparison with Catullus, Sappho was 'a little, just a little Swinburnian?' But these latter days of the paper belonged to Eliot, who had for the first time a ground on which to express his opinions.

These opinions were strongly yet warily stated. Unlike Pound and Lewis, Eliot was not verbally aggressive, yet a strong sense of the reviewer's intellectual superiority to the material under his hand comes through in most of the discussions of new poetry. The true Georgian tone is said to be one of infantile simplicity, and the comments on *The New Poetry*, a collection edited by Monroe, are so dulcetly destructive as to sound complimentary. A new anthology, Eliot said,

> ought not to contain many good poems, but a few; and it ought to embalm a great many bad poems (but bad in a significant way) which would otherwise perish. Bad poems, from this point of view, need to be as carefully chosen as good; Miss Monroe and Mrs Henderson have chosen wisely.[48]

Sometimes Eliot used his name or his initials, sometimes called himself Apteryx or T. S. Apteryx. On one occasion he printed letters written by him under various names, including one protesting about his own review of Brooke, whose dross, Eliot as 'Helen B. Trundlett' said, had been 'purged away in the fire of the Great Ordeal which is proving the well-spring of a Renaissance of English poetry'.[49] This was almost the only reference to the war or politics ever to appear in the paper. In disparagement of *Georgian Poetry 1916–1917* Eliot said that 'Mr Gibson asks "We, how shall we . . ." etc. Messrs Baring and Asquith, in war poems, both employ the word "oriflamme". Mr Drinkwater says "Hist!" '[50] The Sitwells' anthology *Wheels* is said to be a more serious book, but does not get much kinder treatment. Amy Lowell is dismissed as a Director of Propaganda, and the all-American propaganda in her *Tendencies in Modern American Poetry* condemned. In this book Lowell discussed Frost, Masters, Sandburg, Edwin Arlington Robinson, and under the heading 'The Imagists' dealt with H.D. and Fletcher. She modestly excluded her own work from discussion, and similarly excluded Pound. She committed herself to the view that Fletcher was more original than Pound, and likened H.D.'s poetry to the cool flesh of a woman bathing in a fountain. Eliot did not comment on these excesses but said with unusual impercipience that the only negligible poet among Lowell's chosen six was Robinson.

Eliot's contempt for most current poetry is apparent both in his letters of the period, and these reviews. The most extreme of them is a passing comment in the course of 'Observations', made in May 1918:

> I have seen the forces of death with Mr Chesterton at their head upon a white horse. Mr Pound, Mr Joyce, and Mr Lewis write living English; one does not realize the awfulness of death until one meets with the living language.

That detestation of Chesterton would have been shared by Lewis and Pound, but these were not the three musketeers, nor a mutual admiration society. In the years ahead Lewis and Pound had hard things to say about particular works by their coevals, yet the friendship between the three never faltered. Pound especially brooded more and more in old age on the distant past and its people, described the wariness of the Possum as he had named Eliot, asserted that nothing of the past was lost:

> Gaudier's word not blacked out
> nor old Hulme's, nor Wyndham's[51]

In the late forties, Lewis nearing blindness, Pound incarcered in St Elizabeths Hospital, the two old men exchanged chuckles about Eliot and Joyce, not always without envy. Pound said he had more sympathy than most with Possum's 'later marsupial habits' because he remembered 'the headlong impulses (now ALmost incredible) of MiLord the rizen TOM'.[52] Lewis reminded Pound of the service he had done to our 'not very deserving kind' by selling the idea of Joyce to Harriet Shaw Weaver, 'which was the nearest approach to supernatural experience James J. ever knew'.[53] Joyce, among the four, was always the odd man out.

5. THE MAKING AND BURNING OF *Ulysses*

In 1906 Joyce had the idea of a short story to be called 'Ulysses' about a possibly Jewish figure roaming around Dublin. He told

Stanislaus that this figure would resemble an Irish Faust, but the story got no further than the title.[54] The book he began writing in 1914, however, also had in mind a journey through Dublin, with the episodes bearing a relationship to those in the *Odyssey*. There were eventually eighteen episodes, designated only by numbers, and one of the problems in discussing the book is that commentators almost invariably refer to the Telemachus, Hades, Wandering Rocks or Oxen of the Sun episodes, where readers will find only the numerals 1, 6, 10 and 14. Joyce himself used the Homeric references in letters, and avoidance of them in the episode headings is one of the barriers (a peculiarly unnecessary one) raised between the reader and the work. Either the implicit comparisons with the *Odyssey* are of very minor importance, as Pound believed, or they are vital structural elements, in which case they should surely appear as chapter headings. There is no doubt that they seemed vital to Joyce, increasingly so as the book developed. The relationship between Homer's tale and Joyce's fiction is much closer in the latter part of the book than in the earlier, and the author himself offered all sorts of explanations of what he was doing which became more complex, and more dependent on apparently unrelated juxtapositions, as the work progressed. Chords or motifs, Joyce came to believe, could be incorporated in a book as in music, with the references reverberating with increasing plangency.

In its early sections especially, *Ulysses* is overwhelmingly a book about Dublin, its places and people, with the Homeric parallels very much in the background. They become more obtrusive, and the narrative less literal, in the course of the work. More precisely, *Ulysses* is a re-creation of Joyce's youth, compressing several years of his Dublin life into a single day through the lives of Stephen Dedalus and Leopold Bloom, who represent the intellectual and sensual halves of the novelist's nature. In 1915 he told Pound that the work was a continuation of *A Portrait*, but he was then no further advanced than the third episode, and the range of characters was much enlarged later. Joycean scholars have identified characters, scenes and dates with the assiduity of dung-beetles, the interest of these discoveries being confined to showing the astonishing accuracy of the author's memory, and emphasising the fact that he was a romantic whose imaginative life ended with his departure from Ireland.

It was through such voluntary exile that he was able to view the past so vividly, but the enthusiasm of Pound, then of Weaver and others, was a great spur to continuation of the book. The financial support given by Weaver relieved him of urgent worries, and to this support was added early in 1918 the news that another unknown donor was putting 1000 francs a month to his credit. These comparative riches lasted only for eighteen months, after which his benefactress, who had revealed herself as a rich American named Mrs Harold McCormick, suggested that Joyce should be analysed by Jung. His emphatic refusal prompted the cancellation of her support.[55] The subsidies enabled him to concentrate on his work, with little concern for exterior events. From early on in the war he had been indifferent to the result of the conflict, and after it was over he said casually that he understood a war had been going on in Europe. In neutral Switzerland it was easy to feel unconcerned, and his attitude was expressed in a verse of his version of 'Mr Dooley':

> Who is the tranquil gentleman who won't salute the State
> Or serve Nebuchadnezzar or proletariat
> But thinks that every man has quite enough to do
> To paddle down the stream of life his personal canoe?[56]

This was Mr Joyce as well as Mr Dooley.

The international atmosphere of Zurich was congenial. In the Café Odeon Joyce may have met Lenin, although the conjectural meeting is not likely to have made either man's pulse beat faster. Several experimental writers were living in the city, and it has been suggested that their activities may have affected *Ulysses*, but this is unlikely. It is not recorded that Joyce was in attendance at the Terrace café on 8 February 1919 when Hans Arp, with a roll of bread stuffed up his left nostril, heard Tristan Tzara pronounce the word Dada for the first time, nor was he present when Tzara and two other Dadaists read their poems simultaneously. He was not a contributor to Cabaret Voltaire, and it is unlikely that the nihilism of Dada exploited there and elsewhere would have appealed to him.

It is more likely that Joyce's increasing delight in playing games with words was connected with his worsening eye condition. He had refused to wear glasses in youth, but accepted the need for pince-nez in his early twenties and some years later replaced them by spectacles. After the severe attack of glaucoma in 1917, Joyce's

sight constantly worsened, although with intervals when his condition appeared stable. In August 1917 he suffered such severe pain as
to necessitate an iridectomy, the first of eleven eye operations. Early
in 1919, just after the completion of episode 9, he suffered an attack
in his good eye, and another in the following year. Thereafter he
underwent all kinds of operations and treatments, none of them fully
successful. The idea that the steady increase of technical innovation
in Joyce's work was linked to his eye troubles has been called an
insult to the creative imagination,[57] but it is hard to see that an insult
is involved in the suggestion that an artist's work may be affected by
his physical condition.

At all events, there is no doubt that there are stylistic changes
within *Ulysses*, which can be clearly seen if the first three episodes
are compared with the last six, these latter begun in the fall of 1919
and completed by October 1921. Before *Ulysses* Joyce's stylistic
innovation, as we have seen, had been confined to the substitution of
a dash for inverted commas when printing dialogue. Now he used
puns, neologisms, outrageous metaphors, casual references at one
point in the narrative just as casually picked up a hundred pages on
and then given a sidewise glance after another hundred pages –
and the interior monologue, instantly famous for Molly Bloom's
immense uncompleted sentence that makes up the last episode, but
present also in many of Stephen's and Bloom's thought processes.
The idea of an interior monologue was not new, but no other
exponent had used it in Joyce's way, to convey the fluid discon-
tinuous dream-like nature of thought. Sixty years on, this way of
rendering thought as it randomly enters the consciousness does not
seem 'truer' than the more humdrum way that shows a character
thinking 'I must let the cat out when I get home' or 'I wish I hadn't
eaten those kidneys', but to say that is not to deny Joyce's supreme
originality. The development is that between the easily intelligible
extract from Stephen's journal at the end of *A Portrait* and the
immense interweaving of interior references in *Ulysses*, some to be
interpreted through puns and neologisms, others by knowledge of
Irish history and legend, an intimate knowledge of Dublin, even an
understanding of the author's origins and friendships. The full
impact of all this becomes apparent only gradually. The passages of
interior monologue in the first two episodes (Telemachus and
Nestor in Odyssean terminology) need little more interpretation

than Stephen's journal. As the day in Dublin develops and the pebbles of memory accumulate, and Joyce takes more and more pleasure in conjuring with them, at the same time keeping up a tremendous flow of Irish patter and Irish spirit, indulging himself in mock-pedantry which is half-serious, making Rabelaisian lists, parodying a variety of literary styles – why, then one has a work which, one of the first and best commentators on it said, 'not only seems obscure but is also somewhat inaccessible'.[58]

Little of this was apparent when Pound received the first episode in December 1917. He had been a tireless propagandist for *A Portrait*, and now was astonished by what he read. This first instalment seemed to him too serious for minor criticism, and he moved into an early version of American Poundese. 'Waal, Mr Joice . . . I recon' this here work o' yourn is some concarn'd litterchure. You can take it from me, an' I'm a jedge.'[59] He thought the *Little Review* might be suppressed if the first instalment was printed as it stood, but said it was a risk worth taking. As he received episodes month by month, and sent them across the Atlantic, he admired the monumental scope of the book and said Bloom was a great man, but became concerned with what he regarded as a tendency to the excremental, and said some things in the second episode were simply bad writing.

Joyce had sexual desires and torments which he expressed with unusual frankness in the letters he wrote to Nora in 1909 about his delight in seeing her stained bloomers, his longing for her to write wicked words like *arse* and *fuck*, and his desire to be flogged by her and see her eyes blazing with anger. Among Bloom's several incarnations in the brothel episode of the book he turns into 'a charming soubrette with dauby cheeks, mustard hair and large male hands and nose, leering mouth', and is subdued by the whore-mistress Bella Cohen who has become a man and enunciates or enacts fantasies for the pleasure of masochistic Bloom. He is told among other things that he will 'souse and bat our smelling underclothes also when we ladies are unwell' and 'empty the pisspots in the different rooms . . . and rinse the seven of them well, mind, or lap it up like champagne'. There is nothing very unusual about such fantasies, or even about turning them into reality – H.D. indulged the desire of Havelock Ellis to be sprayed with what he called the Fountain of Life, or in other words to be urinated on by a woman[60] – but for a serious novelist to write about them was unknown.

Such matters belonged to the latter half of the book. The first episode contained nothing more disturbing than the sea described in colour as snotgreen and in coldness as scrotumtightening, and a joke about making tea and making water in the same pot, although there were other phrases that could be regarded as blasphemous or distasteful. The second episode sees Bloom at stool easing his bowels quietly, worrying about the possible return of piles, tearing the story he is reading to wipe himself, thinking of the destruction of Sodom and Gomorrah in terms of 'the grey sunken cunt of the world', and seeing his penis in the bath, 'a languid floating flower'.

Some of this disturbed Pound, who advised Joyce to leave the stool to George Robey. Anderson and Heap were quite unfazed by the possibility of a second prosecution since they wished for nothing more than martyrdom in the cause of art, but Quinn was alarmed. To the *Little Review*'s subtitle 'making no compromise with the public taste' should be added, he said, 'or commonly accepted ideas of decency and propriety'.[61] He objected to scrotumtightening and snotgreen, and to other things also as he read on. Pound deleted a few lines here and there on his own responsibility, and tried to soothe Quinn by saying strong medicine was needed in America, while at the same time telling Anderson and Heap that Quinn was not the artistic Philistine they thought him. He had bought the Lewis pictures and was providing 'the Spondos Oligos, which is by interpretation the small tribute or spondooliks wherewith I do pay my contributors'.[62] At this time Quinn was contributing £150 annually to the magazine, of which Pound kept only £60 for himself, and it was only admiration for Pound that restrained Quinn's frequent annoyance with the hopelessly unbusinesslike behaviour of Anderson and Heap. However, the first instalments of *Ulysses* in the *Little Review* passed unscathed in America.

In England things went much less smoothly. In September 1917 Harriet Weaver understood from Pound that *Ulysses* was likely to be finished in the following January. Simultaneous publication in the *Egoist* and the *Little Review* was suggested, and she offered £50 for this, but warned Joyce that 'if by any unfortunate chance the printers should insist on making any deletions we should be powerless to do anything'.[63] In January 1918 she announced the first instalment for

March, but it was January of the following year before it was published, and then it was only a fragment of the third part in the first episode. In the end four such fragments, from different parts of the book, were all that appeared in the *Egoist*. It had proved impossible to find a printer who would contemplate the work, even with deletions. Printers objected to what they regarded as blasphemy and bad taste (like Stephen's nose-picking), as well as to sexual references.

At first Harriet Weaver found the book bitter and difficult reading, but as she saw more of it each month these feelings changed to total admiration. After reading the ninth episode, 'Scylla and Charybdis', she was unable to sleep, and after the twelfth, 'Cyclops', found it 'difficult to speak straight and to avoid interlarding one's words with the favourite and quite unladylike adjective employed so constantly by the figure who is the narrator of the episode!'[64] The difficulties made her more than ever determined to publish the completed work, and she remained unmoved by Marsden's opinion that Joyce was appallingly obscene, and that 'if the British public will struggle with this production it is equal to anything Fate could have in store for it'.[65] Leonard and Virginia Woolf had acquired a printing press, and in April 1918 Weaver went to see them, taking with her the first two episodes, all that was in her hands at the time. The meeting was not a success. Virginia Woolf found Harriet Weaver to be of a domestic rectitude and ordinariness perfectly symbolised by her neat mauve suit and the grey gloves put beside her plate, and wondered how she had ever come into contact with Joyce and his like. 'Why does their filth seek exit from her mouth?'[66] The work was politely declined, with reasonable remarks about its length making publication by a small private press impossible.

A few months later Woolf met Eliot, whom she found polished and cultured but suspected of intolerance and of strongly-held views far from her own. She remarked, and deplored, his admiration for Joyce, Lewis and Pound.[67] They became friendly over the years, but she seems always to have felt uneasily that behind his invariable politeness lay contempt for Bloomsbury in general and little regard for her own works, which he rarely mentioned. She felt ambivalent also about the work of Joyce, calling the completed *Ulysses* diffuse and pretentious, yet fearing at times that some of the things she was

[103]

trying to do had already been done by its author.[68]

Censorship of magazines in America was generally more severe than that of books. The eighth instalment of *Ulysses* survived its first mailing to subscribers, but the Post Office told Anderson and Heap that they must send no more copies by mail. The next instalment, 'Scylla and Charybdis', had as its basis the views about Hamlet propounded by Stephen, but contained words, phrases, ribald fragments ('First he tickled her/Then he patted her/Then he passed the female catheter') certain to cause trouble. The editors made some cuts, but the issue was stopped by the Post Office, and three later issues suffered the same fate. Pound pleaded with Joyce to delete what he called arseore-ial obsessions, deprecated the fart that ended the eleventh episode 'Sirens' and, as he told Quinn, took the responsibility of drying Bloom's shirt in the episode which closed with Bloom's involuntary orgasm. All in vain. The secretary of the New York Society for the Prevention of Vice swore a summons against the Washington Square Bookshop for selling this issue of the magazine. In 1920 *Ulysses* came to court.

This was just what Quinn had been trying to prevent. He had no sympathy with Anderson and Heap, although he still found Anderson disturbingly attractive. He had no doubt, however, that *Ulysses* was a work of genius, wanted to see it published as a book, and knew that a court case must greatly damage the chance of book publication. His strong distaste for sexual material and obscene words gave him considerable sympathy with the prosecution, and he had no intention of trying to defy the law by suggesting that a work of genius should not be subject to it. Although it was inevitable that Quinn should conduct the defence, for these reasons he was not an ideal counsel. Perhaps his attention to the case was less than it might have been because at this time his choleric temperament was in a particularly sanguine phase. In 1920 he fired five of his law partners, and some of his letters to Pound show the least pleasant side of his character as he rants against New York's million Jews, as well as its dagos, Slovaks and Croats. If fuel was needed for Pound's own anti-Semitism, Quinn provided it. He called Anderson and Heap, along with their 'Jew lawyer' and the bookshop proprietors, to a conference where he told them they had got what they deserved. When they spoke of the need to broaden the public, he said they would be 'broadening the matron at Blackwell's Island one of these days', and it would serve them right. His fury extended to Pound, whom he told not to write again complaining about the illiberality of the US laws. He made some tentative plans for a privately printed edition of the book, and wanted to keep it out of court so that such an edition could appear without any likelihood of legal trouble. He asked Joyce for approval of his tactics and received a reply which said that Joyce read nothing in the *Little Review* except his own work, and suggested that Quinn's fears about the effect of a prosecution on book publication were exaggerated. Quinn rightly saw the letter as an evasion and in effect disregarded it.

Quinn's attempts to avoid a prosecution by doing some kind of deal were gall and wormwood to Anderson and Heap. He gave lunch to John S. Sumner, secretary of the prosecuting Society, told Sumner that he regarded Joyce as a genius, and offered to guarantee that if the case was dropped no more of the book would appear in magazine form. Sumner was agreeable, but the District Attorney refused to drop the charges. In court Anderson and Heap, when required only to accept the summons to appear, made speeches justifying what they had done, and saying that prosecution would be immensely helpful to their magazine. Quinn ensured that they had no chance of repeating the performance by waiving their examination. When the case came to the Supreme Court he produced the defence he had adumbrated earlier, that if the 'average reader' failed to understand the passage about Bloom's orgasm it could not corrupt him, and that if he understood it he might be amused or bored, but again not corrupted. He started to make a case for Joyce as a serious artist and not a pornographer, but was soon told that such matters were irrelevant. The intellectual calibre of the judges was not high. When one witness said the Bloom passage was not aphrodisiac, a judge said he should speak plain English if he wanted to be understood. The objectionable passages were read in court, and the judges found them incomprehensible. Quinn immediately said he agreed, and that Joyce's experiments had gone too far. This deliberate appeal to the judges' ignorance failed. Anderson and Heap were fined, and it was decreed that no more of the book must appear in the magazine.

This result left Joyce disappointed and the editors indignant. Anderson believed that if she had been allowed to take the stand she could have made Joyce's motives clear, but it is most unlikely that she would have been allowed to do this. Her attitude, and Heap's, was expressed in an editorial in which she said she disagreed with everything done in court. 'I do not admit that the issue is debatable.'

After the trial Quinn continued his efforts on behalf of Pound and his literary stable. He gave financial backing to the publication, anonymous at this time, of Eliot's brochure 'Ezra Pound: His Metric and Poetry', and Eliot's letters constantly refer to the lawyer's generosity. He expressed himself as freely to Quinn at this time as to anybody, telling the sympathetic businessman that he would sooner be in a bank than depend on journalism for a living, extolling Pound and Lewis, telling Quinn of his instant antipathy on meeting Dora Marsden, expressing intense admiration of Joyce and regretting that he could find so few people in London to share it. He also, rather surprisingly, asserted his political liberalism and opposition to the British government's policies. He gave Quinn a free hand to make any arrangement he wished about his own poems, saying it was obvious he would not be published in America without the lawyer's help.[69] Again Quinn encouraged his correspondent's nascent anti-Semitism as he told him of the 'dirty piece of Jew impertinence' played on him by the publisher Horace Liveright in asking for a total guarantee against loss if he published Eliot. 'That is the way that type of Jew bastard thinks that he can impress his personality.'[70] In the end, as has been said, the poems were published by Knopf, a Jewish publisher.

Quinn bought more Lewis paintings, remained in friendly correspondence with Pound, stayed faithful to Joyce. He always preferred to conceal his generosity by asking for some return and for years supported Arthur Symons, who called Quinn the most generous man he had ever met, by buying his manuscripts. In part to help Joyce, in part to satisfy his collector's instincts, he arranged to buy the manuscript of *Ulysses*, paying for it in instalments. Joyce, in spite of Quinn's warnings, was still looking forward confidently to publication of the book by Huebsch, who had published *A Portrait*. He was deceiving himself. Quinn's warnings about the long-term effect of losing the court case were entirely accurate, and *Ulysses* was not to be sold openly in America for twelve years after the condemnation of individual passages by the Supreme Court.

CHAPTER FIVE

The End of the Beginning

Lewis had become an officer, been heavily shelled during the battle of Passchendaele, then assigned to join the Canadian War Memorials scheme as a war artist. Eliot had made determined but unsuccessful attempts to get a commission in various departments of the Army when America entered the war, asking for help from Quinn among others. To Pound, however, the war had been no more than a minor inconvenience. Indeed, in May 1918 he went to Paris with his wife, professing to have business there, although they spent much of their time on a walking tour through Provence with rucksacks on their backs.[1] They returned in September, and as the war ended and soldiers were demobilised Pound noted that Lewis and Edward Wadsworth were in town, 'Fat Madox Hueffer in last evening'.[2]

Yet all was not as it had been. This was a different world, and Pound's emotional antennae sensed it as such. At times he became weary of the struggle to make a living – he was upset when in October 1918 he was appointed to the well-paid post of drama critic on the *Outlook*, then summarily sacked after writing two pieces. He thought of trying his luck again in America, but Quinn advised strongly against it. Money was short, but it was not lack of money that made Pound feel it was time for him to leave England. He had a strong sense of disillusionment with the country's intellectual life, expressed in a series of articles on 'The Revolt of the Intelligence' written for the *New Age*, in which he attacked in vague terms what he summed up as suffrage, vegetarianism and eugenics. One of the problems in reading Pound's critical prose is that, while it is easy to catch the general drift, he proceeds by leapfrog jumps from one point to another, so that any particular article is likely to be written with an end in mind which is never actually stated. Aldington, one of the last to be demobilised, found Pound violently hostile to English literary life. He tapped his Adam's apple, reiterating to Aldington that the English stopped there, they had no brains.

In the spring of 1920 Pound and Dorothy left for a holiday in Italy. In Sirmione he met Joyce for the first time after their long correspondence. Joyce's arrival was preceded by a letter, written from Trieste, explaining with much elaboration his financial difficulties, and telling Pound that a train accident had prevented him from setting out. Pound sympathised, although he mentioned that they had waited dinner in hope of Joyce's arrival. Joyce then decided that he must make the effort to meet his benefactor, started out, changed his mind and turned back, and finally undertook the train journey accompanied by his fourteen-year-old son. The two men were pleased but not enchanted by each other. Pound suspected, not without justice, that the real Joyce was the Irish romantic who had written *Chamber Music,* and that *A Portrait* and *Ulysses* were what he called the registration of realities on that Irish temperament. Joyce called Pound a miracle of ebulliency, gusto and help, but suspected that the American had been disappointed in him. He may not have been altogether wrong: but still, when the Joyce family moved to Paris in the following month, Pound was there to help them settle in, and in December he and Dorothy also left London for Paris. The final decision may have been prompted by his abrupt dismissal from another job as drama critic, this time on the *Athenaeum.* Orage, editor of the *New Age,* said that by working for the advancement of intelligence and culture Pound had made more enemies than friends, and certainly much of the press was now closed to him, and his poems were ignored or received with hostility. Pound himself told an American paper that he found the decay of the British Empire too depressing a spectacle to witness at close range.[3] He mentioned the ideas of Major C. H. Douglas about a new credit system as the only contribution to creative thought in the past five years, an ominous sign of the turn his mind was taking.

Pound's instincts had not misled him. Most of the literary activities of pre-war days were finished. Although Lewis said he was planning a third issue of *Blast,* to embrace some of the material that a little later was included in his pamphlet *The Caliph's Design,* plus a story by himself and a long poem by Eliot, this never appeared.[4] The Group X Exhibition of 1920, in which half-a-dozen Vorticists exhibited beside other artists alien to their intentions, was rightly assessed by critics as a move away from the angular abstractions of the past, and the Vorticist interest in machinery. (The war had inevitably caused some artistic disillusionment with machinery.) Etchells recalled that Lewis had spent nearly a week trying to persuade him not to give up painting,[5] but like most of the others Etchells had abandoned the technique of Vorticism, and the ideas behind it. Twenty years later Lewis said that 'In me you see a man of the *tabula rasa*, if ever there was one ... My mind is *ahistoric*, I would welcome the clean sweep.'[6] But really such possibilities were ended by the war.

At the end of 1919 the *Egoist* gave up publication in order, it was said, to 'concentrate our energies upon book production exclusively'. Meticulous to the last, Weaver repaid unexpired subscriptions, although she was able to do so often in the form of Egoist Press publications. These continued until 1922 and included volumes by Aldington, Marianne Moore, H.D. and the young American Robert McAlmon, as well as those already mentioned. The final publications were the two issues of Lewis's new magazine venture, the *Tyro*. None of these publications showed a significant profit, although none involved a loss of more than £40.

Before his departure Pound published his farewell to England, the poem which is for this reader his most completely successful achievement, 'Hugh Selwyn Mauberley (Life and Contacts)'. In a technical sense the poem, with its quickly shifting styles, rhythms and subjects, is the justification of Pound's rejection of what he called the 'whakty whackty whatky whatky whak' of pentameter, and the exemplification of his belief that 'lots of lines with no variety won't do'. A rhythm is no sooner established in the poem than it is changed or broken, subjects are commented on rather than examined, the language is pedantic, obscure, colloquial within a few lines, and as often is spotted with references to other times and cultures. The technique, handled here with the utmost delicacy, is wonderfully appropriate to its subject, the story of Pound's attempt – and as he sees it, failure – to come to terms with British intellectual society, although this is more grandiloquently put:

> For three years, out of key with his time,
> He strove to resuscitate the dead art
> Of poetry; to maintain 'the sublime'
> In the old sense.

He had run counter, the poem says, to the contemptibly vulgar demands of 'the age' which wanted 'chiefly a mould in plaster/Made with no loss of time/A prose kinema'. In sections none more than a few lines in length, Pound glances (no time for a long look) at the failure of religion, the tragedy of death in war, the ghostly pre-Raphaelite idols of his youth, the nineties as discussed by a poet of the period, Mr Verog. There are glimpses of the condescending best-selling novelist Mr Nixon who says 'give up verse, my boy/ There's nothing in it', of a literary stylist who 'offers succulent cooking' beneath the sagging, leaky thatched roof of the cottage where he lives with his mistress. Much of this calls for explanation that it does not receive, yet it is not really important to the poem that we should identify the stylist as Ford, Mr Verog as the nineties poet Victor Plarr, Mr Nixon as probably Arnold Bennett. Nor does it matter greatly whether we identify the snatches of translation from Gautier, Rémy de Gourmont and others dotted about the poem, maddening as these often are. Pound denied any personal identification with Mauberley of the kind assumed here and said the character was no more than a dramatic device, a mask of the self, but the poem makes too many direct references to things that have no meaning except as events in Pound's life for this to be accepted. It makes little sense for an imaginary Mauberley to have visited an imaginary literary stylist in his leaky and draughty cottage and discovered that he was a good cook, nor for the first poem in the series to be called 'E.P. Ode Pour l'Election de son Sepulchre'. One of the problems Pound never really confronted was the contradiction between the extremely personal nature of much of his poetry, including 'Mauberley' and the Cantos, and his deprecation of a personal approach by critics to his work. But then Pound never accepted that such contradictions were important, never attempted coherence. There is no writer who better exemplifies Nietzsche's dictum that there must be chaos in the mind if we wish to breed a dancing star. Out of such chaos came 'Mauberley', a testament of his life and beliefs up to the time it was written. It was, he said in a footnote to an American edition of *Personæ* when the poem appeared, 'so distinctly a farewell to London' that a reader concerned with American matters might skip it. The footnote was later deleted, but it told the truth. 'Mauberley' is a disconsolate and defeated farewell to a city in which Pound had hoped to be accepted as a sage, but found himself after the war more and more isolated.

Lewis and Eliot too, for different reasons, found adjustment to post-war life not easy. Lewis was profoundly affected by his exposure to death and arbitrary devastation during the war. The experience led him to the not unusual conclusion that such conflicts must be avoided if civilisation and art were to endure, thence to the view that they could best be preserved through an aristocracy of intellect, which in turn implied a society the reverse of democratic. Much of his pre-war thinking had also suggested such a society, which he expected to be less philistine than the democratic regimes ruling most of Europe. When his mother died early in 1920 Lewis inherited a small legacy and, with this as basis, embarked on a course of social, philosophical and political study designed to enable him to produce a comprehensive work about the nature of modern society and the place of the artist in it. He published little that he wrote and found it hard to sell paintings and drawings. His one-man exhibition, 'Guns', of 1919 was reasonably successful because of Quinn's slightly reluctant purchases of seven drawings, but after that there were not enough commissions to live on. The enmity of Roger Fry, and later of Clive Bell, were partly responsible, but Lewis contributed to his own troubles by his quarrelsomeness and arrogance.

In 1921 Sydney Schiff, a wealthy friend and admirer who wrote novels under the name of Stephen Hudson, put up money for Lewis's *Tyro*, and so did Wadsworth, but this successor to *Blast* was interesting only for the reproductions of Lewis's own 'Tyro' paintings and some contributions by Eliot, including a poem under the pseudonym of Gus Krutzsch. Pound wrote from Paris that the paper was of no interest outside Bloomsbury. Eliot rebuked Lewis for associating his name publicly with those of inferior artists and said he should separate himself from other British painters, as well as from what Eliot considered the tainted company of the young.[7] The paper, conceived in part as a counterblast to Fry, never fully engaged Lewis's energies and died after a couple of numbers.

A year earlier Lewis had lost his principal patron. John Quinn had become disillusioned with almost all the work he had bought through Pound's agency. In vain Lewis told Quinn that Pound was writing a book about him (if completed, it was never published) but refused to reproduce in it anything but abstract pictures. Perhaps

The Founding Fathers

Quinn might be interested in other work? He was not. Quinn was determined to have no further involvement with modern British painters. He told Lewis that if he could paint as well as he wrote he would be one of the great painters of the time, and later signed off as a patron by saying: 'I shall buy no more of your work at the present time. I am through with buying tentative work.'[8] He told Pound he would be happy to sell all of his Johns and most of his Epsteins for fifty cents on the dollar (later he reduced it to twenty cents). As for Lewis, he would like to send back everything he had bought, as testimony of Pound's monumental folly and his own monumental stupidity.[9] Pound returned a soothing reply, and Lewis took his dismissal with good humour.

Eliot's problems were poor health and low spirits. Vivien was often ill with a mysterious nervous condition, and his own health was wretched. His letters to friends were much concerned with illness, strain, nervous tension. His literary reputation grew slowly. In 1917 'Prufrock' was ignored, or dismissed as having no relation to poetry, and *Poems*, published in 1919 by the Woolfs, was not much more warmly received, but the poems collected and published in America as *Poems* and in Britain as *Ara Vos Prec* gained a good deal of critical attention in 1920. 'When two people are discussing modern poetry together the name of T. S. Eliot is sure to crop up,' as Desmond MacCarthy put it.[10] Quinn, who had bought thirty-five copies to give to friends, called a review in the *Dial* by the young E. E. Cummings a piece of impertinence, and Louis Untermeyer still found Eliot's work lacking in 'the exaltation which is the very breath of poetry', but the American reviews were generally friendly. The evident seriousness of Eliot's critical stance, now on display in the *Athenaeum* and *The Times Literary Supplement*, had an effect, and his enjoyment of social occasions played a part in ensuring his acceptance. Pound might be thought conceited and Lewis arrogant, but Eliot maintained an invincible social politeness. Among the Eliots' friends or friendly acquaintances were several denizens of Bloomsbury, as well as the Huxleys, the Schiffs and the Sitwells. Osbert Sitwell would have been surprised by the harsh references to him in Eliot's letters, and Richard Aldington might not have been entirely pleased to know that Eliot thought him one of the few whose writings might count, especially since the reference was to his prose rather than his poems.[11] If the recently founded *London Mercury* succeeded, Eliot said, it would be impossible to get anything good published. His dislike of its editor, J. C. Squire, exceeded anything he felt for Osbert Sitwell.[12] Yet Eliot was ready not just to submit his work for consideration by the few whose opinions he valued, but to make alterations as a consequence of what they said. The humble admiration he often expressed for Lewis and Pound went along with contempt for some established reputations. Ford he found parasitic, Santayana essentially feminine (no recommendation), Middleton Murry lacking respect for reason.[13]

In the summer of 1920 Lewis and Eliot went on a bicycling holiday in France. One of the things Eliot found attractive in both Lewis and Pound was the expansiveness of their personalities, and the two got on very well. Eliot told Schiff that Lewis was an enjoyable companion and there was nobody with whom it was more profitable to talk. In Paris they called on Joyce, who had arrived only a few weeks earlier, and Pound's three modern masters were in each other's company for the first, and as it proved the only time. The occasion was almost ruined by Pound's well-meaning tactlessness. He had given Eliot a parcel for Joyce, which turned out to contain 'some nondescript garments for the trunk' and 'a fairly presentable pair of *old brown boots*'.[14] Pound had no doubt borne in mind Joyce's letters emphasising his poverty, especially perhaps one written just before their meeting in Sirmione in which Joyce said he had no clothes, could not afford to buy any, and was wearing his son's boots which were too big for him. The unwrapped parcel caused Joyce only momentary dismay. His reaction was to insist on being the host wherever the three went during their stay, in restaurants, cafés, even taxis. Joyce and Lewis, both hard drinkers and genial talkers, got on extremely well. Eliot's reaction was more careful. He detected insincerity in Joyce's politeness, self-importance in his quiet manner, and although he told Quinn that Joyce was charming, expressed reservations about him to Schiff. The reservations were personal and did not affect his admiration for *Ulysses*.

With the *Egoist* finished, Vorticism over, Pound self-exiled from London, Lewis almost silent, Eliot faintly praised, *Ulysses* effectively banned from publication, it must have been tempting to think in 1921 that what its enemies regarded as the lunacies of modernism were over. Certainly it was easy to think this in Britain, where the *London Mercury* was launched in November 1919 with a rousing editorial by Squire attacking 'experiments, many of them fore-doomed to sterility . . . dirty living and muddled thinking . . . fungoid growths of feeble pretentious impostors . . . platitudinous rubbish . . . hectic gibberish', all of them leading to 'the pitiful madhouse of moral antinomianism'. The impostors remained unidentified, but the poets who contributed to the magazine's first issue were familiar Georgian names: Turner, Sassoon, Shanks, Freeman, Davies, Binyon, de la Mare. Modernism, so far as the *London Mercury* was concerned, did not exist. Yet the years after the war ended were for the modernists in fact an interregnum, a prelude to triumph. A summary of what had been achieved may be useful, even though at the time the achievement was neither understood nor acknow-ledged.

The mould of poetic language made by the Lake-poets had been broken. It was a mould worn very thin and showing obvious cracks after the turn of the century. 'The Love Song of J. Alfred Prufrock' and 'Portrait of a Lady' surprise one nowadays by their nostalgic romanticism – how can their writer ever have been regarded as outrageous or coldly classical? But at the time the colloquialisms, the ironic juxtapositions, the deliberate drops into unpoetic language, startled and shocked. That Prufrockian fog able to rub its back and muzzle on the window panes and then to lick the corners of the evenings – could such anthropomorphised fog belong to poetry? Was it possible to make poems, not comic but serious and even in tone tragic, from the smells of steak in passageways and a woman clasping the yellow soles of her feet in soiled hands? For Marsh, Squire and their legions, for Untermeyer and some others in America, the answer was a decided 'No'. They found equally distasteful the later Eliot poems written in tight quatrains, introduc-ing a figure named Sweeney who seemed the essence of moronic Philistinism and who was evidently sexually involved with dubiously respectable women. Shocking also were the sacrilegious poems comparing the activities of the Church with those of the hippopota-mus, and in 'Mr Eliot's Sunday Morning Service' mixing up a religious theme with sensual Sweeney in his bath. The remarkable accomplishment of these quatrains, and their extreme nervous energy, escaped those whose ears were accustomed only to nineteenth-century tunes. They did not understand that they were in the presence of a revolutionary approach to the style and substance of poetry.

Pound's approach was less original, and indeed the extravagant language and tone of his early poems do much to justify Eliot's condemnation of him in 1914 as touchingly incompetent.[15] As a poet Pound was so greatly influenced by whatever course of foreign reading engaged him that his poems often read like translations even when they are original, and Eliot's remark that Chinese poetry in English had been invented by Pound is evasive in its praise. To say as Eliot did that Pound had influenced all the writers who had influenced him – Chinese, Provençal, Italian, 'not the matter *an sich*, which is unknowable, but the matter as we know it' – is to misuse the word influence. Pound at this time always needed some model to work away from: yet the best of the poems in *Cathay* and *Lustra* are unlike anything else being written at the time. Odd and charming little splutters, dry as their author's characteristic small cough, they make witty, sad, ribald or elegant comments on people and things. A cake of soap glistens, 'like the cheek of a Chesterton', a poem called 'Coitus' begins 'The gilded phaloi of the crocuses are thrusting at the spring air', many other short poems charm, irritate, amuse. Pound's contribution to the breaking of an old mould and the making of a new one was a minor one compared to Eliot's, but it was real.

The originality of the new prose, as represented by *Tarr* and the fragments of *Ulysses* that had appeared, was more generally recognised. *Tarr* had a respectful although not wholly enthusiastic press. Rebecca West called it a beautiful and serious work of art, the *Morning Post* said it represented 'the extreme of claims already staked out for our newest fiction'; it was praised for avoiding 'the illogical impertinence of a set plot', attacked for daring, frankness, brutality. Dostoievsky's name was often mentioned, although Eliot, giving a whole page to the book in the *Egoist*, observed that other novelists had evidently admired Dostoievsky, to no good effect. 'Mr Lewis has made such good use of Dostoievsky ... that his differences from the Russian must be insisted upon. His mind is different, his method is different, his aims are different.'[16] He remarked on the book's overflowing humour, and ended with a faint Eliotian note of qualification. 'Mr Lewis is a magician who compels our interest in himself: he is the most fascinating personality of our time rather than a novelist.'

[115]

The Founding Fathers

Was he a novelist? Certainly *Tarr* is not a perfect novel, in the sense that *Middlemarch* or *The Great Gatsby* may be regarded as perfect. It has little shape, no carefully devised form, and the author's opinions and personality often obtrude. The book's virtues, however, are so unusual that they make such criticism unimportant. They include the vitality of a prose wholly original in twentieth-century fiction, 'thick and suety, clogging the whole intestine', as Eliot put it.[17] He linked it with *Ulysses* as a terrifying book, and said that the capacity to invoke such terror was the test of a new work of art. This thick and suety prose is not always easy to read. It tends at times towards the near-abstraction of Lewis's drawings and paintings of the period, or strives towards their equivalents in print, with the help of the = sign which Lewis sometimes used in the book as in his correspondence, instead of a full stop. Yet the difficulty was necessary, as can be seen from the 1928 revised version, in which a smoother texture has been achieved at the cost of some loss in power. The conflict between Tarr and Kreisler, between (putting it with crude simplicity) art and life, thought and action, the intellect and the senses, requires the rough grain it was originally given to be fully effective. Kreisler, the exemplification of German philosophy in action, a figure in whom thought has been transformed into lust and purposeless rage, energy incarnate, is one of the great creations in modern fiction. And the book's psychological subtlety was not appreciated, either at the time or more recently. It is suggested in Eliot's remark that events are not seen wholly from Tarr's viewpoint, as is frequently said, but also from those of Kreisler and Bertha. It is possible that Lewis did not intend such shifts of viewpoint, probable that at times he was in less than complete control of his material, yet the book's power and subtlety are enhanced by the occasional rasping dissonances that result. Not all of this, perhaps not much of it, was apparent to reviewers in 1918, but they uneasily grasped that *Tarr* was the work of an alien and in some respects inhuman consciousness. The Lewis who wrote it was indeed 'a man of the *tabula rasa*'.

The originality of *Ulysses*, as already suggested, was of a different kind. It is in conception a perfect complement or opposite to *Tarr*. Tarr's belief, like that of his creator, was that it is a condition of art '*to have no inside*, nothing you cannot see' Joyce's greatest achievement, by contrast, is the rendering of interior feelings and emotions

[116]

as nearly as possible in the free, unorganised, sometimes incoherent flow of their occurrence, rather than in the elaborate Homeric parallels he so much enjoyed inventing. Joyce was much concerned with dreams, including his own, although he denied any interest in psychoanalysis, or that it had influenced him. His imagination grew when he read Vico, he once said, but not when he read Freud or Jung. Perhaps he protested too much, but in any case the soil that nurtured his book came from the Viennese school's investigation of sexual psychology and its origins. If Joyce was not familiar with their theories, the shape of his narrative was ordered by the discoveries of psychoanalysis, and so was some of the language he used. Several sources have been suggested for the basis of his interior monologue, including even a passage from Stanislaus's diary, but its merit did not rest in novelty. It had been used by Dorothy Richardson in the series of twelve novels called *Pilgrimage*, the first of which appeared in 1915, and in modified forms by other writers. Richardson, however, did not approach Joyce in the attempt he made to render *everything*, disjunct thoughts and physical actions, through the device. Her use of the interior monologue (she never strayed into random thoughts) shows only that events seen continuously through the eyes and mind of a single character can be both evasive and intensely boring. To read Richardson is to see Joyce's originality more clearly, for her Miriam Henderson is all mind and no body. We need not wish to see her like Bloom evacuating or masturbating, to realise that an interior monologue concerned only with mind and emotion is evidently incomplete. And although Virginia Woolf was briefly influenced by Joyce in *Jacob's Room* (1922) and perhaps the later *Mrs Dalloway*, she too shuddered away, in fiction as in life, from acts she had no wish to describe. One of the things that overwhelmed the early readers of *Ulysses*, even those as circumspect as Weaver, was that it seemed to be creating three characters, Stephen Dedalus, Molly and Leopold Bloom, more fully than human beings had ever been drawn before in fiction. An awareness of feelings similar to those experienced by Joyce's characters, and the freedom to acknowledge them brought by the overturn of much established sexual and mental orthodoxy through the war, assured Joyce of a responsive audience if his work was ever published free of censorship.

PART TWO

Modernism Becomes American

CHAPTER SIX

Meanwhile in America . . .

If America was a literary desert in the early years of the century, green shoots showed in several places during its second decade, shoots that sprouted into plants and flowers of a distinctively national kind. Suddenly, Conrad Aiken found, poetry was everywhere, Boston as well as Chicago reverberated with it, and there was a demand that this poetry – and imaginative prose as well – should owe as little as possible to Europe, be both American and new.

What, in a literary sense, did the words mean? In prose they represented a rejection of what was cosmopolitan, consciously sophisticated, stylish – Edith Wharton, Ellen Glasgow, James Branch Cabell – in favour of Theodore Dreiser, Sherwood Anderson, Sinclair Lewis, writers who were unmistakably national, owed nothing to Europe. Almost everything of literary interest, H. L. Mencken said, now originated in Chicago. *Poetry* lived in Chicago, the *Little Review* was born there, to Chicago came writers like Anderson, Carl Sandburg and Edgar Lee Masters, happy to accept the label *provincial* fixed on their prose and poetry. A number of energetic literary journalists were ready to give the new American writing columns of praise in the *Chicago Tribune* and elsewhere. Literary activity bubbled away furiously in the city, rather differently from Boston where the fire under the pot was stoked chiefly by Amy Lowell. Her money, her powerful physical presence, the readings of her own work at which she instructed the audience to clap or hiss but *do* something, the magisterial manner in which she paraded and praised her six chosen poets in *Tendencies in Modern American Poetry*, combined to make readers pay attention when she said the country was on the eve of an artistic and poetic renaissance. Bostonians who visited Chicago sometimes felt themselves less than welcome. Fletcher found Harriet Monroe cold, dry and aloof, and Aiken paid an uncomfortable call on Anderson and Heap, hearing behind him as he went down the stairs 'peals of uncontrollable and derisive feminine laughter'.[1] New York's Greenwich Village was full of aspiring poets, novelists and painters, although its most representative magazine, *The Masses*, edited by Max Eastman from 1912 to 1917, was primarily political. The city's literary magazine in the period was *Others*, founded in 1915 by Alfred Kreymborg.

Kreymborg had, as he said himself, little education and in a technical sense equally little knowledge of poetry. What he called his tone-poems or 'mushrooms' were rejected with such unanimity that he founded a magazine to publish his own work and that of 'men and women who were trying themselves in the new forms'.[2] He was a conscientious bohemian, as careless about his appearance as an independent hobo, looking for 'rhythmic patterns akin to music', which may sound like Swinburne but was not, for he hoped to find 'a type of equivalent language' to music rather than writing what Swinburne would have regarded as musical verse. In this desire that poetry should be expressed in terms of another art Kreymborg was a precursor of much more extreme writers. In his case the experiments got no further than poems spoken by Earth, Moon and Wind voices about a pantomime of beads, the whimsical little play 'Manikin and Minikin' in which the characters are two figures on a mantelpiece, and other plays written for miming. Kreymborg ran *Others* erratically until 1919 and later became a more conventional poet, although never an interesting one. In 1930 he compiled *Our Singing Strength*, a selection from the national poetry of the preceding three centuries, in which two-thirds of the work included had been written in the previous twenty years.

The national quality of this new writing, its rejection of European models as irrelevant to American life and landscape, and the anti-intellectualism that became its hallmark, can be seen clearly in the work of two poets and a prose writer: Edgar Lee Masters, William Carlos Williams and Sherwood Anderson. Others in the period, including Sandburg and Vachel Lindsay, could equally well be used to exemplify the need that was felt to produce work owing no debt to Europe in theme or language.

The poems in Edgar Lee Masters's *Spoon River Anthology* appeared from week to week in *Reedy's Mirror*, run by the liberal journalist William Marion Reedy. Masters was a lawyer living in Chicago who had produced several books of poems and a verse play about the Emperor Maximilian of Mexico without success when, in his middle forties, the Spoon River poems rocketed him to fame. As collected in volume form, they consisted of epitaphs for some two hundred and fifty inhabitants of a small town in the Midwest. All were in free verse, a kind of writing he had encountered first in the pages of *Poetry*, and they represented a break from all of his earlier poetry. It is unlikely that Masters thought of himself as a verbal pioneer, yet even today the best of these poems seem markedly original, and the relaxed form of these short pieces, able to accommodate varying lengths of line and changes of tone within a single poem, was perfectly suited to the material. The epitaphs are by turn savage, sentimental, realistic, ironic, pawkily funny, the best of them vivid character sketches. Often the images are crude, as in Robert Fulton Tanner's likening of life to a gigantic rat-trap or the Widow McFarlane's comparison of it to a loom with an unseen pattern, but such crudeness does not much mar the final effect. The range of characters is large – con men, doctors, judges, bank president, lawyers, local poets, tradesmen, artisans. Frank Drummer tries to memorise the *Encyclopaedia Britannica* before being hanged, Sam Hookey runs away to join the circus and is eaten by Brutus the lion, but most of the lives are humdrum. Violent events, murders, suicides, abortions, are recorded with a flatness more effective than any possible rhetoric. If there is a prevailing tone it is that of Mrs Williams the milliner, meditating on adultery and divorce:

> Well now, let me ask you:
> If all of the children, born here in Spoon River,
> Had been reared by the County, somewhere on a farm;
> And the fathers and mothers had been given their freedom
> To live and enjoy, change mates if they wished,
> Do you think that Spoon River
> Had been any the worse?

The combination of such flatness with intensity of feeling gave *Spoon River Anthology* its unique, and uniquely American, flavour. In theory it is possible to think of a British equivalent, but no British poet of the time could have written with Masters's awkward simplicity, his rawness, his combination of affection and hatred. Masters was never able to understand the reason for the success of the collection, nor to repeat it.

The popularity of what had first been weekly space-fillers was immediate and overwhelming when the space-fillers appeared as a volume. Masters found himself hailed as a great American poet. 'It has been insisted over and over again', Lowell said, 'that here was the great American poet, this verse was at last absolutely of America, that not since Whitman had anything so national appeared in print.'[3] Masters, along with Sandburg, was labelled a revolutionary poet, although the word had no political or literary application to either. The only 'revolutionary' thing about them was the crudeness of their language, which for a brief period helped to energise American poetry. For a brief period only. *Domesday Book* (1922) and *The New Spoon River* (1924), in which Masters used again the biographical approach of the original collection, are almost entirely unsuccessful, and most of Sandburg's later work offers less vivid and energetic variations on his poetry before 1920. Both men, as they became established literary figures, lost the intensity and energy that had made their poems memorable.

If Masters, and Sandburg in his *Chicago Poems* (1916) and *Cornhuskers* two years later, were wholly American poets, Sherwood Anderson was their prose counterpart. The appearance in 1919 of *Winesburg, Ohio*, 'A Group of Tales of Ohio Small Town Life', brought Anderson instant celebrity. He was in his early forties, a small-town boy like Sandburg and Masters, who in 1912 had abandoned wife, family and job as paint-factory manager, and made his way to Chicago to live the literary life. He contributed to the first number of the *Little Review*, was part of the city's rather genteel literary bohemia, but remained little known until the publication of *Winesburg*.

Anderson is little read today, and it is difficult now to understand why Hart Crane said that *Winesburg* was a book that Americans should read on their knees, Irving Howe felt it opened a new world for him, or the youthful Lionel Trilling found everything Anderson wrote a revelation. It is equally hard to appreciate the force of the remark made by the critic Ernest Boyd when he said Anderson's writing represented the 'revolt against the great illusion of American civilization, the illusion of optimism'.[4] At this distance of time, and from across the Atlantic, Winesburg looks very much like Spoon River done into prose. The model was the small town of Clyde where Anderson had spent his childhood, and the short sketches are joined only by the presence of the young local reporter George Willard. The incidents, mostly too slight to be called stories, deal with 'characters', the drunken doctor with very few patients who expects to be crucified, the closet homosexual teacher driven out of town, the girl in the family way, the sex-obsessed clergyman. Some of these themes were thought shocking, as readers were shocked by Masters's rapes, seductions and murders, but the sensational element in the stories was only a minor element in their success. Anderson said that in these stories he had made his own loose literary form, but in fact they have no form at all. The style is obviously indebted to Mark Twain rather than William Dean Howells, Anderson was in the over-simple definition a Redskin and not a Paleface, but his homespun manner also has a mock simplicity reminding us that he was much excited by Gertrude Stein's early writings, combined with a mock energy apparent in phrases like 'All over his body Jesse Bentley was alive' or the sentence telling us that Tom Foster when drunk 'was like an innocent young buck of the forest that has eaten of some maddening weed'. Anderson felt a mystical identification with the America of his youth where, as he said in a letter, men alone in the fields and the forest 'got a sense of bigness outside themselves that has now in some way been lost' and 'mystery whispered in the grass, played in the branches of trees overhead, was caught up and blown across the American line in clouds of dust at evening on the prairies'.[5] Such phrases would have made Eliot and Pound shudder.

Lowell and Kreymborg, Masters and Anderson and many others: modernism in America was fashionable, and commercially success-ful. It was a different kind of thing from the modernism practised and advocated on the other side of the Atlantic. Joyce, Eliot and Lewis, even Pound, were 'difficult' writers, all in greater or less degree with a contempt for populism, the 'ordinary man', the 'mob'. Many American writers, however, felt they belonged to that very mob and were delighted to discover how easy it was to be a poet or a story writer. American modernists had no truck with what most would have found the unpleasant or unintelligible ideas of Hulme. They did not particularly want to link modernism in art with any kind of development in society, but if pressed to do so would have pronounced it democratic. Just as Lowell had cried out that she too was an Imagiste, so a hundred young men and women felt all they

[125]

had to do was to rake up a few memories of childhood and youth and put them down in the simplest possible prose like Sherwood Anderson's, or set down their thoughts and emotions in unrhymed lines written in vaguely modern language, to be prose writer or poet.

From the beginning such easy modernism was open to exploitation by jokers. One of them emerged in 1916 with the publication of *Spectra*, 'A Book of Poetic Experiments', by Emanuel Morgan and Anne Knish. Morgan mostly used rhyme, Knish wrote always in free verse, and the preface to their volume said that Spectrism, the movement of which they were a part, was based on theories about 'the insubstantiality of the poet's spectres' which nevertheless contained 'the manifold spell and true essence of objects'. The collection was warmly greeted. Masters wrote an enthusiastic letter to Morgan, Fletcher praised both poets, Don Marquis in his newspaper column asked 'Are you hep to the Spectric Group?' Monroe accepted several of Morgan's poems, all of which were untitled, called only 'Opus' followed by a number. Monroe asked for a number of poems, she later said, because one would not give the flavour. The *Little Review* printed 'Opus 96', and in January 1917 *Others* gave a complete issue to the Spectric School. Morgan, Knish and the third Spectrist Elijah Hay never appeared in public, but the movement lasted for some eighteen months until one of its most persistent critics, the poet Witter Bynner, was challenged during a lecture and asked if he was not Emanuel Morgan, and Arthur Davison Ficke Anne Knish? Bynner replied simply: 'Yes.' It should be added that some work by Morgan and Knish seems to have qualities not present in that of Bynner and Ficke (for Ficke in his own person see above, page 22), but that is something not unknown in literary hoaxes. Nevertheless, the Spectrist poems were deliberate fakes, and they deceived many, though not all critics, because of American devotion to the new.[6]

The most categorical demands for a specifically American literature, and the most complete rejection of intellectual, or European, modernism, came now and in the following years from William Carlos Williams. Pound's dismissal of Williams's early poems has been mentioned, and for some years he was evidently unsure of what kind of poetry he wished to write. Although he only gradually freed himself from the English poetic locutions and manners he had been taught at school and college, Williams was from youth, and almost instinctively, inclined to dislike and distrust the literature of Europe. When he was studying pediatrics in Leipzig he wrote home to his brother of longing for the freedom of his own country, and he seems to have gained assurance as both person and poet when he returned home to set up as a family doctor in Rutherford, New Jersey, where the rest of his life was to be spent. In his first year of practice, 1911, he made $750 and bought his first Ford.

Williams's comfortable living as a physician meant that he had no need to worry about a financial return from his writing, and was even able to subsidise it. Before the publication in 1925 of *In the American Grain* he had never been paid for a book. Apart from two visits to Europe in the twenties Williams spent his life in the United States in a small town that when he was growing up had no sewers, water supply, gas, electricity or telephones, and even during the twenties remained a small American town, with all that implied of disregard for literature. In old age Williams said Rutherford had been a bad environment for a poet,[7] but it was the town in which he voluntarily lived, and there must have been much in it that was in tune with his increasingly aggressive anti-intellectualism. Free verse appealed to him at once because it was not bound by the rules he associated with English poetry. In a letter to the *Egoist* he proclaimed the beginning of a new era because free verse was now discussed everywhere, and in a running debate with Monroe he attacked her for failing to run a magazine where poets could write uncensored by rules. He objected also to her replacement by capitals of the lower-case letters he had used at the beginning of lines. He told Lowell, in relation to her Imagist anthologies, that apart from what she had stolen from Pound her venture was worthless. Her quarrel with Pound apart, Lowell was for Williams far too much influenced by Europe. Kreymborg, it is not surprising to learn, he found very congenial, and he was closely associated with the publication of *Others*. Kreymborg and his wife moved out of New York to New Jersey, not far from Williams, and Williams now for the first time actively participated in the editorship of a magazine. When Kreymborg's *Mushrooms* was published he praised it, not only as poetry but as a triumph for America, and he was enthusiastic about Sandburg for the same reason. Sandburg knew his America, Williams said, and was getting it into his poems. Should no European influence ever be accepted?

[127]

Only if it was changed, transformed. Laforgue would be a new Laforgue for Americans.[8]

Williams was to become an extreme example of the determination to write specifically American poetry. In 1920 his ideas were still in the process of formulation, but he already felt a distinct discontent with existing American magazines, even with the *Little Review*. He visited Anderson and Heap, who in 1917 had moved from Chicago to New York, and was impressed by their great bed hung by four chains from the ceiling, but regretted the frequency with which the magazine looked towards Europe. In company with young Robert McAlmon he founded a magazine of his own called *Contact*. McAlmon, who made a living posing in the nude for art classes, fascinated Williams. Two issues of *Contact* appeared, and then McAlmon contracted an extraordinary marriage and went to Europe. Williams was, as he said himself, heartbroken. Why did Americans want to go to Europe, why couldn't they stay home?

CHAPTER SEVEN

Paris Our Dream

I. ROBERT McALMON, REPRESENTATIVE MAN OF THE TWENTIES

Pound's role as public relations man to other modernists was almost over, but his sensibility did not deceive him when he chose Paris as a place to live rather than London. After the war young literary Americans flocked to the French capital. They went because of the shattering effect wartime service had on them, the feeling that 'all our roots were dead now, even the Anglo-Saxon tradition of our literary ancestors, even the habits of slow thrift that characterised our social class'.[1] They went to escape from the puritanism and philistinism of a country run by what Mencken called the booboisie, from Prohibition and President Harding. They went looking for freedom, sexual, alcoholic and literary, and for many of them these freedoms were complementary. They went because the strength of the dollar meant that France, like the rest of Europe, was a cheap country in which to work and play.

They went to Paris instead of London because many of them admired French rather than British literary models, because Flaubert and Stendhal, Laforgue and Baudelaire and even Huysmans interested them more than any British nineteenth-century novelists or poets. They went because James Joyce lived in Paris, and the subterranean fame of the book he was writing spread, so that it was believed this work would probably change the form and scope of the novel. They went because Gertrude Stein was there, and Sherwood Anderson had said her writing had made him feel he was entering a country where everything was wonderful and strange. Paris was to them a dream of civilisation. They went to absorb it, but also to turn that civilisation to American literary uses. Some visited but did not stay, like Williams. Most of those who stayed moved around the twin suns of Joyce and Stein, and produced and wrote for the short-lived little magazines that sprang up every quarter. A few were writers of genius, like Hemingway and Djuna Barnes, most had minor talents or none at all. The minor talents were mostly extinguished in a search for newness that became increasingly desperate as the decade went on. One of those minor talents, a figure representative of the decade, one of the lost men of the American Renaissance Pound had announced in 1913, was Robert McAlmon.

In March 1921 the *New York Times* carried a story headed 'HEIRESS' WRITER WEDS VILLAGE POET with sub-headings 'Greenwich Circles stirred by The Romance of Robert Menzies McAlmon' and 'Girl Proposed, Is Report'. The girl, the story said, had produced 'a book of self-revelation under the *nom de plume* of Winifred Bryher', but was really Winifred Ellerman, related to shipping magnate Sir John Ellerman. The bride in this case had proposed to the groom 'because she became enthralled and entranced with a poem that appeared in one of the Greenwich Village publications'.[2] The story was reasonably accurate. The penniless model for art classes had married into a very rich family. What the story did not say was that Bryher was a lesbian, was in love with H.D., and that her marriage to the homosexual McAlmon was purely one of convenience. When the couple sailed for Europe after the wedding, H.D. and her daughter Perdita accompanied them. Bryher, according to McAlmon, was not allowed to travel freely unless she married, and the marriage was 'legal only, unromantic, and strictly an agreement'.[3] He was given an allowance, and the two only occasionally lived under the same roof although they remained friendly until 1927 when, partly because of the violent scenes McAlmon made when drunk, they were divorced. McAlmon was given a handsome settlement, which caused him to be named Robert McAlimony.

Like many of those who lived the literary life in Paris, McAlmon came from the Middle West. He was born in Kansas in 1896, the tenth and last child of a Presbyterian minister. The family moved around from town to town in South Dakota, and when Robert was in his early teens they went to Minneapolis. McAlmon had what he remembered as an unhappy childhood, in which he was often at odds with authority. He played truant from school, stole bread from the baker, and when he left home worked on surveying gangs, on a newspaper, in advertising. Early in 1918 he joined the air force but was never posted overseas. He enrolled at the University of Southern California, but soon became impatient with the courses, and went to New York. There for the first time he made serious attempts to write, and there also met Winifred Ellerman, who called herself Bryher.

McAlmon spent a short time in England after the marriage, and passed muster in family eyes as Bryher's husband. He met Eliot whom he found cautious and governessy, and Lewis who was at first waspish, but later became a congenial drinking companion. In appearance McAlmon was of medium height, 'a coldly intense young man, with hard blue eyes', as Williams called him.[4] Others admired the neat regularity of his features, and thought him beautiful. There is no doubt of his suspicious and quarrelsome nature, aspects of his personality emphasised in a drawing of him done by Lewis in 1922. Very soon he left England and Bryher and settled down in Paris to café life, disregarding Eliot's advice that the city was valuable to a writer as a place and a tradition, not for the futile and time-wasting people one encountered. McAlmon enjoyed the people, loved the life of argument and boozing, and became the leader of what he called 'the crowd'. In between drinking sessions he used the allowance given him to found a publishing firm called Contact Editions. Their first publication, in 1922, was a volume of his own short stories called *A Hasty Bunch*, followed in the next year by a dozen books including two of his own, Hemingway's first publication, *Three Stories and Ten Poems*, and work by Williams and Marsden Hartley. Like the editors of the *Little Review* McAlmon was 'not concerned with what the "public" wants . . . These books are published simply because they are written, and we like them well enough to get them out.'[5] Only three hundred copies of each book were printed, with one or two exceptions, and Contact Editions ceased publishing in 1931. McAlmon chose well. In combination with a journalist interested in printing named William Bird he published Pound's first sixteen Cantos in book form, Hemingway's *in our time*, Mary Butts's first novel *Ashe of Rings*, and (the last publication) Nathanael West's *The Dream Life of Balso Snell*. He also gave generous support to friends who were hard up.

Between drinking bouts and private and public quarrels, which he conducted in pungently offensive language, McAlmon did a surprisingly large amount of writing. His poems are negligible. The best of his short stories, however, are remarkable. Like Anderson and Hemingway he was in a literary sense uneducated, and in part this lack of literary education gave his writing freshness. He became increasingly concerned with writing that was in theme autobiographical, in approach documentary, and the best things he wrote are bits of his life imaginatively transformed, impressing through their creation of a place and a way of life, successful through use of the plainest possible style and avoidance of any contrived shape. They are less flowery than Anderson, original as early Hemingway. Among them are 'Potato Picking' and 'The Jack Rabbit Drive' which are in effect reminiscences of childhood, and 'Blithe Insecurities' which is about 'a hobo following the seasons', moving from place to place as McAlmon did in youth.[6] There are ten or a dozen stories on this level. Most of the rest are part of what he called a transcontinental novel, bits of which appeared in many *avant-garde* magazines. They fail because of his inability to co-ordinate his material, and his chronic carelessness. His talent was for the short story and was hopelessly unsuited to the grandiose design of a book in which he hoped to symbolise the nature of two continents through the account of a single wandering life. He summed up his own inadequacies early on, when he said, 'I don't know, can't care, must write any way, nothing else I want to do.'[7] His erratic life and talent have a symbolic quality. He was the leader and also the truly representative figure of 'the crowd', an American crowd that came to Paris in the early twenties.

2. JOYCE: THE GROWTH OF LEGEND

Joyce, his biographer Richard Ellmann has said, came to Paris for a week and stayed twenty years. He loved the city, but enjoyed even more the fame that *A Portrait*, and much more the published sections of *Ulysses*, brought him. Constant financial difficulties were just as constantly eased by Harriet Weaver, and at last he was valued by others at something like his own estimate. This was high: when asked by an American woman to name the greatest living author writing in English he replied: 'Aside from myself, I don't know.' The family moved from one apartment to another, most of them small and uncomfortable, but much of Joyce's time was spent in cafés. There he received admirers, talked to them about the progress of his book, and by August 1921 was planning the final section, conceived originally as a series of letters written by Molly Bloom but changed to the monologue which had, he said, four cardinal points, *breasts, arse, womb* and *cunt*, expressed by the words *because, bottom, woman, yes*.[8] Within a few months of his arrival he had become a legend among literary people in Paris.

He had also found a publisher. This was, like most of his benefactors, a woman. Sylvia Beach, daughter of a Presbyterian minister in Princeton (there had been nine ministers in twelve generations of her father's family), broke with family tradition by opening in November 1919 a bookshop in Paris which she called Shakespeare and Company. It was in the rue Dupuytren, just round the corner from the bookshop owned by her friend Adrienne Monnier. Sylvia at this time was thirty-one, Monnier five years younger. The shop, founded with money given by Sylvia's mother, was devoted almost entirely to writers in or related to the modern movement. From the beginning it was a success, and within a couple of years had become a place of pilgrimage, particularly for Americans. Perhaps the success came partly because she was so unbusinesslike. She ran a financially unprofitable lending library, marked no prices on books, and preferred visitors to sit down and look at books before buying them. Shakespeare and Company became a place for people to meet and chat.

Joyce was, Sylvia Beach said, one of the three loves of her life. (The others were Monnier and Shakespeare and Company.) She met him in July 1920, at a party given by the poet André Spire. She already knew Pound, who was present, because he had come in and mended one of her chairs, but when she learned that Joyce was there she wanted to run away. However, she talked to Nora, who said that they spoke Italian at home and she couldn't understand a word of French, and after supper encountered Joyce himself in the library. 'Is this the great James Joyce?' she asked. He replied 'J. J.,' and gave her his limp handshake. She noted the fine delicate features, well-shaped nose and narrow lips, and discovered the light of genius in his eyes, even behind the thick lenses of his glasses.[9] Joyce became a frequent visitor to the shop and a few months later, on hearing from him that yet another American publisher had declined to print *Ulysses* as it stood, she offered to publish the book. (Or in her later recollection, asked if Shakespeare and Company 'might have the honour of bringing out your *Ulysses*.')[10] Weaver had given up hope of printing in Britain, but said she would publish an English edition from the French plates, and took the opportunity of sending Joyce an advance of £200 on royalties – this in response to one of his frequent, frantic requests for money. The terms proposed by these ladies enamoured of genius were remarkable. Beach offered Joyce sixty-six per cent of the net profits, Weaver ninety per cent of them. The printer chosen by Beach was Maurice Darantière of Dijon, and of course there was no question of censorship in France. Weaver sent over the names of bookshops and individuals in Britain who had enquired about the book, and a four-page pamphlet was produced inviting subscriptions. André Gide brought in his subscription in person, and Pound one from Yeats. According to Beach's records Winston Churchill subscribed, unlikely as that sounds. The most vivid refusal came from Shaw, who said the fragments he had read in serial form were 'a revolting record of a disgusting phase of civilization', and added that the 'Dear Madam' to whom he addressed himself was probably 'a young barbarian beglamoured by the excitements and enthusiasms that art stirs up', but he knew the streets of Dublin and had taken part in the conversations of young men 'drivelling in slackjawed blackguardism'. He ended by saying that if she imagined any Irishman would pay 150 francs for a book she did not know his countrymen.[11] Shaw's view of what he might then have seen seems oddly uninformed. Perhaps he had read the whole book when, later, he said he could not have brought himself to write down such words on paper.

Joyce's typists were similarly shocked. Nine of them refused to work on the 'Circe' (or brothel) episode, one threatening to throw herself out of the window, while another flung the manuscript on the floor in Joyce's flat and left before he could pay her. He appealed to Sylvia Beach, who got most of the typing done, although Joyce's difficult handwriting and the amount of material he added piled practical problems onto moral ones. Still, these were not absent. The wife of a British Embassy employee was typing a passage when her husband read some of the manuscript and threw it into the fire, burning several pages. Quinn had another draft of 'Circe' and an appeal was made to him to replace the lost material, but Quinn was in a bad mood. He told Joyce that he rather admired the husband and that the wife should have been pleased by the fact of his disapproval. He peremptorily rebuffed Beach and refused to have anything to do with her. Eventually he had the sheets photographed and enlarged and sent to Joyce direct. Quinn was annoyed by the way in which his generosity was taken as a matter of course and told Pound he was through with Joyce, although he soon changed his mind.[12] In spite of these problems, the large number of errors in the proofs, and the fact that Joyce complicated things further by making dozens of additional changes on the galleys, printing progressed.

It was inevitable that McAlmon should become a habitué of the shop. Beach deprecated his heavy drinking, but thought for a few days that she might be in love with him, much to McAlmon's concern. However, he was one of the favoured few who had their mail addressed to the shop and put into a pigeonhole box ready for collection. And if Beach liked McAlmon, she liked Bryher even more, delighted by her lack of makeup, nondescript clothes, and avoidance of femininity. Very soon McAlmon knew Joyce, either introduced by Beach as she said, or by his own account presenting a letter of introduction from Weaver. It was at once apparent to both men that they had in common a natural bohemianism and a liking for drink. McAlmon and the French writer Valéry Larbaud often spent evenings with Joyce, and one morning brought him home in a wheelbarrow. When Lewis visited Paris in the early summer of 1921 he and Joyce had what Joyce called several uproarious all-night sittings together, sometimes in McAlmon's company. Lewis told Harriet Weaver of these evenings, saying that Joyce often ended up extremely drunk. She was horrified, as Lewis perhaps intended she should be, for her emotional primness would not have appealed to him. Obscene words not previously known to her were one thing, drunkenness quite another. She wrote Joyce a letter about the evils of drink which became a little sermon. His reply, sent after consultation with his old friend Frank Budgen, was a masterpiece of evasion, listing twenty different rumours about him of a more or less ridiculous kind, and not exactly denying but certainly not admitting anything Lewis or McAlmon might have said about his drinking habits. He ended by saying, 'it must now seem to you a waste of rope to accomplish the dissolution of a person who has now dissolved visibly'.[13] When McAlmon came to England, deputed by Joyce to see Weaver and smooth things over, he told her that Mr Joyce was only relaxed by drink, held it properly, and was always a gentleman. With that she had to rest content.

McAlmon became something more than an acquaintance for Joyce, although less than a close friend. When problems arose about the typing of the last section of the book, he undertook it, working from the written script plus four notebooks containing phrases to be inserted in places marked in red, yellow, purple, blue and green on the script. At first he took pains to put these phrases in their proper places, but his natural impatience supervened so that he put them in wherever he happened to be typing, feeling it was of no importance when Molly had this or that particular thought. Joyce said years later that he had noticed the changes but did nothing about them because he agreed that the order of Molly's thoughts was not important. McAlmon also became one of Joyce's benefactors, lending him $150 a month, not all of which was repaid. He spent generously the considerable Ellerman allowance, often playing host to 'the crowd'.

Joyce found McAlmon a more congenial companion than Pound. The meeting in Sirmione had shown both men that their relationship was happiest when it was postal. Joyce seems always to have regarded Pound as an entrepreneur working on his behalf rather than a fellow-artist, and one night had a dream in which Pound appeared as one among a group of American journalists. Pound on his side was happiest in the role of advocate shouting defiance against the booboisie. He was full of admiration for *Ulysses* but was not prepared to worship Joyce nor to spend drunken evenings with him. His own life was frugal, and he disapproved of the way in which Joyce squandered money and then cried out for more. He was an absentee from a spectacularly successful session at Shakespeare and Company when Larbaud lectured on Joyce. The shop was packed by two hundred and fifty people, mostly American admirers and French literati, as Larbaud, primed by Joyce's key to the book which referred each episode to a Homeric parallel and attributed to each a colour, symbol, time, and art or science, stressed the relationship of *Ulysses* to Homer. The book was now finished, and Joyce, whose interest in dreams and astrological symbols was intense, insisted that it must appear on his own fortieth birthday, 2 February 1922.

In the summer of 1921 Quinn crossed the Atlantic, principally to look at pictures and talk to art dealers. In the course of the visit he saw Pound and also met Joyce for the first time. They met in Larbaud's luxurious flat, which Joyce and his family occupied from time to time. Both men were touchy about Joyce's request relating to the burned pages, and Joyce still thought Quinn's methods in the *Little Review* case had been mistaken. However, the meeting was friendly enough for Quinn to give Joyce 2000 francs, which he regarded as a further instalment on his purchase of the *Ulysses* manuscript. He had not long returned from this European trip when he received an appeal from Beach that he should send Joyce money. Quinn, who had had enough of literary women, told Pound that he would send money if Joyce was starving but was damned if he would do it at Sylvia Beach's request. Pound told him Joyce was not too badly off, and Quinn held on to his money. Joyce's lack of warm feeling towards Quinn may be gathered from his brisk cable when *Ulysses* was published. 'Ulysses published. Thanks.' It was not much of an acknowledgement to a man who had given money, time and enthusiasm over the years to advance his work.

Joyce's anxiety to have the book published on his birthday was literally fulfilled. The printer sent two advance copies from Dijon to Paris, Beach met the train, kept one copy to exhibit and gave Joyce the other. That night the Joyces dined with friends at an Italian restaurant, a toast was drunk, and the superstitious author was pleased by the coincidence that the Duke of Tetuan, mentioned in the book, was then in Paris. It was weeks and not days before the whole edition was ready. Joyce was in the shop every day, wrapping copies himself, suggesting names of possible reviewers, and assuming when individuals at *The Times* and the British Museum ordered copies that the book might, after all, be published freely in Britain. He waited fretfully for reviews.

3. 'THE BEGINNING, REALLY THE BEGINNING OF MODERN WRITING'

Joyce met Gertrude Stein only once, after *Ulysses* had become famous, when he said it was strange that they lived in the same quarter but had never met, and she rather doubtfully assented. She did not care for Joyce's name to be mentioned in her presence and transferred her library subscription from Shakespeare and Company to the American Library as a mark of her displeasure with Beach for being so much concerned with Joyce's work, when her own thousand-page *The Making of Americans* was 'the beginning, really the beginning of modern writing'.[14]

She had come to live in Paris with her brother Leo as long ago as 1903. The Stein family emigrated from Germany to America in the 1840s like many other German Jews, and in the sixties her father Daniel set up a successful clothing store in Pittsburgh with his brother Solomon. Gertrude was born in 1874, the youngest of five surviving children. Her first years were spent in Europe, but when she was six her branch of the family settled in California where she grew up, greatly attached to Leo, who was two years older. Leo, a bright student, went from the University of California to Harvard, and Gertrude enrolled as a student of philosophy at Harvard Annex, later Radcliffe. She lived in the shadow of brilliant Leo, sharing a house with him in Baltimore, listening while he talked or echoing what he said. In 1900 he left America to study art in Europe, met and became friendly with Bernard Berenson and settled in Paris. There Gertrude joined him, and there, at 27 rue de Fleurus, was established a salon at first presided over by Leo but later ruled by his sister.

Their apartment had four small rooms plus kitchen and bathroom and also 'a very large atelier' at first separated from the rest of the apartment but later joined to it by a tiny hall passage.[15] To Leo's Saturday evenings came the artists he admired and whose work he bought, Matisse, Picasso, Marie Laurencin. Leo became a propagandist for modern art. He told a friend that the 'Big Four' were Manet, Renoir, Degas, Cézanne, and added to them Matisse, Picasso and others. But there were limits to Leo's appreciation of the modern. He was enthusiastic for the Fauves, claimed to be the only person who in those days liked both Matisse and Picasso, but rebelled against modernity with the advent of Cubism. In 1908 he bought his last Matisse, in 1910 his last Picasso, and a few years later in an anti-modernist gesture he sold some of his Picassos to buy another Renoir. The change in Leo's attitude involved a change in his relationship with Gertrude. He had been the unquestioned leader, she had voiced his opinions, but now Gertrude admired the Cubist paintings Leo execrated. In 1907, after the publication of her *Three Lives*, she began to dominate the Saturday evenings. When a young woman named Alice B. Toklas, slight and dark, almost oriental in appearance and dress, joined the household and became Gertrude's lover, she flourished as Leo faded. There was no open quarrel, but in 1914 they divided the books and pictures they had bought (he took the Renoirs and a Cézanne, she the Picassos), and Leo left Paris for Florence. 'I hope that we will all live happily ever after,' he wrote to her, but his own health and spirits deteriorated, so that in 1922 he assessed his life as having been an utter failure. More than a decade later he summed up their characters in a letter to a friend, saying that she was basically stupid and he basically intelligent. Perhaps he was right, but it was Gertrude Stein who lived happily ever after.

The course of her life was affected by her relationship with Leo, but the nature of her writing was ordered by her physical make-up and her student experience. She had been from childhood large, placid, a hearty eater, a child who liked to be cosseted and cuddled, and as she grew up she remained slightly childish in her habits and forms of speech. When she became an adult, friends called her darling baby, lovey, and baby woojums.[16] Her splendid head and great treetrunk legs belied her disposition. She was, in the expressive cliché, a child at heart. At Harvard this large child took the philosophy classes of William James. He considered her one of his brightest students, she on her side worshipped him. As part of the course, she conducted with a fellow-student experiments in automatic writing, and together they produced a paper on 'Normal Motor Automatism' which much impressed James and others. The paper contains examples of automatic writing which prefigure the later work of Gertrude Stein.

She and Leon M. Solomons, her partner in the experiment, began by such simple approaches as writing the letter 'm' while reading an interesting story. They found that some of the words in the story were being written down also, as it seemed automatically. They went on to what they called spontaneous automatic writing, controlled, the experimenters believed, by the movement of the arm rather than the sound of a word. They called this unconscious writing, although it was 'broken into every six or seven words by flashes of consciousness'. The conscious self, as Stein put it, alternated with the automatic writing. Here is a fragment she wrote:

> Hence there is no possible way of avoiding what I have spoken of, and if
> this is not believed by the people of whom you have spoken, then it is not
> possible to prevent the people of whom you have spoken so glibly

And another:

> This long time when he did this best time, and he could thus have been
> bound, and in this long time, when he could be this to first use of this
> long time

Stein said she was a total failure as a subject for automatic writing
after she had been strapped up and her arm thrust into a big glass
tube. She was, she implied, too vehement an individual to be able
to make herself the necessary perfect blank. Her practice during
the experiment, however, belied what she said. What she wrote
'automatically', with its repetitions that made only an approach
to coherence, was to become the basis of what she produced
deliberately.

There was, however, no hint of automatic writing in her first
approaches to literature. She went from Harvard to Johns Hopkins
to study medicine and while there fell in love with a fellow-student
named May Bookstaver and wrote in 1903 a novel called _Q.E.D._
which she made no attempt to publish. _Q.E.D._ is about a lesbian
triangle consisting of Helen, 'the American version of the English
handsome girl', slightly decadent Mabel Neathe, and innocent
Adele. The style is ponderous, neo-Jamesian, at times absurd.
'Forgive the indecency of my having allowed the dregs of my soul to
appear on the surface,' Adele says to Helen, and when she receives a
friendly reply, goes on: 'I never expected to find you one of the most
gentle and considerate of human kind.'[18] The lesbian connotations
are no more than implicit. Adele is 'intently kissed on the eyes and
on the lips' by Helen, and later there is reference to 'the relations
existing' between Helen and Mabel, but it is not clear what these
are. The approach here, and in _Fernhurst_ of the same period, is that
of an adolescent, but at this time Stein was a woman – in a mental
and perhaps also physical sense a very innocent woman – in her late
twenties.

The first appearance of an approach to automatic writing in her
published work came in 1907 when, after the three long short stories
she called _Three Lives_ had been rejected by several commercial

firms, she paid for their publication herself. The repetitions, not yet extreme, give the effect of a story told by a child with a small vocabulary, or more exactly of an adult deliberately simplifying a story to meet the understanding of a child. In 'The Good Anna', derived in subject from Flaubert's '*Un Cœur Simple*' which Stein had translated, the heroine reflects that 'a girl was a girl and should always act like a girl, both as to giving all respect and as to what she had to eat', and remarks of a maid that 'Sallie's chief badness besides forgetting all the time and never washing her hands clean to serve at table, was the butcher boy.' 'Melanctha', the tale of a black girl and her lover Dr Jeff, has the same deliberate repetitiveness, accompanied by the double negatives that Stein seems to have regarded as a necessary feature of Negro speech ('I certainly never did see no man like you, Jeff'). Like all repetitions these add emphasis, and they give the stories an air of truthfulness, but it is hard to say much more about tales which in terms of narrative interest hardly exist. 'Narrative interest' was, however, the last thing that concerned Stein. She was moving towards a kind of writing in which effects would be obtained solely through the repetitions of words and phrases. The words and phrases themselves would always be simple, be written in the continuous present. One piece of writing of this kind is very much like another. Here are the first sentences of two sketches of people, 'Julia Marlowe' and 'Four Protégés':

Some are ones being very successful ones in being ones being living ('Julia Marlowe')

Four certainly are not going to be succeeding in living, not really succeeding in living ('Four Protégés')

These opening sentences are then elaborated on, varied, lengthened, so that near the end of 'Julia Marlowe' we have advanced to: 'The one succeeding in being one being living was not one who was one any one could easily be convincing that the one married to her was one coming to be one completely not remembering that she was existing.'

Such writing bears a relationship to the deliberate splitting up of literal pictorial reality by the Cubists, Futurists and Vorticists. The difference between *looking at* a painting and *reading* Stein is, however, great. As she enlarged her experiments in apparently automatic writing that was in fact contrived, she found what she was doing easier and easier. What she wrote could be as brief as the two pages of 'Julia Marlowe', as long as *The Making of Americans* which she began in 1903 but put aside for some years. The point at which the writer stopped was purely arbitrary.

In 1912 the 'Portraits' that have been quoted appeared, and in 1914 came *Tender Buttons*, a series of descriptions of objects (a box, a red stamp, another box, a plate, a seltzer bottle, eye glasses, a cutlet, etc.) which impressed and influenced Sherwood Anderson. These descriptions, again, are both literary and childish, some no longer than a couple of lines, others like 'rooms' extending to several pages. Sometimes the descriptions are literal, rather more often fanciful. A good deal of space is given to 'food', in which Stein was always interested. The few reviews that appeared were contemptuous or parodic, but she did not change her style. As she said much later, when she had become internationally famous:

> No one is ahead of his time, it is only that the particular variety of creating his time is the one that his contemporaries who are also creating their own time refuse to accept . . . Those who are creating the modern composition authentically are naturally only of importance when they are dead because by that time the modern composition having become past is classified and the description of it is classical.[19]

By 1922 Stein's position as a Parisian landmark had been acknowledged, and was known to young Americans.

CHAPTER EIGHT

1922: The Year of Triumph

1. THE RECOGNITION OF *Ulysses*

Any hopes Joyce had that *Ulysses*, now a book bound in the blue and white Greek colours that he considered both appropriate and personally lucky, would be universally greeted as a masterpiece were quickly shattered. Since the book was evidently obscene, some literary editors may have thought, what was the point of reviewing it? But still, some reviews did appear. In America Gilbert Seldes praised it, and Edmund Wilson greeted it as providing a standard and a stimulus. In England there were articles by Arnold Bennett and Middleton Murry. Pound wrote some columns of praise in the *Dial*, in which he played down the Homeric correspondences but invoked the names of Henry James and Rabelais and said the book had more form than any novel by Flaubert. Eliot said that Joyce had killed the nineteenth-century novel stone dead and added that the handlings of the parallels between Homer and twentieth-century Dublin had the importance of a scientific discovery. As usual, however, his praise was sprinkled with ambiguities and qualifications, whether he was writing to Joyce that he wished he had not read the book or saying that the interior method in general and Bloom in particular told one nothing about human nature.

Unfavourable comments much outweighed admiring ones and were often passionate in denunciation, especially in Britain. No doubt it did not matter that the *Sporting Times*, better known as the saucy 'Pink 'Un', said that the book was enough to make a Hottentot sick, or that James Douglas, who a few years earlier had condemned *The Rainbow*, called *Ulysses* the most villainously obscene book in ancient or modern literature, or that the *Teachers' World* said it was an immense mass of clotted nonsense. Joyce was distressed by all unfavourable reviews, but these were mere scratches. Wounds came later when he learned, as he must have done, that George Moore said he had read a little here and there but found it impossible to plough through such stuff, and of Edmund Gosse's view that he was 'a literary charlatan of the extremest order'. Gosse said this in a letter to a French critic who proposed to write an article about Joyce in the *Revue des Deux-Mondes*, adding with what one can only call a display of ignorance that Joyce was 'a sort of Marquis de Sade, but does not write so well'.[1] Nor did the reactions of friends and family make Joyce happy. His father stared at some passages through his monocle and then said that James was a nice sort of blackguard. Stanislaus offered qualified praise, but called many of the innovations technical monstrosities. Nora certainly never read the book in its entirety. Irish friends were chiefly concerned to know who was in it, to which the reply was, roughly, everybody.

Three months after publication Joyce suffered an agonising attack of iritis and rejected advice that he should have another operation. An American endocrinologist recommended by Pound said that all Joyce's teeth should come out, but he managed to postpone this until early in 1923, when he also had an eye operation called a sphincterotomy involving a muscle surrounding the eyelid. This, however, gave only temporary relief. In August he came to London, met Harriet Weaver for the first time and was no less charming than she had expected. If she noticed that he always took taxis rather than buses she did not remark on it, and the fact that he had a sudden relapse of his eye condition made her more than ever determined to continue her financial support of a genius. Support was always needed. Although he passed several of his thirty-three days in London confined to his hotel room, Joyce and Nora managed to spend some £200.[2]

The fame of *Ulysses* spread, not least as that of an obscene book. An Irish priest who came into Shakespeare and Company to buy it asked Beach if she had any other spicy books. Most of the copies sent to the original subscribers got through without trouble, but the Customs authorities in both America and Britain began to impound and destroy all copies found in baggage, and there was no prospect of the work being sold openly in bookshops. Beach and Weaver, those two respectable ladies, set out to smuggle and distribute the book illegally. Beach used an advertising man named Barney Braverman, who worked in Canada but had an apartment over the border in Detroit. Copies arrived safely in Canada, and Braverman, keen to circumvent what he called the Methodist smut-hounds, persuaded the Canadian Customs inspector that this was a consignment of cheap novels, and so paid only a few cents duty per copy instead of the $750 properly due. He then smuggled the work copy by copy on his daily ferry trip to Detroit, passed through without question by US Customs officials, and posted the copies to subscribers and to highbrow bookshops prepared to sell them under the counter, often at an exorbitant price. There were catastrophes – some four hundred copies were intercepted and destroyed by US Customs – but most of the copies got through.

In Britain things went differently. At first Weaver sold a few copies to bookshops, but when the condemnatory comments came in this was no longer possible. The manager of Bumpus bought three copies secretly, but could order no more because his partner objected to having the book on the premises.[3] Weaver had made these sales under the mistaken impression that only the publisher was liable to prosecution but now learned that any agent or bookseller was equally vulnerable. Dora Marsden, whose militant feelings had been roused by the hostile press, planned to abandon her work on the relation of the atomic weights of the chemical elements to the complexity of their atomic structure, come to London, mount a campaign for open publication, and then fight the inevitable prosecution. This came to nothing, and when Joyce visited London he was depressed both by the fact that there seemed little prospect of an English edition which would correct the many typographical errors of the French printer, and by Weaver's news that booksellers were asking up to £50 for a copy of Darantière's edition.

In the end John Rodker, who aspired to poetry and the novel but was most successful as publisher of handsome limited editions, arranged to go to Paris, deal with Darantière, and hold in Paris the bulk of a new edition of 2000 unnumbered and 100 numbered copies. This second edition of the book, because of the haste necessary in production, contained no revision of the text but only an errata slip. Weaver had no part in the production, although it was said to be published by the Egoist Press. Much of the edition was successfully smuggled through to America, some copies by ship and others by stripping the book into sections for rebinding on arrival.

Other copies crossed the Channel without trouble. Weaver dealt with the London orders herself, keeping some of the stock in the wardrobe of her flat and delivering copies to bookshops in person.[4] She might at any time have been raided and prosecuted, but in fact was not. Early in 1923, however, disaster struck when 500 copies of a further edition were seized by the Customs at Folkestone and destroyed. A single copy had been impounded earlier at Croydon and pronounced *prima facie* obscene, and Weaver thought it useless to try to fight the case in court. Now that the book had been officially pronounced obscene, booksellers were much more wary of it. Far more copies of these first two editions got through to America than to Britain, although throughout the twenties passengers returning to Britain from France would bring tucked away in their suitcases a bulky brown-paper-wrapped parcel and lend the book it contained to friends in school, university or club. *Ulysses* was not on public sale, yet there were plenty of copies available, not to be bought but to be passed from hand to hand. Throughout the twenties its fame grew steadily.

What did the readers make of it? Like other modernist creations *Ulysses* is easier to look at than to live in. To understand the book's general course is easy, to catch more than a small fraction of Joyce's jokes and jumps and juxtapositions needs a mind as full of references, as overwhelmingly literary and obsessed with language as Joyce's own. Failing the ideal condition of being an Irishman, it would help if you were thoroughly acquainted with Irish history and customs. The readers who came to the book in this decade might be divided into several groups. First, those who opened it for the sake of words and phrases not then to be encountered elsewhere, who would have been sadly disappointed. Second, those who had been told that this was something new in literature, many of whom would have read with increasing incomprehension and probably given up after a hundred pages. And third, a large minority, most of them young, who were looking for a fiction that, by breaking away from the customary restraints and practices of the novel, represented something like the breaking of restraints in their own lives. Those who taught school and those who were learning in university or college, those who had read much or a little Freud and were eager to look for motive behind action and gesture, those who wanted to break the bonds of their own and their parents' respectable lives, those irritated by the hypocrisies of British tradition and American Prohibition and felt the censorship of this book to be a good particular ground on which to base their general frustration – these, as well as the tiny minority actively concerned with fictional techniques and the still smaller one interested in the Homeric parallels, were James Joyce's readers. They grasped enough of the book to know that this new way of writing a novel, this delving into subconscious motive and the rendering of it in a manner naturalistically disjointed, had important reference to the way they wished to live their own lives. And in the lustrum succeeding its publication the book's fame was swelled by critical articles in magazines whose respectable character could not be doubted. No book banned from open circulation has ever been so much written about.

Not all of the comment was adulatory, even among friends and admirers. Hemingway in Paris told Sherwood Anderson in America that Joyce had written a most goddamn wonderful book, but McAlmon decided finally that only what he called Joyce's Irish wit and Irish twilight saved *Ulysses* from being dull, inanimate and pretentious.[5] Joyce was perhaps more upset by this lack of enthusiasm in a friend than he allowed to appear. When, a decade later, McAlmon read to him the manuscript of his own rambling autobiography Joyce laughed and said the book's title should be *Advocatus Diaboli*, but to others he called the book the office boy's revenge. Stein admitted that Joyce had done *something*, but pointed out that *Three Lives* had been published fourteen years before *Ulysses*.

Joyce and Stein: their names were bracketed by the earnest or flippant young men and women who came to Paris to worship, learn, and in some cases go away and write under Joycean or Steinian influence. Yet the use of language by these two was very different, and in some ways contradictory.

In *Ulysses* Joyce was moving through the invention of words into the expansion of language he sought to achieve in *Finnegans Wake*. McAlmon went to hear Joyce reading 'Anna Livia Plurabelle', one of the simpler sections of the book then called *Work in Progress*. It contained, Joyce said, the word 'peace' in twenty-nine languages and the names of hundreds of rivers. McAlmon made no more of it than that it evoked thoughts of night and deep dark rivers. He looked at the other listeners, who included Beach and Hemingway, and saw their faces set in grave expressions, so that it would have been 'cruel to ask them to crack the wax or break the mask with a natural grin'. When Joyce laughed during the reading they permitted themselves strained smiles, although McAlmon felt sure that none of them got more than he did out of the reading.[6]

If Joyce was concerned to emphasise the importance of words by inventing new ones, Stein wanted to downgrade them. One has the impression that she would have liked to eliminate them altogether. In the late twenties Lewis analysed the Stein manner, emphasising its deliberate infantilism and its destructive effect on language, and condemning it as dead. 'We can represent it as a cold suet-roll of fabulously-reptilian length. Cut it at any point, it is the same thing; the same heavy, sticky, opaque mass all through, and all along.'[7] Laura Riding, whose early work shows some traces of Steinian influence, called her language primitive and abstract. Moving on from a remark of Eliot's that if Steinian language was the future, then that future belonged to the barbarians, Riding suggested that only Stein 'had been willing to be as ordinary, as simple, as primitive, as stupid, as barbaric as successful barbarism demands ... She uses language automatically to record pure, ultimate obviousness.'[8] One could put it differently (Riding ended by praising Stein's clarity and simplicity) by saying that what Stein deliberately left out of her work was everything that makes a book worth reading. She would no doubt have approved of Basic English, which became fashionable in the thirties, except that she might have thought its 850-word vocabulary too large. 'The Autobiography of Rose', a work of the thirties, is put down with elephantine childishness:

> There there is a little boy
> Here there is a little girl
> There his name is Allan
> Here her name is Rose
> It is interesting

Interesting is just what it is not, as it continues through five pages. The beginning of 'Money', of the same period, puts the facts on the line: 'Everybody now just has to make up their mind. Is money money or isn't money money.'

Stein's writing was too simple to be understood. Readers looked for what was not there, failing to realise that her statements were mostly of infantile simplicity. Friendly comment had necessarily to be opaque, or what would there have been to say? 'In structurally spontaneous composition in which words are grouped rhythmically she succeeds in giving us her mathematics of the word, clear primitive and beautiful',[9] was a typical contemporary comment. Yet to say that her writing is worthless is not to deny her influence, nor that in some cases it was beneficial.

Pilgrims came to the rue de Fleurus and were welcomed graciously. Carl van Vechten, a young journalist and neo-Firbankian novelist, praised Stein's head of bronze, eyes dancing with merriment or steeped in ironic scepticism, the intense care she gave to rearranging a box of buttons. *Three Lives*, he said, was a masterpiece.[10] The most interesting of Stein's disciples was Ernest Hemingway. Anderson, who met Hemingway in Chicago, urged the young man, then a journalist with literary aspirations, to read *Tender Buttons*. Anderson was at the peak of his fame, and the young man was properly worshipful as he listened to talk about Twain and Whitman and the importance of becoming not just a writer, but an American writer. In Hemingway's early stories Anderson discovered the influence of Kipling and O. Henry.[11] When the young man and his newly married wife Hadley contemplated living in Italy, Anderson urged them to go to Paris. The modern movement was in Paris, Joyce, Picasso and Stein were in Paris, Paris was the place for a young writer. To Paris the young man and his wife dutifully went.

This was not the swaggering Hemingway of later days. Anderson had written about him to Stein, saying with some exaggeration that the young man was in touch with everything worth while in America. Hemingway and Hadley went to tea, and admired the atelier that he later said was one of the best rooms in the finest museum. He listened when Stein told him that the young Americans who served in the war were a lost generation, and soon learned that it was unwise to mention Joyce in her presence. He showed her the stories that were blends of other writers, although their dialogue was often lively. She criticised, he rewrote. Whether or not he read *Tender Buttons*, the rewriting showed the influence of Stein. Through her example he learned the value of keeping the writing simple and emphasising points through repetition. For her the repetitions themselves were enough, she would have felt reference through them to exterior events was specious, but Hemingway used them to make social or sexual or other physical points, as in Nick Adams's realisation of sex:

> It was liking, and liking the body, and introducing the body, and persuading, and taking chances, and never frightening, and assuming about the other person, and always taking never asking, and gentleness and liking, and making liking and happiness, and joking and making people not afraid.[12]

Some of these stories began to appear in magazines, and Hemingway expressed his gratitude. His writing had been bad before he met her, he said, and although it was awfully bad now, it was a different kind of bad.[13] Stein was not his only mentor. He became friendly with Pound, after a chance meeting in Beach's bookshop. They played tennis and boxed with each other. Lewis's first sight of Hemingway was in Pound's flat where the young man, tall, handsome and serene, was repelling Pound's hectic assaults. 'After a final swing at the dazzling solar plexus (parried effectively by the trousered statue) Pound fell back upon his settee.'[14] Hemingway told Anderson that Pound led with his chin and was willing but short-winded. Pound also was shown Hemingway stories, and blue-pencilled the adjectives.

With the aid of these nurses a truly original talent emerged from the unpromising Lardner–Henry–Kipling chrysalis. Would it have appeared in the same form if Hemingway had gone to Italy instead of Paris, and not been exposed to these mentors? It seems doubtful. Hemingway was in a literary sense a quick learner and adapter, but his natural inclination was towards the sentimental, the sensational, the physically lyrical. The restrictive influences of Stein and Pound were enormously beneficial. The tautness of his style sprang partly from the demands of his work in journalism, particularly on the *Toronto Star*, but it was refined and shaped by what he learned from his mentors about the value of phrases repeated and of things left unsaid.

The very short stories, some almost factual journalism, that he wrote in 1922 and 1923, were published as *in our time* in the following year, after *Three Stories and Ten Poems*. They caused a stir among American expatriates in Paris, a sound whose echoes crossed the Atlantic, so that a commercial publisher produced *In Our Time* in 1925 to a chorus of praise. The two works are by no means identical, the factual sketches of McAlmon's publication of *in our time* being interspersed between the Nick Adams stories in the later book. Hemingway's intentions in this odd construction were that the factual nature and deadpan impartiality of the sketches should contrast with the intensely personal and often physical quality of the Nick Adams stories, so that the effect would be like that of looking at a scene from a distance and then seeing it in close-up, or living in it. Few readers are likely to have been affected in that way. Immediately obvious, however, were the sparseness, intensity and originality of the prose. Edmund Wilson, as usual, was first off the mark, reviewing the two Paris-published works in the *Dial*, commending Hemingway's prose as of the first distinction, and saying that Stein, Anderson and Hemingway might be said to form a school marked by 'a naiveté of language . . . which serves actually to convey profound emotions and complex states of mind'.[15] He added that this development was distinctively American.

Hemingway wrote a suitably modest acknowledgement of the review. Within a very few years, however, the modesty was replaced by a spitefulness that led him to write a savage parody of Anderson (*The Torrents of Spring*) and, for no obvious reason, to quarrel with Stein. He remained on good terms with Pound, however, throughout his life.

2 THE *Dial* AWARD TO *The Waste Land*

Among Quinn's manifold benefactions to Eliot and Pound was an arrangement he made in 1920 that Eliot should write a regular London Letter and Pound a Paris Letter for the *Dial*. This was a long-established magazine of a kind Quinn respected. It was literary but decorous, with no Washington Squareitis about it, nothing about refusing to compromise with the public taste. In 1919 two rich young men, Scofield Thayer and James Sibley Watson Jr, took over and transformed the magazine, retaining its staidly elegant appearance but playing host to a variety of writers, painters, anthropologists, philosophers and psychologists who had interesting new theories and ideas about life and art in the twenties. Yet their enthusiasm for the new did not exclude respect for the conventional and established. In a typical period of six months (January–July 1921) they printed poems by Williams, Mina Loy, Kreymborg, Aiken – but also by Harold Monro, John Drinkwater and Witter Bynner. Thayer, like Eliot, had attended Milton Academy, Harvard and Oxford, and the two knew each other, although not well. Thayer was a self-consciously sophisticated aesthete, with a strong interest in all modern art that stayed this side of abstraction, and what might be called decisively moderate opinions about modern literature. He called Pound's early Cantos unbelievable rot, and regarded Anderson as of no interest except as a short story writer. There were those who thought Thayer affected, but a more friendly view was that 'what were taken for affectations were mannerisms indigenous to his character ... He was ice on the surface and molten lava underneath.'[16]

Eliot thought little of the new *Dial*, but said it might be toned up by a London editor, no doubt having himself or Pound in mind. He was, he told Quinn, worried about what was to become of Pound. At much the same time Pound was expressing to Quinn his indignation that Eliot should be spending eight hours a day in a bank. Partly through Quinn's advocacy, generous offers were made by Thayer to both men, and were promptly accepted, Pound's in a six-page letter that took the form of a rambling lecture on literature and criticism. Quinn's injunction that Pound should behave with tact and discretion in dealing with Thayer went unheeded. Pound also was not over-optimistic about what could be done with the *Dial*, telling T. E. Lawrence that he hoped to ginger it up to 'something approaching the frenetic wildness of the *Athenaeum*'.[17] Nevertheless, both men enjoyed themselves, Eliot particularly. In one of his Letters he denounced once more what proved to be the last of the Georgian anthologies. Its dullness, he said, was original, unique, its audience that offensive part of the middle class which thought itself culturally superior to 'the decent middle-class mob'.[18]

Thayer and Watson had no intention of risking censorship troubles and would never have considered publishing the extracts from *Ulysses* that brought prosecution on the *Little Review*, but the encouragement they gave to modern literature, and especially to American writers, was constant. From 1921 onwards a yearly award of $2000 was made for services to American letters. The first recipient was Sherwood Anderson. The second, Eliot learned from

Quinn in August 1922, would be given for *The Waste Land*.

The history of the poem, often told, must be briefly repeated here. In 1921 Eliot suffered the kind of emotional collapse evasively described as a mental breakdown. He was told in September that he must go away at once, and alone, for three months, and was given paid leave by the bank to do so. The trouble, he told Aldington a little later, was not overwork but 'an *aboulie* and emotional derangement which has been a lifelong affliction',[19] although Aiken suggested it might have been caused by the severe strain of being an Englishman. He was able, however, to work on a poem. In November he went to Lausanne, spent some weeks there in the care of Dr Roger Vittoz, who seems to have prescribed a fairly simple form of psychological therapy, and in January 1922 returned to London. Both on the way to Lausanne and on the return journey he stayed briefly in Paris and showed the poem to Pound. This was *The Waste Land*. Pound advised many changes, perhaps the most important being the deletion of the first fifty-odd lines, a pub and brothel scene, and of what Eliot afterwards called an excellent set of couplets. Pound said, however, that Pope had done this kind of thing so well that it could not be done better. Near the end of his letter Pound said 'Complimenti, you bitch. I am wracked by the seven jealousies,' and in relation to what he called his obstetric efforts wrote some verses ending

> If you must needs enquire
> Know diligent Reader
> That on each Occasion
> Ezra performed the caesarean Operation

Eliot accepted almost all of the suggested changes, asking for further advice from *Cher Maître*, and saying that he wanted to use Pound's verse in italics before the poem. This was not done, but *The Waste Land* was dedicated to Pound.[20]

So far the history: but the poem can, and should, be seen also as a summary of and comment on Eliot's mostly unhappy life, in particular his married life. Vivien wrote to the Schiffs that she could hardly bear the thought of seeing the poem in print,[21] and in view of the problems in their marriage there is a poignancy about one of the suggested changes she scribbled on the draft. 'What you get married for if you don't want to have children?' she wrote in reference to

[153]

Albert and Lil in 'A Game of Chess'.[22] The line was used, replacing
the weaker 'You want to keep him at home, I suppose'. The
technique was that used in many of the earlier poems, the sudden
shifts of tone and tempo derived chiefly from Laforgue, the ironic
juxtapositions (more marked before Pound's excisions), the classical, historical and literary references and quotations, which called for
dozens of notes at the end. Aiken found several passages he had
read in unpublished early poems, and there were one or two Eliotian
jokes like use of the name Gus Krutzsch, the pseudonym used in
Eliot's *Tyro* poem. For Eliot the poem was both the culmination and
the close of a period in his poetry. Late in 1922 he told Aldington
that he was feeling towards a new form and style. He was never
again to use that elaborate framework of cultural reference, and the
ironic juxtapositions, too, were almost eliminated from his later
poems. In old age he was inclined to deprecate *The Waste Land* as a
work that was simply an expression of personal unhappiness, and in
1959 he was depressed by rumours that the original manuscript had
been found.[23] He also referred to his notes with retrospective
harshness as a 'remarkable exposition of bogus scholarship',[24] and
it is true that anybody who came to them in hope of finding an
explanation of the poem's form would have been disappointed.

In 1921, through Sydney Schiff, Eliot was introduced to Lady
Rothermere. She was prepared to back a new literary review, and
appoint Eliot as editor. The negotiations were lengthy, and included
at one time the idea of close links with the *Dial*, something wisely
avoided, since Thayer's eclecticism would never have suited Eliot's
desire to produce a magazine with Hulmeian tendencies. In the end
the name *Criterion* was agreed, and Eliot burdened himself with the
duties of running a book-sized quarterly (later for a brief time a
monthly) review. The money he received as editor was nothing like
enough to enable him to give up his job at the bank, and payment to
contributors was at best, as he told Aiken, exiguous. In spite of the
financial stringency, to which was added Lady Rothermere's desire
for something more fashionable and less heavyweight than Eliot
produced, he was delighted to have his own magazine. It must have
added to his pleasure that Vivien helped with such practical matters
as typing, and contributed several short pieces under pseudonyms.
The Rothermere connection was never a happy one on either side,
and in 1927 she withdrew her support and was replaced by the

publishing firm of Faber & Gwyer (later Faber & Faber) which Eliot had joined in 1925. All this was in the future. The first issue of the *Criterion* came out in October 1921, and in it appeared *The Waste Land*.

The story of literary modernism in its first two decades was the story of little magazines, because only such magazines were prepared to consider writing new in language and conception. Were the *Criterion* and *Dial* little magazines? In the sense of making a deliberate appeal to a minority audience the *Criterion* filled the bill, since the circulation was never more than a few hundred. The *Dial*, on the other hand, had a circulation of 10,000 at the end of 1921,[25] although it still lost money, in part because both staff and contributors were reasonably and regularly paid. Argument about the precise definition of a little magazine will never be resolved, but it was partly the size and nature of the *Dial*'s readership that caused doubt to arise about Eliot's acceptability as a recipient of the award. The *Dial* was devoted to a particularly American spirit of modernism which would 'convey that special serum of the imagination with which Thayer hoped to revive the true American spirit'.[26] That Eliot's poem, or his general approach to literature, should have been thought to contain that serum is odd indeed. He may have seemed to the British obviously American, but he had decisively turned his back on the kind of work his compatriots (with a very few exceptions) were producing. The *Criterion* rejected the deliberate simplicity that marked American poetic modernism, so that when Aiken suggested articles about Williams and Marianne Moore he was told 'candidly' that the magazine could not use anything long about either of them.[27] To Thayer's doubts about the poem was added an argument about payment, Thayer offering $150, and Eliot asking for something like $4000, a considerable sum even now, and then a small fortune. Thayer had made his offer sight unseen, and when he read the poem he was disappointed, thinking it inferior to Eliot's early work. Others, including Watson, were enthusiastic, and eventually Thayer conquered his doubts about the poem, and about Eliot's cosmopolitanism, and decided to use the award to *The Waste Land*, and the poem itself, as proof of the maturity of American literature.

Eliot left the negotiations to Quinn, who arranged for book publication of the poem with Boni & Liveright, although he thought its readers would be confined to 'the select few or the superior guys.'[28] When Quinn learned that it would receive the *Dial* award he realised that he could now negotiate from a favourable position, and in the end the magazine agreed to pay for the poem at its standard rates (plus of course the award), and also to buy 350 copies of the book for sale to their subscribers. Boni & Liveright, on their side, delayed publication until the *Dial* had appeared.[29] It was an ideal arrangement for Eliot. He expressed himself overwhelmed, and insisted that Quinn should accept the manuscript of the poem as a gift. Thayer and Watson agreed that the little-known Eliot must be publicised, and George Saintsbury was invited to write an essay on him, a suggestion which shows some ignorance of English literary attitudes to modernism. Saintsbury duly declined, and they approached Edmund Wilson, whose long article 'The Poetry of Drouth' is one of the most perceptive pieces ever written about the poem or indeed about Eliot. The poet's first small volume, Wilson said, had stirred only a few ripples, but was now 'found to stain the whole sea'. He paid considerable attention to the poem's symbolism suggested through Jessie L. Weston's book, said that Eliot 'uses the Waste Land as the concrete image of a spiritual drouth', and went on to a detailed explanation of the poem's individual parts. He listed most of the things said at the time and later against Eliot (his borrowings, his distaste for the physical, his constricted emotional experience), and dismissed them because in the end 'Mr Eliot's trivialities are more valuable than other people's epics'. Wilson later expanded this view of Eliot, but never improved on it.

The poem was warmly received rather than universally acclaimed. Most of those who praised it did so on Wilson's lines but less coherently, as the poetic expression of a widespread disillusionment with the material world, a search for faith. Adverse views were sometimes based on the poem's unintelligibility, sometimes on the passages of coarsely colloquial language. Aiken called it a brilliant and kaleidoscopic confusion. Privately he said it cancelled any poetic debt he owed to Eliot. 'I seem to detect echoes or parodies of Senlin, *House, Forslin* in the evening at the violet hour, etc, Madame Sosostris, etc.'[30] and there are certainly some distinct rhythmic similarities, in particular between Eliot's poem and Aiken's 'Senlin'. Harriet Monroe reviewed the poem, along with *The Box of God*, 'an outdoor man's poem of faith' by Lew Sarett, rather to the advantage of the latter. Untermeyer, that old opponent of modernism, said the award had 'occasioned a display of some of the most enthusiastically naive superlatives that have ever issued from publicly sophisticated iconoclasts'. Harold Monro, in the course of an imaginary dialogue with Eliot, said that in England the poem had been regarded 'chiefly with indignation or contempt'. That was hardly an overstatement. J. C. Squire said that 'a grunt would serve equally well', F. L. Lucas that 'among the maggots that breed in the corruption of poetry one of the commonest is the bookworm', with the implication that Eliot was one of the maggots, the *Manchester Guardian* that the poem was so much waste paper. Clive Bell, with a sideswipe at 'the lamentable Ezra Pound', convicted Eliot of a lack of imagination, and Edgell Rickword in an unsigned review in *The Times Literary Supplement* called the poem an ambitious experiment, with the implication that the experiment was a failure.

It is easy to understand some of this criticism, and right and reasonable to ask whether all the allusiveness was necessary, not only the scraps of foreign languages but the lines taken from here and there (as faithfully recorded in the notes), the disjointedness of the various pieces in relation to the whole, the undoubted facts that as Aiken pointed out the symbols did not always quite belong where they had been put and the positioning of the parts in the poem was not inevitable. If the order had been inevitable Pound could not have made his changes, some ruthless, without severe damage to the whole. It is possible, indeed, to consider *The Waste Land* as not one but a series of poems, Eliot's 'Mauberley'. Pound seems to have regarded it rather in that way, although he approved of what was evidently a change in order by which Eliot, on Pound's second sight of the work, had 'put the remaining superfluities at the end'. These were presumably the short poems that appear at the end of the facsimile version. Pound thought they should be omitted, and they were, but their very existence shows that the poem was not conceived as a single entity.

Yet all this matters very little. If the poem had been printed in its original entirety, without Pound's deletions, or if the five sections were printed in a different order, the effect would not be much changed or the poem's power lessened, because it is primarily an expression of Eliot's sensibility, and only secondarily a logical progression in terms of theme. And the shifts of tone and style were not an ambitious experiment but the elaboration of similar shifts in

'Prufrock' and 'Gerontion'. They are justified in terms of what 'the age demanded' in a changed poetic approach, a changed language. To express the despair that is the poem's ultimate message in language used by the Georgians – and still used in America by many contributors to *Poetry* – would have been like trying to write poetic drama in Elizabethan blank verse, something which the Georgian Lascelles Abercrombie did in fact attempt. Eliot's poem, like *Ulysses* and *Tarr*, was part of a revolution that was a social and aesthetic recognition of contemporary reality. And like other great writers who have borrowed themes and phrases, Eliot transformed what he took over into something that belonged to himself.

The Waste Land triumphed over the hostility of most British critics and the half-heartedness of some Americans, so that Eliot's influence on young poets was, as Malcolm Cowley said, omnipresent.[31] To some degree this was attributable to the attraction held for university students by his use of jazz rhythms and his vision of urban life, but probably more was due to the *Dial* award and the continued existence of the *Criterion*. The *Dial* was no fly-by-night 'revolutionary' magazine. It was run by rich young men, contained serious and sober articles, looked and was immensely respectable. By the end of 1923 the editor announced that it had 30,000 readers, and those who had not yet subscribed were urged to 'identify yourself with this country's arts and letters'. Yet although its influence was great, it was not lasting. In 1925 Thayer suffered a 'nervous breakdown' and resigned. Although treated by Freud he never made a full recovery, and control of the magazine passed out of his hands. Thayer wanted the social historian Van Wyck Brooks to succeed him, but Brooks too was having a nervous breakdown and refused. The post went to Marianne Moore, who was already working for the magazine and had received the *Dial* award. Her poetry represented, Thayer said in a compliment that perhaps did not wholly please its subject, 'the informed literary middle-of-the-road', something that might also have been said of the magazine. Although Moore almost always consulted Watson before making any important decision, some found her both finicky and autocratic. Hart Crane, whose early work had been printed, was annoyed when one of his poems was returned with remarks about its 'lack of simplicity and cumulative force', indignant when Moore insisted on changing the title of a poem she accepted, 'and cutting it up until you would not even recognise it'.[32]

1922: The Year of Triumph

Writing to Allen Tate, Crane called the editors of the *Dial* and *Poetry* two hysterical virgins. In 1926 Moore turned down 'Anna Livia Plurabelle', in part because she thought Thayer would not have liked to see it in the magazine, in part because of its length, but also – one is bound to feel – because it would have risked prosecution.[33] In 1929, with the subscription list down to what almost any other literary magazine would have considered the excellent figure of 5000, the *Dial* closed its doors.

One of the reasons for Thayer's mental derangement was the fact that his wife Elaine had fallen in love with his friend Edward Estlin Cummings. When the couple were on their honeymoon Cummings had sent them a sonnet beginning 'O friend who hast attained thyself in her' which Thayer pronounced 'really corking',[34] but the attainment as husband was brief. When the honeymoon ended, Thayer returned to his bachelor's apartment in New York complete with valet, and Elaine rented a place nearby. Thayer condoned his wife's affair with Cummings whom she briefly married after a divorce from Thayer, and it may be that suppressed homosexual feelings, not necessarily for Cummings, were a cause of the breakdown. In any case E. E. Cummings became the *Dial*'s particular poetic discovery.

Like others Cummings volunteered for ambulance work in World War I, and out of his service and temporary incarceration in a French internment camp on suspicion of being a spy, came the remarkable prose work *The Enormous Room*. But his mother had wanted a son who was a poet, and this Cummings became, although he hardly fulfilled her desire to breed a poet resembling Longfellow. At Harvard he was much impressed by *Tender Buttons* and a little later by Pound in his *Cathay* period, especially by the novel (as they still were) arrangements of lines. By 1916 he was experimenting with attempts to render street talk in verse, and by the very early twenties had developed the poetic styles that he never changed or much expanded. The styles varied, but all had their basis in a desire to change the uses of parts of speech and use typographical devices to make visual jokes. His various styles show no particular poetic influences, but he was prone to an extravagance of language that sometimes gives the impression of verbal delirium. The Introduction to his *Collected Poems* (1938) is an example:

The now of his each pitying free imperfect gesture, his birth or breathing, insults perfected inframortally millenniums of slavishness.

A thunderstorm is conveyed in one poem by effects of visual onomatopoeia, an impression of people getting drunk in a speakeasy rendered in another by running words together and then verbally stumbling over them.

The tricks Cummings played with language were very varied, and the effects could be comic, dramatic, satirical or indignant about cruelty, as in the famous poem that begins 'i sing of Olaf'. Yet even in this poem there is something jarringly self-conscious and mock-modestly parodic about that lower case 'i'. This jaunty little 'i' played a large part in Cummings's creation of himself as a slightly pathetic, Chaplinesque figure. In verse his I was never a powerful capital, always a little i:

> o by the by
> has anybody seen
> little you-i
> who stood on a green
> hill and threw
> his wish at blue

If we make allowance for the avoidance of capitals and the poet's determination to play around with tenses and meanings, one of Cummings's manners is ecstatically lyrical as Keats or Shelley, another genially or coyly obscene, and yet another might be the work of a clever little boy writing for other children. It will seem heresy to Cummings's more fervent admirers to say that he wrote most effectively when working away from the freedom of poetry, under the constraints of factual experience put down in prose, as in *The Enormous Room* or the weeks in Russia that prompted the writing of *Eimi* (1933), a book where the textual difficulties do really seem justified. The jolts and jumps of the prose give an impression of the writer's reactions to the Soviet Union in a way that an account called 'My Travel Diary in Soviet Russia' could never have done.

Cummings was also a visual artist, but *vision*, the seeing of things, is just what his poems lack. He was undoubtedly original, for nobody else then or later juggled with words in quite the same way, but the originality is either used to make jokes or is at the service of a personality that wanted to write lyrical sonnets, but took off the edge of sentiment by playful confusions. To write 'My father moved through dooms of love/through sames of am through haves of give' is an evasion of the poet's desire to write seriously in praise of his father, leaving us saying instead: 'Haves of give, now, isn't that really *clever.*' What Eliot said of Poe, that to take him wholly seriously was to be less than serious oneself, seems particularly true of Cummings. Always amusing to read except in his most serious style – the style, naturally, most favoured by the *Dial* – Cummings never developed as a poet beyond being little you-i. Content with his repertoire of tricks, he became the Ogden Nash of modernism.

The *Dial*'s circulation when it closed would have seemed handsome to Eliot, but he would have regarded it with suspicion, feeling that a taint must always be associated with such popularity. During its sixteen years of life the *Criterion* was an expression of the editor's blend of caution and daring, and it is possible that nothing in his literary career gave him more pleasure than the editing of what, once clear of the Rothermere entanglement, might have been called Eliot's Magazine. In 1926 his editorial, 'The Idea of a Literary Review', laid down guidelines: a magazine should not announce a programme but exemplify a tendency, and it should not be a mere miscellany, 'the feeble reflection of the character of a feeble editor'. Intellectually the Eliot tendency was in the most literal sense reactionary, the reaction being against political and social liberalism. Wells, Shaw and Bertrand Russell were dismissed as 'that part of the present which is already dead'. This was Eliot daring, for he was by now firmly settled in England, and English literary life was dominated by the liberal intellectuals he despised. But cautious Eliot was there too, for the periodical never launched the attacks on those dead parts of the present one might naively have expected. The dead were classified as such, with no need felt for post-mortems.

The *Criterion*'s politics swam against the tide in favouring authoritarian governments based on Christian tradition, 'a right theology' being essential. In the thirties no attitude to Nazism was announced, no books about it reviewed. In relation to social and ethical questions the magazine was narrowly, although not feebly, edited. In relation to literature, especially poetry, daring Eliot ruled. He printed much work by writers whose attitudes and approaches must have been uncongenial to him, like Crane and, later on, Auden's 'Paid on Both Sides', and early Dylan Thomas poems and stories.

Contributors living in or near London met regularly at the Cock Tavern in Fleet Street, in a private room at a Soho restaurant, and at a pub in South Kensington. They included Harold Monro, Flint, Herbert Read, Bonamy Dobrée, and among others occasionally Fletcher and Aiken. The meetings were sprightly affairs, full of good fellowship, and almost all of those who attended looked up to Eliot as their intellectual leader and also, as one admirer said, a gentleman in the best sense of the term. The group did not consist of followers but of those who, as Eliot put it to Herbert Read, had an impersonal loyalty to a faith not antagonistic to his own. Such a solemn remark did not reflect the general atmosphere of jokes and jollity. At one meeting a catch was sung for three voices. Two of them said, 'Who's this Eliot anyway?' 'Well, from all I hear, he's a personal sort of beggar', while a third sang

> I like young Eliot, he's got style
> But I ask you, is it po'try?[35]

There were some who felt that these lunches and dinners were not only social occasions, that people were there to be assessed, reputations to be made or destroyed. Fletcher and Aiken thought so. Fletcher said the meetings 'constituted a deliberate and Machiavellian practice of power-politics', and Aiken remarked that he and Fletcher were allowed to review books 'or even, when an assassination was in order, invited to place the tormenting banderillas, or use muleta and sword', but were never of the inner circle.[36] Both men were perhaps jealous, and Aiken certainly exaggerated the periodical's influence by saying that it became in the end omnipotent. It is true, however, that the *Criterion* was one of the principal stepping stones in Eliot's rise by the end of the twenties to a position of acknowledged literary supremacy.

3. ELIOT, POUND, LEWIS: CHANGING RELATIONSHIPS

Pound had been immensely helpful to his friends in years when such help was most important, but his continued attempts to assist Eliot and Lewis in the twenties were embarrassingly crude and foolish. Quinn was not the only person to whom Pound deplored Eliot's subordination to an office job – and one in a bank, which from

1922: The Year of Triumph

Pound's point of view made things worse, since he was developing theories about economics and usury in which banks were among the chief villains. In 1922 he conceived a scheme which he called Bel Esprit, the immediate object of which was to find Eliot an income of £300 a year. If thirty donors would each give £10 a year the thing would be done. In Pound's mind Eliot would be only the first of several beneficiaries. The long outline of the scheme he sent to Williams began, 'There is no organised or co-ordinated civilization left, only individual scattered survivors,' and envisaged the 'release [of] as many captives as possible' from the bonds of working for money. Williams might be the second to be freed, Marianne Moore the third, and any donor was free to start a group for his own choice.[37] Full of enthusiasm, Pound put an announcement of the appeal in the *New Age*, and had printed a four-page pamphlet containing a pledge form. Quinn offered to take six or seven shares, and Pound quickly got promises of about two-thirds of the money, although it is not clear whether some of the guarantees were for more than a single year. There were a few caustic or facetious comments, like that of Lytton Strachey: 'It has been known for some time to Mr Lytton Strachey's friends that his income is in excess of his expenditure, and that he has a large balance at the Bank . . .'[38]

Pound said nothing to Eliot about Bel Esprit. The putative beneficiary's reaction when he heard of it was the moderate one that the plan bordered on precarious and undignified charity. What really upset him was a story in the *Liverpool Post* which said that £800 had been collected and presented to him, and that he had said the money would be put to good use, but he liked the bank and had no intention of leaving it. Eliot could no doubt have sued for libel but did not. He wrote a letter saying the story was a fabrication and that the Bel Esprit scheme 'is not in existence with my consent or approval'. The paper printed a grudging apology. The affair did nothing to help Eliot's mental or physical condition, and his correspondence at the time shows the strain it put on him. The hostile reception of *The Waste Land* in Britain, the labour of editing the *Criterion* in his sitting room in the evenings, his wife's and his own ill-health, seemed at times too much to bear. He told Quinn in 1923 that he could not go on and contemplated a course of psychoanalysis. But still he did go on, stayed in the bank, and showed no personal resentment of Pound's foolish secrecy.

[163]

Yet their relationship was not what it had been. Pound thought the *Criterion* dull, 'heavily camouflaged as Westminster Abbey',[39] and often said so. He was caustic when invited in the thirties to write an article about the poet he called Rabbit Britches, but still Eliot did not take offence. He printed some of the Cantos, and when established at Faber published them in book form. But he submitted no more manuscripts for Pound to read, realising that their views on poetry were moving so far apart that any comments would not be useful. With the exception of *Sweeney Agonistes*, the dramatic fragment which he worked on in the early and middle twenties, Eliot had abandoned after *The Waste Land* the form and language of modernism. The verse plays, *Four Quartets*, other individual poems, contained no shocking or outrageous language, presented no problems of meaning. Nothing in them would have shocked Squire, although that is not to say they would have pleased him.

Eliot also published Lewis in the *Criterion* and paid for what he published. Lewis was not an easy contributor. He had, in his own phrase, gone underground during the early twenties (although surfacing often for dinner parties) to work on the vast philosophical, social and politico-artistic work which he called 'The Man of the World'. The scheme was never completed, but parts of it were published in book form during the decade, most notably *The Art of Being Ruled* and *Time and Western Man*. Allied to them were *The Childermass* and *The Apes of God*, in which several of Lewis's enemies and some of his friends were savagely satirised. When, late in 1923, Eliot received a section of *Apes* he called it a masterpiece and said it was worth running the periodical to publish such work. But there were problems as always with Lewis, problems about recognisable portraits, and the sections that might have caused the most trouble never appeared in the *Criterion*.

Lewis was suspicious of the Rothermere connection, but Eliot assured him that she did not interfere in any way. This was not quite true, for it was in response to her urging that he reluctantly printed a piece by Stein. When Lewis's 'Mr Zagreus and the Split-Man' appeared there were cautionary words from some who still counted themselves among Lewis's friends. Osbert Sitwell, in a gently chiding letter, said that in the attack on 'us apes, dear God', Lewis had put himself into the bad company of the gutter press and had ignored the fact that 'some of my Simian family happen to have written rather good books'.[40] Their relations remained friendly, however, until the appearance in 1930 of *The Apes of God*.

As Lewis told Eliot, he had quarrelled with almost everybody in order to get the money and time to write his survey of modern society. He quarrelled with admiring friends, resenting the fact that he was in a position to need their charity and also their ability to play a part in supporting him. He quarrelled with Schiff, with Wadsworth and his wife who administered a monthly allowance he received, with Richard Wyndham whom he had taken under his wing as a painter. '*Money* spoils many things,' he wrote to Wyndham, 'for it seems to most people who possess it so much more important than their poor humble selves, that they cannot believe, or trust their judgment to believe, that it does not overshadow them: and when their personality is called upon to compete with it (as is I suppose always the case with a wealthy person) they feel that it will master them forever.'[41] He did his best to quarrel with Eliot. The ostensible cause was the acceptance of a long piece by Lewis for the *Criterion*, advertisement of its prospective appearance, and delay in publishing it. Eliot said he had been ill and harassed, the piece had been too long for inclusion in a single issue, the advertisement had slipped through in error, but Lewis was not appeased. He withdrew various parts of books in Eliot's hands and said that 'should any of these fragments find their way into other hands than yours before they appear in book-form, I shall regard it as a treachery rather than a harmless trick, or as the inadvertence of a harassed man'.[42] In reply Eliot stressed the importance of the maintenance of a modernist united front of himself, Lewis and Pound. Any public disagreement between Lewis and himself, he said, would please their enemies and be harmful to the public good.[43] Lewis remained unforgiving. He countered, as it were, Eliot's pleas of illness with the fact that he had three writs out against him, and the exasperated Eliot said it was a pity they did not have a higher view of each other's characters. In the end, after repeating vainly that he was not 'the tool or the operator of machinations against you', he wrote despairingly, 'I simply do not understand you at all . . . [There is] no malevolence on my part. *I simply don't understand.*'[44] Eliot's patience during this correspondence might reasonably be called saintly.

Lewis's quarrelsomeness sprang from the paranoiac suspiciousness that marked and marred his life, but also from a determination to cut loose from his early work, although not to disavow it. Purely abstract painting no longer appealed to him. He now allowed rein to his skill as a portraitist, and although this was done to earn money, his other graphic work shows recognisable figures and shapes. The various pre-war movements, he said, had done the Columbus work of discovering a new world, but now the *Blast* days were over. 'All these movements now have to set about construction and develop-ment, and evolve a new world of art out of the continent their enterprise has acquired.'[45] He felt dissatisfaction not only with the visual art he had produced, but with his prose writing. *Tarr*, as has been mentioned, had its rougher edges smoothed for reprinting, and during the twenties his writing became more restrained in metaphor, less inclined to gnomic Nietzschean phrases. There are exceptions, particularly in *The Childermass*, but the development of Lewis's style was towards the removal of the barbed wire fence he had put between his writing and any imagined 'intelligent reader'. This was replaced by a technique of description similar in effect to a slow-motion camera, and a rendering of dialogue with all the hesitations and repetitions that occur in nature but are rarely put down on paper. Such adaptations of modernism led him slowly, at the time perhaps imperceptibly, away from purely verbal experi-ment. He was in the process of cutting himself off both from the ideas of modernism and from nine-tenths of its practitioners.

None of this was understood by the well-meaning Pound. In Paris Pound was uneasy. If he had expected to enjoy a position of influence, he was disappointed. Visitors came to the flat in Notre Dame des Champs, admired or were amused by the home-made furniture, the tea-table made from packing cases painted scarlet, the armchairs constructed out of rough boards and canvas, but few accepted him in the role of dominating teacher. Most of the visitors left to worship at the shrines of Joyce and Stein.

In Paris, then, Pound was a celebrated but also slightly comic figure. He decided to write an opera, undeterred by inadequate musical knowledge. If *Pelléas et Mélisande* was the result of know-ledge, he said, ignorance could hold no terrors. He settled on Villon as a subject, found that 'hunting around with one finger on a keyboard instrument was not perhaps the best method of composition',[46] and bought a bassoon on which he made sounds that horrified his hearers. McAlmon said that Pound was virtually tone deaf. Nevertheless the opera was written, the subject Villon's Testament, from which the songs were taken, as Pound told Yeats, 'strophe by strophe'. The drama, he said, was OK, 'greek model, one act, and final tableau'. The decor could be any old thing, but there must be masks, a small orchestra, four bass singers, two tenors, two contraltos. If he came over to Ireland, would the Abbey Theatre be available?[47] The opera was not performed at the Abbey or else-where, but various pieces and songs were played at the Salle Pleyel, the audience mostly American Paris literati. Eliot was seen to be present but slipped away before the end.

Pound contributed notes on music to the short-lived *Transatlantic Review* edited in Paris by Ford, supervised a series of booklets issued by McAlmon's publishing collaborator William Bird, wrote his Paris Letters for the *Dial* from which an irritated Thayer eventually sacked him, discovered or publicised a young American composer named George Antheil, was briefly associated once again with the *Little Review*, which Anderson and Heap had brought to Paris. Anderson had become converted to the mystical ideas of George Gurdjieff, and Pound worked chiefly with Heap. He ate a meal cooked by Gurdjieff, commended the bright yellow Persian soup and said that if the mystic had had a few more things like the soup in his repertoire he might have made another convert.[48]

All this activity still left him restless and discontented. Perhaps Paris had never been the place for him. In October 1924 he and Dorothy left France and settled in Rapallo. There they were followed by Olga Rudge, a violinist who played two pieces at the Salle Pleyel performance. In 1925 Pound had a daughter by Olga Rudge, in the following year a son by Dorothy. The girl Mary was brought up on a farm in the Tyrol by a local peasant, the boy Omar Shakespear was raised by his grandmother in England. Like Lewis, Pound did not want children around him, although he took an interest in both his own children later in life. From 1924 until the end of World War II Rapallo remained his home.

His random energetic goodwill was directed at Lewis as well as Eliot. Almost from the time of his arrival in Paris he peppered Lewis with well-meant suggestions for publicising his work and earning him money. Would Lewis agree to having articles reprinted, would he send some illustrations to appear in the *Little Review*, what about a special Lewis number of that magazine? Confident that this attraction was irresistible he actually announced in autumn 1922, 'Next – Wyndham Lewis Number'. Lewis rejected such blandishments, as he rejected the attempt made by Schiff to arrange a one-man show for him in Paris. To Schiff he gave all sorts of excuses and evasions.[49] Did he have in mind Eliot's advice not to get mixed up with the clever second-rate men in Paris, did he resent Schiff's attempt to be helpful, was he afraid that a Paris show might fail? All of these explanations are possible. He also resisted Pound's tentative arrangements for him to have an exhibition in the Libreria del Convegno in Milan. His response was to ask, three times in a single letter, to be left alone for a while, perhaps for a year. Pound, however, was incapable of leaving Lewis alone, or of believing that anybody could reject the blessings of publicity. He continued to offer suggestions and make tentative arrangements about portraits to be painted and material to go into the putative *Little Review* issue. Either Lewis ignored most of these letters, or his replies have been lost.

In 1924 John Quinn, who had been a benefactor to all four of the founding fathers of modernism, as well as to many other artists and writers, died in his middle fifties. Acerbic and optimistic to the end, he blamed the partners in his law firm for not allowing him to take a vacation and refused to believe his cirrhosis of the liver was a mortal illness. Shortly before his death he told his mistress: 'My girl, when I get out of this I'm going to live. I have never lived.'[50]

By the time of Quinn's death the links between Eliot, Lewis and Pound had not been broken but were under some strain. Lewis's intransigence, Pound's crassness, Eliot's ill-health, were chiefly responsible. Joyce continued to the end of his life to be grateful to Pound, without having any wish to see him. Joyce and Lewis enjoyed each other's company, but although Lewis signed himself 'your devoted friend' and thought Joyce 'a tremendously gifted individual' he called *Ulysses* 'a masturbatory, historico-political Irish fairyland'.[51] Eliot and Joyce barely knew each other, but Eliot's admiration of Joyce carried more and more qualifications as time passed. The year of triumph for European modernism written in English was 1922, *Ulysses* and *The Waste Land* its great achievements. In the following years Eliot, Joyce, Lewis were all changing their attitudes and their approaches to writing. Only Pound remained in relation to literature a pure revolutionary, what Lewis called 'a Trotsky of the written word' (although Trotsky wrote some words too), looking eagerly as he had done since the days of Imagism and Vorticism for ways to make it new. Only Pound among the founding fathers was in tune with the developing American modernism.

CHAPTER NINE

The American Way of Modernism

I. WILLIAM CARLOS WILLIAMS AND THE VARIABLE FOOT

William Carlos Williams was from the early twenties onwards the most passionate spokesman for an American way of modernism. Publication of *The Waste Land* changed Williams's instinctive distrust of a modern movement based on European culture into outright opposition. The poem's appearance, he said later, had set him back twenty years. Eliot had returned poetry to the classroom just when poets in America were moving towards a new art form rooted in their own home ground. Eliot could have become 'our adviser, our hero', and what had he done instead? Walked out on his native traditions. When Williams saw the *Criterion* he recognised that there was no place in it for him 'or anything I stood for'.[1]

Eliot's poem had at least the benefit for Williams that it clarified his feelings about the kind of poems he wanted to write. They would be in a language and rhythms specifically American, and of course with no whiff of classroom scholarship. He determined also to have nothing to do with symbolism or metaphor. It was not until the publication in the forties of his long poem *Paterson* that he voiced what was to become a famous dictum, 'No ideas but in things', but it was implied in his poetry from *Spring and All* (1923) onwards. This adherence to 'things' did not mean that Williams deprecated feelings. On the contrary, the forthright doctor-poet addressed by Pound variously as Dear Bull, Old Sawbukk von Grump and Old Hugger-Scrunch was passionately romantic in his approach to everything – life, literature, nature and history. Just how romantic can be seen in the prose lyric about American history he called *In the American Grain*. Some of the heroes involved in writing that moves from fuzzy rhodomontade ('If men inherit souls this is the colour of mine') to the chatty, colloquial and rawly funny (as in the anecdote of the man who abandoned his wife when she had twin black babies but discovered 'there had been a darky in *his* family six generations before'),[2] are Columbus, Ponce de Leon, Raleigh (embarrassingly invoked), Poe and Lincoln. Alien to Williams are any who contributed to 'the niggardliness of the damning puritanical tradition'. In its openness and frequent flowery absurdity this is almost Williams's most characteristic work.

To say there are *no ideas but in things*: is that a sensible remark? It is one that contradicts any intellectual conception of the world, for ideas are evidently not things, although they may be *about* things. Ideas are abstractions, what is abstract belongs to the intellect, and as one of Williams's severest critics said, Williams was not just anti-intellectual, but did not know what the intellect was.[3] *No ideas but in things*, when applied to the writing of poems, involves the consideration of the 'thing' as a thing-in-itself, something having an existence outside anything else in the world. And that was in fact this poet's intention, a desire to see in any individual poem 'the world contracted to a recognisable image'. The poet regards this image and puts it down on paper, but Williams's assumption is that it exists without him. The poem would not exist without the poet writing it, that is true, but what he records has, according to Williams, an independent existence, and the recording should be testimony to that.

The result is poems much simpler than the metaphysical attitude from which they spring, very often poems about trees, flowers, insects, common objects. 'The Red Wheelbarrow' is considered here because it was well regarded both by Williams and by critics, and because it is very short:

> so much depends
> upon
>
> a red wheel
> barrow
>
> glazed with rain
> water
>
> beside the white
> chickens

The poem is rather like a naive painting, it creates a crudely simple picture. 'Creates a picture', however, is a phrase that would not do for a follower of Williams. He would say this was not *a picture*, with the artificiality implied in that word, but a poem given over wholly to wheelbarrow, rainwater, chickens, perhaps quoting Williams's own assertion in relation to his similar 'Chicory and Daisies' that the poet 'gives his poem over to the flower and its plant themselves', concerned to 'borrow no particle from right or left'.[4]

Certain things should be obvious about this and the dozens of similar poems Williams wrote in the twenties and thirties, of which 'The Red Wheelbarrow' is unusual only in its brevity. One is the similarity of such poetry to Imagism, another the debt that its childish simplicity owes to Stein, a third that the thing-in-itself objectivity of wheelbarrow and chickens is a deceit.

The Imagist connection has sometimes been remarked, for instance by Wallace Stevens when he called one of Williams's poems an addition to Imagism. Williams himself called his 'By the road to the contagious hospital' 'a pure imagistic poem – if such a thing exists'.[5] He replaced the idea of the Image as a thing-in-itself to which additions of metaphor and simile would be useless ornaments, by the Object viewed in the same way. But the Image as seen by Aldington, H.D., and the few other poets who genuinely tried to adhere to the principles of the Imagist manifesto, was most often of something seen as beautiful. For Williams, however, the Object was a subject for poetry simply by *being there*: the red wheelbarrow was unique like everything else in the world, and the poet's awareness of it was neither subjective nor objective but both at once, so that for the time of the poem he both became and observed the red wheelbarrow. To copy nature, Williams said, was a spineless activity, the important thing was to *become* nature 'and so invent an object which is an extension of the process',[6] the poem being the object.

Williams's likeness to Stein is apparent in his insistence on using simple words, and viewing things as a child might. No complex thought or observation is permissible, the effect in Stein being one of repetition, in Williams an appearance of complete banality or foolishness. 'January!/The beginning of all things' one poem begins, another 'When I was younger/it was plain to me/I must make something of myself', a third 'In brilliant gas light/I turn the kitchen spigot/and watch the water plash/into the clean white sink'. There are many similar passages. In some of them the poet keeps his eye on the Object (the kitchen spigot, the water, the sink), in others it strays into social observation or moral reflection. The effects obtained were certainly very different from those of European modernists. At best they may be thought trivial, at worst null.

It would be wrong to deny that such poems are expressing *something* through their bareness, their mock or real simplicity, their sense of colour, awareness of flowers, fruit, trees, animals, their struggling inexpressive awkwardness and determined lack of sophistication. 'Aw, shucks,' many of them seem to be saying, 'I'm just putting down things the way I see them, and if you write them down true, what else is there to say?' It is very much the spirit in which Stein wrote at the beginning of the first draft of *The Making of Americans*: 'It has always seemed to me a rare privilege that of being an American, a real American and yet one whose tradition it has taken scarcely sixty years to create.'[7]

No doubt Williams thought it a rare privilege too, and as the years passed he gathered disciples, became the patron saint of a movement called Objectivism, and codified his distrust of European sophistication into a creed which condemned for modern use any and every formal poetic structure because it belonged to a British, not an American tradition. Americans had to begin, he said, by understanding that they spoke a distinct and separate language, which was not English. The English language denoted English prosody, which was no use to Americans. A good piece of advice to a young American poet, he told the young American writer Kay Boyle, would be: don't write sonnets. Anything good in the sonnet had been said in twelfth-century Italian. (In his youth Williams had written a sonnet a day for a year.) Eliot was finally and definitely dead, 'his troop along with him', and in any case there was no need for Americans even to consider English poets. 'English writers I exclude axiomatically.' Even some Americans, Robinson Jeffers among them, had been unable to 'overcome poetic diction'.[8] When, shortly before his death in 1963, he was asked what he had done of special interest to new or future poets, he replied: 'The variable foot – the division of the line according to a new method that would be satisfactory to an American.' An American had to write in 'language modified by *our* environment; the American environment'.[9] What was the new method? He never defined it, beyond making some remarks about the breathing habits of Americans being different from those of the British, and it would seem that the variable foot in Williams's own work varied just as he felt at any particular moment. Yet even those in a later generation of American poets not persuaded by his dogmas are respectful towards Williams. Robert Lowell said that his style was almost what Williams had claimed for it, the American style. He added that Williams was a poet who could be imitated anonymously.[10]

Over the years the imitations have proved all too easy. Since Williams never constructed or defined a metric and would presumably have rejected the idea of doing so, his view of poetry in effect gave licence to name anything a poem if its approach could be certified 'objective'. The form it took was not important, since Williams thought no workable form existed any longer; the vital thing was to write with your eye upon the object. Because Williams's sensibilities were more delicate than his letters suggest, his susceptibility to nature and seasonal changes acute, he produced some touching, observant poems. The early 'Young Sycamore', the late 'Asphodel, That Greeny Flower', have been generally admired, but they are poems that succeed in spite of their formlessness, not because of it. Williams's influence, as it grew in the thirties and later, became a main factor in the endorsement of a poetry perhaps American in language, undoubtedly anti-intellectual in tone, opposed to any formal constraint on the length or rhythm of a poetic line. He was the Father of the Generation of the Variable Foot.

2. 'WHY DON'T YOU GET AMERICANISED?'

This was the question young Matthew Josephson asked a fellow-student whom he found reading a Yiddish paper at their public school in Brooklyn. Josephson, whose parents were Romanian and Russian Jews, was typical of a group who took to literature as the latest, really exciting thing. At Columbia in 1916 he discovered Amy Lowell and Imagism, sent her some poems after attending a Lowell lecture, and received a cautiously phrased letter of approval. But Josephson did not stay long with Lowell. He took a look at Greenwich Village, wrote poems which appeared in *Poetry* and the *Little Review*, had a brief attachment to the French Symbolists, and then on holiday in Maine became converted to Dadaism. In 1921, seeking not fortune but sophistication, he left New York for Paris in company with his young wife. The couple rented a room off the Boulevard Montparnasse, and Josephson found that by doing occasional translations for the *New York Herald* and selling a few articles here and there, it was possible for an American to survive quite reasonably in Paris. He wrote home to his friend Malcolm Cowley that he was attaching himself to the Dadaists. There would be no more reading poems to old ladies (a glancing look at Lowell's typical audiences); instead he and others would 'go forth into the streets to confront the public and strike great blows at its stupid face'.[11]

But was Dadaism really where things were at? Within a few months Josephson had given it up, and become co-editor first of *Secession*, then of *Broom*. The contributors to these magazines (neither lasted more than a couple of years) were almost all American, although the periodicals themselves were published at various times from Vienna, Berlin, Florence and Rome. In loud-voiced editorials Josephson proclaimed in turn the merits of Dadaism, of the Machine (some long way after Marinetti and Vorticism), and by way of the Machine, America. Eliot represented for him weary outdated Europe and had, he discovered, been born dead. He praised the prose of 'The Great American Billposter', comparing Keats's 'beaded bubbles winking at the brim' with a soup advertisement praising 'meaty marrowy oxtail joints' to the advantage of the latter, said that 'our Drakes and Marco Polos are in the laboratory or at the sales manager's desk', and dedicated a poem to Henry Ford. In Europe Matthew Josephson became fully Americanised, and within a short time was ready to return home. There he developed into a well-heeled literary man, writing commercially successful biographies of Zola and Stendhal and a lively survey of the American nineteenth-century capitalists called *The Robber Barons*, for which the two years he spent as an account representative in Wall Street gave him particular qualifications.

The absurdities in the early literary career of this ass with no observable ability, as Wilson called him in the twenties, are of interest because they suggest the difficulty of separating real from fake, serious from trivial, in the American literary generation that crowded the Rotonde, the Select and the Dôme. *Secession*

announced itself as interested in writers 'preoccupied with resear-
ches for new forms' and *Broom* had much the same intention. The
writers were said to represent a younger generation in American
letters, and petty squabbles marked the editorial running of the
magazines and their relationship with contributors, most of them
caused by Josephson's antics. Like him, a number of the writers
merely wanted to Make Literature New in what they hoped would
be an American way, but there were others of a very different kind,
including poets like Stevens, Moore, Yvor Winters and Hart Crane,
who can hardly have sympathised with the brash fervour of these
magazines. If they, like some other poets in the period, are not
discussed here in detail it is because most of them were not
modernists, either in the metres and rhythms they used or in their
general attitude to literature.

Stevens is a particular case in point, a poet unconventional only in
the glancing ironies and whimsicalities of his approach. He met and
liked Williams, but as a poet remained content throughout his life to
use the diction and metres condemned by Williams as unworkable
and unAmerican. Stevens's letters show how little connection he
had with the modernist bohemian literary world. After a brief
attempt to make a living as a journalist he asked the question in his
journal: 'Is literature really a profession?', gave a negative answer,
enrolled in the New York Law School in the fall of 1901 and so
began the business career that took him to the Vice-Presidency of
the Hartford Accident and Indemnity Company. He made no
attempt to experiment with language, the difficulties of his poems
resting in the obliquity of their approach. He was discouraging to
those who looked for subtleties of meaning in his work, telling one
correspondent who asked questions about 'Le Monocle de Mon
Oncle' that 'I had in mind simply a man fairly well along in life,
looking over and talking in a more or less personal way about life.'[12]
If he had opinions about Imagism or Vorticism, the allusiveness of
The Waste Land or Williams's variable foot, they remain unmentioned in his letters. He complained mildly when Harriet Monroe
used only four out of the eight sections of 'Sunday Morning', but
insisted only on an order which he said was necessary to the idea.

Moore, similarly, could be considered a modernist only by those
whose ideas about poetry were set in the nineteenth century.
Although Williams called her the saint of American modernism, her

poetry was sedate, and at times almost academic in tone. Her deft small ironies, subdued wit, deliberate avoidance of strong colours and vivid language, are hardly modernist characteristics. The innovatory elements in her work extended little farther than the gently amusing metrical trickery she brought to the observation of elephants and steam rollers, flowers and fish and people. Winters, although not using in the early twenties the traditional metres he adopted after 1928, wrote what seem now rather hesitant poems in a free verse closely connected to Imagism.

If one asks why these poets and others contributed to magazines which they found on the whole alien, it is probably because they were eager to see their work in print. And why did the magazines accept poems so little fitted to their editorial proclamations? Perhaps it can be put down to recognition of talent, as well as to the fact that the demand for verse and prose that broke free of verbal orthodoxy was as yet much less insistent than it became late in the decade. The problem of being an American, and also a poet tuned to modernity but aware of the past, is exemplified in the career of Hart Crane. Born in 1899, the only child of a wealthy candy manufacturer in Ohio who separated from his wife when their son was in his teens, Crane had the openness and vulnerability that seem to Europeans one American trait. When he was twenty he wrote to his mother that for eight years his youth had been a bloody background for his parents' sexual problems, and in the same year openly acknowledged his homosexuality to a sexually conventional friend. The openness extended to literature. Crane rejected the chance of going to college, and from the age of seventeen lived a rackety life, working briefly at a variety of jobs and for a longer period in one of his father's stores. He had been writing poems from the age of thirteen and, with an enthusiasm springing from his lack of academic education, was bowled over first by the Elizabethans, then by modern poets as he discovered them. He was still in his teens when Margaret Anderson, addressing him as 'Dear Hart Crane, poet!!', accepted a poem, and not much older when the *Dial* took 'My Grandmother's Love Letters', and sent the first money he received for a poem.

Crane tried to get into his poems elements of everything he admired. Elizabethan rhetoric necessarily had a major place, and he was overwhelmed when he read Eliot, telling Allen Tate in 1922 that it was a fearful temptation merely to imitate the master, but he

[177]

had discovered an approach which 'goes *through* him toward a different goal'.[13] There were other influences to absorb, modern and ancient: Anderson, whose story 'I Want To Know Why' seemed to the young Crane one of the greatest things he ever expected to read, Rabelais and Villon and Stendhal, Petronius and Dostoievsky, *Ulysses* (the parts printed in the *Little Review*) and *Tarr* and the photography of Alfred Stieglitz, and a good many more, including Americans. Crane, as he told a friend, ran joyfully towards Poe and Whitman. He tried to comprehend in poems not just the spirit of writers he admired, but also the taste, tone and reality of the contemporary America that surrounded him, less the America of his native Ohio and the candy store than the world of the automat, the movies, skyscrapers, radio antennae, subways, dandruff advertisements, traffic lights. Above all of bridges, which were for him emblematic both of city life and of links between one people and another, one time and another. Crane's response to 'Why don't you get Americanised?' might have been that Americanisation need not exclude Europe. In his optimistic youth Crane believed that *everything* could be included in a poetry that would still be unquestionably American. Drink and an unhappy sex life drained his powers quickly, but in the early twenties he made strenuous attempts to fulfil his belief that by ransacking the vocabularies of Shakespeare, Jonson and Webster, and adding 'our scientific, street and counter, and psychological terms, etc', a poet might achieve a total expression of modernity.

It is not surprising that the results were often chaotic, so that even sympathetic readers were baffled by his poems. Williams's wheelbarrow left readers asking 'Is that all?', looking for symbolism where none was intended, trying to understand why anything, let alone 'so much' should depend on a wheelbarrow and chickens. Crane posed quite different questions. His blend of neo-Elizabethan rhetoric with what he called the 'snarling hails of melody' coming from modern America were regarded by many as just unintelligible. When he tried to explain, as he did by saying that in 'Chaplinesque' he had tried to express 'in the buffooneries of the tragedian, Chaplin' his feeling that anybody who wished to present human feelings today must 'duck and camouflage for dear life'[14] in a Chaplinesque way, the explanation often puzzled as much as the verses. The links between separate parts of stanzas of Crane's poems were sometimes apparent only to himself, yet there were images and passages of such evident magnificence that the search for meaning sometimes seemed a secondary thing. He was as much obsessed by the sea as by bridges, and it inspired in the sequence of poems called 'Voyages' some of his finest rhetoric:

> Take this Sea, whose diapason knells
> On scrolls of silver snowy sentences,
> The sceptred terror of whose sessions rends
> As her demeanors motion well or ill,
> All but the pieties of lovers' hands.

A psychoanalyst writing in the fifties said that it was hardly possible to be more explicit than Crane had been himself about the sexual imagery of 'Voyages', but that was not the way it seemed at the time. This series of poems, like 'The Marriage of Faustus and Helen' with its epigraph from *The Alchemist*, its vision of Helen in a street car, and the transference of her court revels to a metropolitan roof garden with jazz orchestra ('Brazen hypnotics glitter here;/Glee shifts from foot to foot'), then appeared too obscure for a meaning to be teased free of the rhetoric. When Crane's first collection *White Buildings* appeared in 1926 with an introduction by Tate, Conrad Aiken dismissed it as high-class intellectual fake, and Wilson, although he conceded that Crane had 'a style that is strikingly original – almost something like a great style',[15] added that this style seemed not to be applied to any subject.

Crane was always ready to explain his poems, sending to Harriet Monroe a two-thousand-word letter in elucidation of the four verses making up 'At Melville's Tomb', and writing an almost equally long letter to the millionaire Otto Kahn, who supported him financially during the writing of his major poem 'The Bridge'. Describing, in the letter to Kahn, the interweavings of modern and historical scenes and themes in the poem, moving from a monologue by Columbus to the 'Harbor Dawn' in twentieth-century Manhattan, Crane told Kahn that the whole was the Myth of America.[16] Yet it was still a myth of America that looked towards Europe, and it is not surprising that in Britain the *Criterion* and the *Calendar of Modern Letters* printed parts of the poem without worrying about the meaning of lines like

> And while legs waken salads in the brain
> You pick your blonde out neatly in the smoke.

Modernism Becomes American

In the late twenties Crane crossed the Atlantic, gravitated naturally to Paris, and there was clubbed into insensibility by the police and arrested, after a fracas in the Café Select when he could not pay for his drinks. His suicide in 1932 was prompted by despair at the wreck of his personal life, which led to increasingly violent encounters with rough trade among sailors. This personal disintegration was linked with his inability to complete or even continue 'The Bridge', which remained a magnificent failure. Perhaps Crane would have achieved more if, like his friend Tate, he had remained aloof from modernism and been less ambitious, but that is asking for him to have been a different kind of man and poet. For a short time no American got nearer to creating a national modernism that still did not turn its back on Europe.

3. THE BLUE EYES OF SUCCESS

The founding fathers of modernism accepted, even welcomed, the fact that their work would not be popular, believing that art of any value in the twentieth century must inevitably be 'difficult'. They looked for financial support from admirers, accepted gladly by Joyce and grudgingly by Lewis, or lived frugally like Pound, or took a daily job like Eliot. They did not expect their work to be understood by the public that richly rewarded Arnold Bennett, Sinclair Lewis and Hugh Walpole, and felt contempt for the values of such a public. Time changed this, made Eliot a celebrated dramatist and Joyce a perfect subject for thousands of student theses, but in the mid-twenties such a prospect seemed so far distant as to be invisible.

Yet there were modernists who felt differently. Stein yearned for popular acclaim, and Hemingway was only one among a generation of American fiction writers who thought of themselves as modernists but also waited eagerly for a kind look from the blue eyes of success. It was a tenet of the founding fathers that what Eliot called the nineteenth-century novel was as dead for modern purposes as nineteenth-century poetic diction. Contemporary fiction, it was felt, must start from Joyce's revolutionary approach to vocabulary and subjects and perhaps must regard also the sexual mysticism of Lawrence. New fiction might be mystical, fantastic or consciously intellectual, but it must inevitably bear no resemblance to the novel of plot and character labelled *nineteenth century*. And of course it was not enough to use Joyce as a model. When Aiken did so in his unsuccessful *Blue Voyage* (1927) he found himself contemptuously dismissed in the *Criterion* as standing in relation to Joyce as an actor 'relying rather too palpably upon the prompter (Mr Joyce) whose tones are clearly audible'.[17] Aiken believed Eliot had written the review.

Among prose writers who disagreed with, ignored, or did not understand such tenets of the founding fathers were Hemingway, John dos Passos and William Faulkner. Hemingway developed a style, and a way of using it, that was modern, individual, and American. Dos Passos and Faulkner turned aspects of Joyce to their own uses. None, however, felt any suspicion of popularity, or any need to reject it. On the contrary, they were eager for the widest possible acceptance of their work. They represented American modernism in prose, as Williams did in poetry.

The very idea of rejecting popularity was one Hemingway would not have understood. In some ways he was out of place among the Americans in Paris, barely tolerating homosexuals, disliking Jews, and suspicious of McAlmon. But still McAlmon was his publisher, and they went together to Spain where Hemingway saw his first bullfight and was entranced by the colour, the violence, the conflict between man and animal, the climax of death. He returned to Spain more than once, and one of these trips was the core of *The Sun Also Rises*. The characters in the novel were easily recognisable to acquaintances in Paris: Duff Twysden, who was being pursued by Hemingway at the time, as Lady Brett (the most imitated, least witty or amusing of bohemian ladies around Paris at the time according to McAlmon), Harold Loeb who was a backer of *Broom* as Cohn with whom the hero fights (although in fact they didn't fight, and Hemingway apologised for his behaviour), Ford viciously carica-tured as Henry Braddocks. Hemingway was disposed to like men physically well set-up. He found Ford's presence, heavy, wheezing and ignoble as he later called it, unpleasant and disliked also his endless, sometimes fictitious stories of the famous men he had known. He had received nothing but kindness from Ford, who had called him the best writer in America, but the kindness contained a hint of patronage which Hemingway found unbearable. He also found it hard to tolerate McAlmon, perhaps because McAlmon had

[181]

been his first publisher or was foolishly free with his money. A tart encounter between them, one of several, began with McAlmon saying: 'If it isn't Ernest, the fabulous phoney. How are the bulls?' and Hemingway replying: 'And how is North American McAlmon, the unfinished Poem?'[18]

The Sun Also Rises, later called *Fiesta* in Britain, is the first major triumph of Hemingway's style, and the first book to make clear his strengths and limitations. The dialogue has developed from *In Our Time*, is sharper when it needs to be sharp, and wonderfully skilful in conveying meaning through hints, gestures, words unsaid. Something like the same style was being developed by American pulp writers in the period, but they used such language to express the nature of people whose lives existed only in relation to violence, Hemingway to convey doubt, tenderness, love. The approach has proved all too easily imitable, not least by Hemingway himself, but its original effect was extremely powerful. It can be understood best by making comparisons – for instance, by looking at Sinclair Lewis's *Babbitt* and *Main Street* beside Hemingway's novel. Lewis's dialogue is adequate, just, in conveying the conversation of the inhabitants of Gopher Prairie and Zenith, but it has the flatness and tedium of their lives. Hemingway's characters may be, as some readers complained, worthless people – although there is an implicit contention in the book that their lives have been ruined inevitably by the war – but the subtleties of the dialogue suggest depths of emotion that Lewis's painstakingly created businessmen and school teachers never possess. *The Sun Also Rises* established Hemingway as an original novelist, a writer whose skills would bring big rewards in the American market place. Some of the short stories he wrote after the book's publication appeared in national magazines like *Scribner's* and the *Atlantic Monthly*. Others went into the little magazines that had nurtured him, but within a few years Hemingway had cut loose from them and was selling stories to *Esquire*.

Did success spoil Ernest Hemingway? In a personal sense, perhaps. Certainly the boastful, quarrelsome, consciously tough figure of the forties and fifties is a much less agreeable personality than the young man who said that he taught Pound how to box and Pound taught him to write. But Hemingway's development shows also the limitations of the style, the things it couldn't do. Prose, he said, was much more difficult than poetry, and he was trying to see 'how far prose can be carried if anyone is serious enough and has luck . . . It is prose that has never been written. But it can be written without tricks and without cheating. With nothing that will go bad afterwards.'[19] The meaning of the statement was perhaps not clear even to its writer. Tricks, whether of a Jamesian or a Joycean kind, are an essential part of the modern novel, and Hemingway's supreme trick was his use of dialogue. The dialogue both revealed and concealed, and one of the things it hid was the sentimentality that was the other face of the deadpan devotee of action. The values of Nick Adams were also those of Ernest Hemingway. They were concerned with the beauty of physical action, with loyalty, tenderness, love, all regarded with schoolboy naiveté. They concerned the writer only and not other people, and they are hardly the values of a great novelist. Whether Hemingway's finest work is thought to be the early stories of *In Our Time*, or *The Sun Also Rises*, or *A Farewell to Arms*, there can be no doubt of his steady decline as a novelist who had no objective view of the world to express but only an ego to indulge and soothe. His reliance on clichés of character became fully apparent in *For Whom the Bell Tolls*, a descent from which he never again looked upwards, at least as a novelist. The skill in dialogue remained, evident particularly in the short stories. And the blue eyes of success smiled on him always, giving money and wives and luxurious homes with servants and swimming pools. The Ernest Hemingway who had these things, however, was a long way from the young man whose years in Paris had been a moveable feast.

The career of John dos Passos shows the heady effects of modernism on a writer basically as conventional as Sinclair Lewis. Dos, as he was known from youth, was born in 1896, illegitimately because his father, a successful attorney, had a mentally ill wife whom he would not divorce. His mother was in her early forties and his father a decade older when Dos was born, and since their relationship was not acknowledged and they could travel together openly only in Europe, Dos had what he later called a hotel childhood, punctuated by boarding at a London school. Later he went to Choate, then Harvard, where he did a lot of reading. His taste at this time was similar to that of the Georgians. He admired Masefield and Francis Thompson, and thought Walpole's *Fortitude* a 'simply ripping' novel. He rebuked a young friend for using the word 'smooth'st' and urged him to write in living language, but there is little indication that he had read much modern poetry or knew of Imagism, although most of his own writing at the time was in free verse. In 1917 he enlisted in an ambulance group like Hemingway, and served in France.

As a writer dos Passos was affected, much more directly than any other contemporary American novelist, by immediate events. *The Sun Also Rises* and Fitzgerald's *The Beautiful and Damned* are in a sense pictures of the post-war world, but they view it indirectly. Dos Passos's inclination was to set things down with the literalness of Sinclair Lewis, so that his war novel *Three Soldiers* (published in 1923 but written earlier) was realistic in the way of Lewis and in the tradition of Theodore Dreiser. The nearest he got to any innovation was a suggestion, based perhaps on his admiration for *Dubliners*, that inverted commas round dialogue should be replaced by dashes before a speech. His concern as a writer was much less with individuals than with the mass of people so that, unlike most of his friends and contemporaries, he could properly be called a social novelist. What should such a novelist do but write directly of what he saw?

Yet dos Passos had become aware that modernism existed, and felt he should be part of it, that it would no longer do to write like Sinclair Lewis, Dreiser or Frank Norris. He was an enthusiastic traveller and a frequent visitor to Paris, although never one of McAlmon's 'crowd'. He visited Stein, who liked his dark gipsyish appearance but pronounced his ideas foolish. In the back room of Shakespeare and Company he shook the limp hand of an uninterested Joyce, and bought a copy of *Ulysses*, which he claimed to have read at one gulp during a bout of influenza on a transatlantic liner. That must have been a big gulp, and since he found some of the book boring he may have skipped parts of it. Dos Passos was too serious for the atmosphere of McAlmon's and Josephson's Paris, too much concerned with social problems to take an interest in Stein. His experimentation in the twenties was linked to expressionist drama like his *The Garbage Man* ('In Act I Death is a lousy little man rather like a doctor . . . in Act II he is the garbage man . . . in Act III he is a very gorgeous person'[20]), and the unsuccessful *Airways Inc* put on by the New Playwrights' Theater. When *The Forty-second Parallel*, the first part of his trilogy *USA*, appeared in 1930 he used several devices relating to modernism, most of them derived from cinema and theatre, others which indirectly owed something to Joyce and even to Amy Lowell.

For dos Passos such devices were always trappings, used in the service of a basically realistic exposure of the way things were for the American working class after World War I and during the twenties. The devices are the 'newsreel', the 'camera eye', and biographies of various historical figures, most of them heroes like Gene Debs, Big Bill Haywood, John Reid and the Unknown Warrior, but not excluding such villains as Pierpont Morgan and William Randolph Hearst. These biographies, which celebrated also an age of scientific miracles exemplified by the Wright Brothers and Henry Ford, were written in something like the polyphonic prose poetry contemplated by Lowell and Fletcher. The purpose of the 'newsreels' was to provide a background of contemporary events, so that they began with the century and ended with WALL STREET STUNNED, PRESIDENT SEES PROSPERITY NEAR and Police Turn Machine Guns on Colorado Strikers. The 'camera eye' is focused on individuals and shows that dos Passos had, after all, taken something from Stein, perhaps at second hand. The portrait of an English 'fashionable lady' who loves bull terriers and loathes children ends:

> . . . and you thought of Dick Whittington and the big bells of Bow, three times Lord Mayor of London and looked into her gray eyes and said Maybe because I called her that the first time I saw him and I didn't like her and I didn't like the bullterriers and I didn't like the fourinhand but I wished Dick Whittington three times Lord Mayor of London boomed the big bells of Bow and I wished Dick Whittington I wished I was home but I hadn't any home and the man in the back blew a long horn.[21]

The biographies, written with lines broken as if they were Whitmanesque poetry, and most of them no more than three or four pages long, are by turns heroic, ironic and sentimental, sometimes as in the account of Theodore Roosevelt all three in the same thumbnail sketch.

The devices are all skilfully, even brilliantly handled, but they are devised to serve only as a framework, and the stories at the centre of them, as we follow the lives of several individuals through the trilogy, take us back to literalness. Dos Passos was a charming and generous man who placed great value on individual friendships, but his concern with the mass when writing fiction led him to create stereotypes rather than characters. A vision of the movement of history swamps the people, so that the time-servers move up in the world and the idealists down, with an effect that is both mechanical and too obviously balanced. The final volume of the trilogy, *The Big Money*, did not appear until 1936 and might have been a savage condemnation of the world that ended with the Wall Street crash, but most of the savagery went into the biographies of Fred Taylor, inventor of the Taylor System of Scientific Management, and William Randolph Hearst. It is the devices derived from modernist originals, not the stories too mechanically demonstrating a view of society in the mass, that one remembers from *USA*.

Dos Passos had met Hemingway briefly in 1918 and became friendly with him a few years later. His wife Katy had been a youthful flame of Hemingway's. Like Hemingway, he did not search for commercial success, but when his novels were bought and read by large numbers of people he saw no reason to question the value of what he was doing. The two men had a good many things in common, beyond a baptism of war via ambulance service and a concern with literary innovation, although dos Passos had no interest in bullfighting or deep sea fishing, and Hemingway did not bubble with concern about social injustice. The friendships among young American writers – Hemingway, dos Passos, Cummings, Scott Fitzgerald, Crane, Josephson, Malcolm Cowley, and others unmentioned – arose in part from shared intentions, a consciousness that their varied literary enterprises were in one way or another experimental. Such shared intentions sprang also from shared experiences. Most of them were deeply affected by the war, though none served for more than a small part of it. Exposure to death, shellfire, and to the alien, astonishing civilisation of Europe, was a shock from which some of them took a long time to recover.

Even William Faulkner, who longed to take part in the war but never succeeded in doing so, was strongly affected by it. He was born in 1897, of the same generation as dos Passos and Hemingway, but brought up in the small town of Oxford, Mississippi, far removed in distance and feeling from the solemn idealism of the Chicago renaissance and Greenwich Village bohemianism. The eldest of four sons, from youth a hard drinker like his erratic father, he mixed with the town drunks, played truant and failed to graduate from high school. When the United States entered the war he

[186]

volunteered as a pilot, but was rejected as too small. He left Oxford for New Haven and then New York where, having added a 'u' to his surname of Falkner, and carrying documents purporting to show that he had been born in England, along with a recommendation from an imaginary clergyman named Edward Twimberly-Thorndyke, he was accepted by a British recruiting officer for pilot training in the Royal Flying Corps. The end of the war found him in Toronto, still training, far from the sound of ack-ack batteries. He made the best of it, returning to Oxford wearing the British officer's uniform to which he was entitled and sporting a limp which he attributed to a crash on a solo flight.

From adolescence he had written poetry of a Swinburnian or ninetyish kind with little success. He was conscious of his literary isolation and left Oxford for New York where he worked briefly in a bookshop, then contemplated a trip to Europe, but got no farther than New Orleans. At last in 1925 he left the American continent for the first time. He walked through much of France, visited Britain, spent time in Paris and went to Shakespeare and Company and to Joyce's favourite café, but made no attempt to present his letter of introduction to Joyce. He was back in Oxford when his first novel, *Soldiers' Pay*, was published in 1926 and tepidly received. The book is an interesting, uneasy work in which the two central characters represent the actuality and the dream of Faulkner's own war experience, the first the young cadet he had been, the second a wounded and horribly scarred RFC pilot. There is little in it to suggest that the author had been affected by the modern movement. Nor was he yet prepared to accept the advice of Sherwood Anderson, who told him that he was a country boy who really only knew about Mississippi.

It was not until three years later, with *The Sound and the Fury*, that Faulkner made full use of modernist devices – discontinuity of narrative, ambiguity of time, abandonment of ordinary punctuation – and put them into the service of a melodramatically romantic view of Southern history and *mores* to create a world and style completely Faulknerian.

On a first reading, *The Sound and the Fury* is a baffling book. We understand that the first part is told by the idiot Benjy, and that there are shifts backwards and forwards in time (and may find it odd that, since Benjy is unable to speak, things viewed through him are

[187]

set down in words), but the number of time shifts is likely to bewilder, and although the change in the second part of the book to the world as seen by Benjy's oldest brother Quentin seems straight-forward, this is deceptive, for the Quentin section is not as it at first appears only an account of events on the day of his suicide in 1910, but also moves around in time. The opening section is dated 7 April 1928, and the action in the present covers only three days in time. If the story had been told from its chronological beginning, as several critics have pointed out, the narrative would have been compara-tively simple. Yet through the time variations the work acquires a richness and poignancy that no mere chronicle history could have achieved. Faulkner's modernist devices are not used to conceal the melodramatic nature of his theme, but to emphasise it. They are not, as in dos Passos, something extraneous to the plot but an integral part of the way it is told – and, as we become convinced, of the way it has to be told. There is no such thing as a typical passage, but here is one from the Quentin section that suggests the use Faulkner made of Joyce. (Elsewhere there are Steinian repetitions.) Quentin's sister Caddy has just returned from making love to her seducer Dalton Ames, and Benjy senses this:

> ... one minute she was standing there the next he was yelling and pulling at her dress they went into the hall and up the stairs yelling and shoving at her up the stairs to the bathroom door and stopped her back against the door and her arm across her face yelling and trying to shove her into the bathroom when she came in to supper T.P. was feeding him he started again just whimpering at first until she touched him then he yelled and stood there her eyes like cornered rats then I was running in the grey darkness it smelled of rain and all flower scents the damp warm air released and crickets sawing away in the grass

This is a straightforward passage, but elsewhere Quentin's thought processes, conveyed through a Joycean stream of conscious-ness, move through half a dozen time shifts in a single page. In Benjy's case, once the technique is understood we can see that one thing reminds him of another, so that when he crawls through a broken piece of fence and catches his clothes on a nail, we move instantly to another occasion when he crawled through the fence with his beloved Caddy and snagged his clothes similarly.

Faulkner said nobody would publish the book for ten years. He was wrong, but although the novel was a critical success it sold poorly, no more than 3000 copies being distributed until the end of World War II. He developed, and in some ways complicated further, devices learned mostly from Joyce, in the books that succeeded *Sound, As I Lay Dying* and *Light in August*, his sense of freedom to experiment all the greater because he had so little connection with the Parisian or American literary scene. *The Sound and the Fury*, however, remained the most successful of the novels written under a modernist influence that faded as his fame increased. Recognition of its importance is reflected in the fact that when the finally corrected authorised text was prepared in 1986, the book had sold 1,500,000 copies in the United States alone. By the time he was awarded the Nobel Prize in 1949 modernism was for Faulkner no more than an approach he had found technically useful and then discarded. In his early career Faulkner, more than Hemingway and dos Passos, wanted commercial success. His own account of planning a novel horrific enough to sell 10,000 copies and then writing it in six weeks is true in spirit, although not accurate in detail. In fact *Sanctuary* took four months to write. It sold extremely well, but although Faulkner later condemned it as a book basely conceived, the novel explored violent themes always interesting to its author, and ended up as something much more subtle than the purely commercial product he intended. It is imbued with the fear and even hatred of women that marks the early novels, Quentin's relationship with Caddy in *The Sound and the Fury*, the equine symbolism exemplifying Jewel's relationship with his mother in *As I Lay Dying*, the horror of menstruation and of the sexual act felt by Joe Christmas in *Light in August*.

Perhaps it should be repeated that the concern of this book is with the relationship of these writers to modernism, rather than with their importance as novelists. If the course of the American novel during the period were being charted, rather than that of modernist literature, then the work of F. Scott Fitzgerald, Willa Cather, Ellen Glasgow, and dandies of the period like van Vechten, Elinor Wylie and Frances Newman would call for consideration, but here they stay on the sidelines. English novelists of the twenties were even less affected by the commotion going on across the Channel. Lawrence, Huxley and Forster owe nothing discernible to Joyce's word association or his use of the internal monologue, and the wayward talent of

William Gerhardi seems in debt to no writer later than Tchekov. Only Virginia Woolf occasionally turned some aspects of Joyce's technique to her own politer purposes. The stylistic example set by Lewis in *Tarr* was followed by very few, chiefly because it was so wholly framed for Lewis's own artistic and social uses that any disciple would probably have been a mere copyist. Lewis's later writing in the twenties looked beyond the bounds of fiction in a way Joyce's never did, so that writers of fiction may have admired his effects from a distance, but made no attempt to emulate them.

The fiction writer of the decade who felt the influence of Joyce most beneficially, and with its help made a masterpiece, was the remarkable Djuna Barnes. Several of the American expatriates who lived in Paris for months or years had money from one source or another. Hemingway worked as a journalist, but his wife Hadley's income meant that they would never starve, McAlmon had his allowance, and others like Josephson scratched a living without much difficulty. Djuna Barnes, however, had from 1914 onwards supported herself and three younger brothers as a freelance journalist. She was born in 1892, the daughter of an unsuccessful artist who was called Barnes, although his name was Budington. Tall, stylish and strange, Djuna Barnes was bisexual from her youth, but by the early twenties had settled for the love of a young American sculptress named Thelma Wood. She was not lesbian, she said on one occasion, it was simply that she loved Thelma Wood. Their affair was tempestuous, full of the rows and unfaithfulness that marked Barnes's love life. Her biographer says that she was basically heterosexual, but Pound's remark about her is no doubt accurate: 'She weren't too cuddly, I can tell you that.'[22] Edmund Wilson was briefly overwhelmed by her. Walter Winchell in his gossip column said she could hit a spittoon at thirty feet.

The impression this may give of an uninterestingly noisy bohemianism is most easily corrected, oddly enough, by looking at the journalism through which Barnes maintained herself. This appeared in magazines as diverse as *McCall's*, *Vanity Fair*, and something called the *Unmuzzled Ox*, and consists mostly of interviews, written with a wit and style that belonged to her rather than to the interviewee into whose mouth it is put. The forgotten playwright and artist Charles Rann Kennedy condemns puritanism by saying 'Our mouths take on the shape of a rubber ring over the iniquity of our neighbors,' actress Lillian Russell offers a Wildean witticism about gilt chairs and the genuine gold of wisdom. There is a brilliant sketch of world boxing champion Jess Willard (1916–19), and his successor Jack Dempsey, who says he likes to hear women howl at fights. 'A woman howls twice as convincingly as a man . . . And then I like to hear the feminine sigh when it's all over; a man just grunts.'[23] Did Dempsey really say that, did Barnes's editor notice the connection made with a sexual climax? It is not recorded that any of those interviewed complained.

Barnes's admiration for Joyce was intense. When she read the instalments of *Ulysses* in the *Little Review* she said she would never have the nerve to write another line. In 1922 she persuaded *Vanity Fair* to commission an interview with Joyce, and produced a most vivid portrait of his physical appearance. Like others she commented on the limp 'and peculiarly pulpy' handshake, and said his characteristic pose was

> that of the head, turned farther away than disgust and not so far as death . . . After this I should add, think of him as a heavy man yet thin, drinking a thin cool wine with lips almost hidden in his high narrow head, or smoking the eternal cigar, held slightly above shoulder-level and never moved until consumed, the mouth brought to and taken away from it to eject the sharp jets of smoke.[24]

She came to Paris in 1919 or 1920, and although she once said that she came to Europe to get culture, and if this was culture she might as well return to America, in fact she stayed. She wrote well-paid articles for American newspapers and magazines, mixed with her compatriots around *Broom*, searched at night in various bars for the constantly straying Thelma Wood, drank hard, occasionally suffered what she called her famous breakdowns.[25] The memoirs of the time show what a powerful impression was made on other expatriates by her tall elegance, her cutting tongue, her wildness. She is glimpsed selling in the street *Ladies' Almanack*, her anonymous book about the literary lesbians of Paris, including the most famous of them, Natalie Barney, and rescuing Harriet Weaver when on her first visit to Paris, she took half a glass of wine at a dinner party and Pound said jokingly that he had never before seen her drunk. Weaver was much upset by the suggestion, and Barnes shepherded her back to her hotel. (After this Weaver dreaded that she might find Joyce drunk when she saw him, but their meeting went off perfectly well. She listened to Joyce reading a fragment of the new work which she had already said she found hard to understand, and his drinking was temperate. She continued to support the Joyce family as various problems assailed them, and gave him permission to cash some of the stock on which he depended for an income, although such disinvestment disturbed her. In 1932, when she said he was throwing away his money by selling stock, he said he needed new false teeth and must provide a tombstone for his father, who had died in the preceding December. Moved by his evident distress, she decided never again to resist a request for the release of further capital.)

Barnes was unusual among the hard-drinking drug-taking ex-patriates in being able to keep her excesses under control, so that the wildest nights searching for Thelma Wood left her competent to carry out journalistic assignments. She was similarly able to control the excesses of her writing when she moved outside journalism. Her natural tendency was to the Gothic, the fantastic, the outrageous, yet she never drifted into surrealism, and her best work leaves vividly uncomfortable pictures in the mind:

> Toward dusk, in the summer of the year, a man in evening dress, carrying a top hat and a cane, crept on hands and knees through the underbrush bordering the pastures of the Buckler estate.

Those are the opening lines of 'A Night Among the Horses', which won an O. Henry award in 1919. They might be by Ambrose Bierce, but some of the images in the story, like 'a grove of white birch shimmering like teeth in a skull', are outside Bierce's concerns. The story's subject, an ostler who has as lover the mistress of the estate, a 'small fiery woman with a battery for a heart and the body of a boy', may remind one briefly of Lady Chatterley and her gamekeeper, but Barnes's subject is not love but death, death mostly seen in a grotesque form. The ostler's evening wear is explained – in Barnes's stories nothing may be reasonable, but everything is explained – and he is killed by a stampede of the horses he cares for. 'The upraised hooves of the first horse missed him, the second did not.'

Anderson and Heap printed several of Barnes's stories but found her personally remote. One would like to think this was because she did not appreciate Heap's conversation, but in fact Barnes told a friend that for some years she had what she called a crush on Heap, which Anderson may have known and resented. The short stories she wrote in the twenties owe something to Poe, Dostoievsky, perhaps German romanticism, but the debts are minor, the effects original. The deaths of animals interested her most, that of men and women almost as much. In 'No Man's Mare' a horse carrying a corpse bolts for the sea and the action of the waves seems to bring the corpse to life; in 'The Rabbit' a little American tailor strangles a rabbit to prove his manhood to an Italian girl. 'The terrible, the really terrible thing, the creature did not squeal, wail, cry; it panted as if the wind were blunt; it thrashed its life, the frightful suffering of the overwhelmed, in the last trifling enormity.' If Poe is the writer she most resembles in these macabre tales, she differs from him in having a base of commonsense, so that one is often aware of an intellectual manoeuvring in her writing, a search for some kind of extreme morality. Nor do the stories lack irony. 'Life is filthy; it is also frightful,' Madame von Bartmann tells her seventeen-year-old daughter in 'Aller et Retour'. God is the light the mortal insect kindles, she says, human passions are only seasoning to life's horror, yet her daughter should have no prejudice against whores or murderers. A few days later the girl tells her mother that she is engaged to a staid middle-aged Englishman.

Barnes was modern in her choice of subjects even though these are in debt to Poe, in her treatment of them although it has echoes of Dostoievsky, in her language which always tries to escape the influence of Joyce and often succeeds. Neither the stories nor the novel *Ryder* (1928) contain much evidence of Joycean wordplay, and if her late verse play *The Antiphon* is impenetrably difficult, it is not because she plays around with word associations but because the many echoes of Jacobean playwrights, along with the use of soliloquy and asides, create a fog through which the motives of the main characters remain obscure. She said, perhaps ironically, that a misreading of the play was not impossible, but the problem is to make the whole meaning intelligible. When *The Antiphon* was given a reading at Harvard in 1956, in the presence of Barnes, Eliot, and the play's keen admirer Edwin Muir, the readers were often unable to read the lines intelligibly and sometimes stopped to ask questions of the author. It should be added that in 1961 the play was presented successfully in Stockholm. Her masterpiece, however, is *Nightwood*, published in 1937 but written over a period of years.

Barnes sometimes used her friends as characters. In *Nightwood* the central figures, Nora and Robin, reflect Barnes's relationship with Thelma Wood, and the most memorable character, Dr Matthew O'Connor, is based on her café friend Dan Mahoney, 'who combined the professions of pathic, abortionist, professional boxer and quasi-confessor to literary women'.[26] Mahoney made a living as an abortionist, was an inveterate pursuer of young men (he called the uncircumcised blind meat) and a great talker – or, as some who did not like him thought, interminably loquacious. Barnes used him in *Ryder* and then greatly expanded and deepened the portrait in *Nightwood*, but the book transcends the minor interest of such identification. This is a work about the nature of religion, and the agonies of belief when contrasted with the impurities of human action. The chief characters each exemplify a form of religious faith, Dr O'Connor Roman Catholicism, Nora Calvinism, another character Judaism, and all are lost as they pursue love through the nightwood of their lives but are granted only sexual pleasure. Religion, one might say, is for these people sexual action purified, a condition they aspire to but never achieve, as they aspire also to bisexuality. Robin is 'a tall girl with the body of a boy', Dr Matthew-Mighty-grain-of-salt-Dante-O'Connor calls himself 'the last woman left in this world, although I am the bearded lady', and laments his penis: 'Oh, that short dangle! We corrupt morality by its industry.'

Nightwood cannot be considered as a novel in the sense that Hemingway, dos Passos and Faulkner wrote novels (or, to change the country, Maugham, Waugh and Priestley). As one critic has said, if viewed realistically the characters are unbelievable, the story concerns the ending of a lesbian love affair, there is practically no action.[27] Its merits are in the subtleties of the metaphysical arguments, and in the writing. Eliot said the book would appeal primarily to readers of poetry, because 'a prose that is altogether alive demands something of the reader that the ordinary novel-reader is not prepared to give'.[28] Most contemporary novels, he added, were not really written. The remark goes to the heart of one distinction between modernist and conventional prose: modernist prose was always in one way or another heightened and stylised. It is because dos Passos's prose is purely conventional in all the narrative parts of *USA* that the book as a whole does not belong to modernism.

Her style in *Nightwood* has the edge of wit that marks all her writing. The passionately snobbish Baron keeps a valet because he looks like Louis XIV and a cook who resembles Queen Victoria, 'but Victoria in another cheaper material, cut to the poor man's purse'. Another character has 'the fluency of tongue and action meted out by divine providence to those who cannot think for themselves'. But it is the rich rambling rhetoric of Matthew O'Connor, at once devout and blasphemous, that stays most disturbingly in the mind, along with the picture of him lying in a narrow iron bed with dirty sheets, wearing a woman's flannel nightgown. Only in *Nightwood* and half a dozen of the short stories is Djuna Barnes seen operating to the limits of her genius.

In the two traditions of modernism defined here, Barnes's is unquestionably European. It is not surprising that of the prose writers discussed in this chapter, she alone received unqualified praise in the *Criterion*. Dos Passos remained unreviewed, and Faulkner was considered only once, late in the thirties, when *The Unvanquished* was said to provide characters all ready for the screen and to be 'the same dear familiar hokum which no true heart has been able to resist since movies began',[29] a judgement not greatly qualified by the comment that Faulkner had rehabilitated melodrama as an art. Hemingway was treated at greater length in a review of *A Farewell to Arms*, which granted him great natural talent but said that 'the workings of a barbarian mind' represented his standard of thought, and that his work showed 'how little of European life this American is capable of penetrating'.[30] The 'barbarian mind' was, of course, just what many American modernists admired.

PART THREE

A Movement in Decline

CHAPTER TEN

Here Comes Everybody, Including Eugene Jolas

In relation to literary modernism, the second half of the twenties differed markedly from the first. The intellectual impulse that had been the movement's mainspring was forgotten, misunderstood or ignored by the young Americans who came to Paris. Without making the distinction between European and American modernism suggested here, they regarded Eliot and Pound as elders to be treated with respect, rather than any longer leaders to be followed. Eliot was on the other side of the Channel and occupied in editing what those Americans in Paris who read it would have found an unexciting magazine, Pound away in Rapallo, self-exiled from the centre of activity. That centre was Joyce, Stein, McAlmon and the Crowd, anything that differed from what had been written last year, last month or last week. Young Samuel Putnam came to Paris, a mid-Westerner longing like many others who thought the Chicago renaissance long over, *Poetry* hidebound and stale, to escape what he called the prairie flatness, the stockyard atmosphere. Putnam, who later started his own short-lived magazine the *New Review*, remarked perceptively that the second flush of American exiles was not like the characters of *The Sun Also Rises*. They were not a lost generation affected by World War I, not disillusioned rebels or really artists, but young men and women looking for excitement. It was understood, of course, that such excitement would have a connection with new literature, a new language, especially the new language of James Joyce.

'New' was not quite the word for the book on which Joyce was working urgently, between drinking sessions with McAlmon, Lewis and others and increasingly frequent bouts of eye trouble. Time and the river and the mountains, he told one friend, were the heroes of the new book, but then he said also that it exemplified the ideas of the Neapolitan philosopher Vico that *events* were merely superficial manifestations of mythological *energies*, something he had found confirmed in the coincidences marking his own life. At other times he made it clear that nothing was alien to the book, it was not merely a work that would embrace the whole history of mankind, but one that could accommodate any kind of random idea or joke. He told Harriet Weaver that if she would order a piece of writing, he would execute the work, and it would be fitted into the whole scheme. Was the scheme a joke, then? Not a joke, but undoubtedly jokey. Remember Laurence Sterne, he said, and sent Weaver a long glossary explaining such words as passencore and wielderfight. 'Passencore = pas encore and *ricorsi storici* of Vico . . . wielderfight = wiederfechten = refight.'[1] Weaver said she would have been lost without the glossary, and suggested that an annotated edition of the new book would be a good idea.

One of the difficulties found in this new work, as in *Ulysses*, was that it was both comic and cosmic. Joyce assured Djuna Barnes that 'on the honor of a gentleman there is not one single serious line' in *Ulysses*, and he might have said the same about *Work in Progress*. Yet at the same time he claimed implicitly or even explicitly that it was a record of all human life and history. This seemed to others, not to Joyce, contradictory. But the primary stumbling block for readers was the language. When Pound heard that Joyce was engaged on something new, he assumed it would resemble *Ulysses* in tone and texture. In 1926 Joyce sent him the chapters dealing with Shaun for interest, approval, and possible publication in a new periodical Pound was planning. Pound was much disappointed. 'Nothing, so far as I can make out, nothing short of divine vision or a new cure for the clap can possibly be worth all the circumambient peripherization.'[2] Almost immediately after this Pound refused to sign an international protest against the pirating of *Ulysses* by Samuel Roth, who operated on the erotic fringes of literature, in a magazine called *Two Worlds Monthly*, which had a considerable sale. Several of those who signed the protest (they included Robert Bridges, Galsworthy, Maeterlinck and Masefield) did so out of opposition to pirating rather than admiration for Joyce. Pound refused on the ground that Roth was only an adventurer taking advantage of the scandalous American law that tolerated the theft of copyright. The protest had no effect. Roth continued to pirate the material, for which he paid Joyce nothing, until October 1927.[3]

Here Comes Everybody, Including Eugene Jolas

Stanislaus, with the brotherly candour he practised, called an extract from the new book unspeakably wearisome, a piece of drivelling rigmarole. Like Pound he wondered whether the writer was fooling or serious, unable to accept that he might be both. Joyce perhaps took his brother's remarks with equanimity and was not much upset by Pound, but he was disturbed when Lewis criticised both his style and his method. In a couple of pages of *The Art of Being Ruled* Lewis suggested that Bloom's thought-processes were abnormally wordy and 'as unreal, from the point of view of the strictest naturalist dogma, as a Hamlet soliloquy'.[4] He followed this up early in the following year with a full-scale view of Joyce as a genial comic writer to be placed somewhere between Stevenson and Sterne, 'if you imagine these writers transplanted into a heavily-grundianised milieu'.[5] While saying that his analysis was not an assessment of the literary value of Joyce's work, Lewis looked at *Ulysses* as a book concerned primarily with what he called the philosophy of space-time and labelled Joyce a master craftsman wholly concerned with his own past. 'It is the *craftsman* in Joyce that is progressive: but the *man* has not moved since his early days in Dublin.'[6] He defended Joyce against the charge of obscenity, but called Bloom a stage Jew, Buck Mulligan a stage Irishman, and Stephen a frigid prig, dismissed the Homeric framework as 'an entertaining structural device or conceit', and made an effective comparison between two passages from Nashe and two from *Work in Progress*.

Weaver would not have agreed with much of this but was increasingly disturbed by what she found the unintelligibility of the new work. Perhaps when it was finished, she said, Joyce would listen to the advice of some of his older friends like Pound, and when he asked wistfully whether she liked nothing at all in *Work in Progress*, responded that of course she did, but she did not care for what she Joyceanly called the output of the Wholesale Safety Pun Factory. Joyce took to his bed, where he got no sympathy from Nora, who asked why he could not write books people would understand. McAlmon reassured him by saying that the new work was just touched enough for genius in the James Jesus Joyce manner.[7]

Lewis's analysis was the longest, most serious view of Joyce's work that had then appeared in Britain or America and might perhaps have been thought welcome, in particular for its praise of the writer's virtuosity and literary scholarship. To be compared with

[201]

Stevenson and Sterne might also be thought complimentary rather than insulting. But Joyce was upset and his Parisian admirers indignant, the idea that his manner resembled that of an Elizabethan and so belonged to the past being particularly uncongenial. Joyce responded with parodies and jokes about Lewis in further extracts of his book, and Lewis in turn parodied Joyce. The affair effectively ended the friendship of the two and also meant that Joyce's more passionate admirers almost automatically disliked Lewis, a feeling he reciprocated.

Conspicuous among these admirers was Eugene Jolas, who had come to Paris in 1924 as a journalist working for the Paris edition of the *Chicago Tribune*. Jolas called himself a man from Babel, and the phrase expresses the polyglot nature of his upbringing. He was born in New Jersey in 1894 of Franco-German immigrants, spent his childhood in Lorraine where he learned both his father's French and his mother's German, at fourteen spent two years in a seminary, and returned to America in 1910. Thereafter he had jobs as delivery boy, bookstore clerk and reporter, was drafted into the armed forces, and discharged in 1920. He worked on several papers but hated the telephones and typewriters of the press room, which he regarded as diabolical instruments the basic aim of which was to destroy the individual's spiritual life.

In person Jolas was short, broad, sturdy, with thick black brows, dark complexion, mouth turned down disapprovingly, and a missing front tooth. He had by one account 'the fine head of a Roman senator and the wild gaze of a poet',[8] and was able to recite Rilke in German, Apollinaire in French. By another account he was shockingly inarticulate, with an English vocabulary limited to three hundred words.[9] In 1926, the year he met Joyce, he married an American music student, a rather plain six-footer named Maria McDonald.

Jolas was eager to start a magazine that would use what he called the catalytic powers of art in support of everything that opposed the mechanisation represented by telephones and typewriters, stressing instead the supreme artistic value of the irrational. He tolerated rather than supported Surrealism (the Surrealist movement never attracted any considerable British or American talent), but *Work in Progress*, which in one aspect was a dreamed fiction, was to him an example and an inspiration. Jolas was joined in his magazine enterprise by two other American journalists, Elliot Paul and Robert Sage. Paul replaced Jolas on the Paris *Chicago Tribune*, and Sage had a review column in it. Both were chiefly concerned with having fun, sometimes of a fairly schoolboyish kind (one of Paul's editorials was headed K.O.R.A.A., the initials signifying Kiss Our Royal American Arse), but Jolas was always serious. His magazine *transition* was to be a laboratory for poetic experiment, and Americans would be the chief experimenters. The result must be romantic, must be irrational, and might perhaps be an 'almost mystic concept of an ideal America'. Mixed with such promises were what sometimes sounded like threats. 'The sensitive man of our age has trusted to pure reason too long . . . a certain kind of barbarism to some seems the only solution.'[10] This was in support of an editorial by Paul announcing 'The New Nihilism' of writers like Lautréamont and Drieu la Rochelle, and saying there was no need to sympathise with it to acknowledge its importance. Lautréamont, Jolas said, 'with magnificent courage chose to hymn the satanic'.[11] Side by side with such suggestions for what was called a new magic went admiration for the originality of recent American writing, and praise from Jolas for *In the American Grain*. The editors were also clear about what was *not* interesting – the written photographic view of events, the silhouetting of facts, the presentation of actual misery, the 'anecdotic boredom' of verse in the usual anthologies.

Who were the new magicians? Joyce, Stein and Crane were said to be showing the way, and Joyce and Stein were at first *transition*'s twin pillars. Joyce contributed sections of *Work in Progress* to almost every issue, and at the end of a list of contributors Stein was placed by herself, with the Stein-style comment:

> Whenever she pleases, GERTRUDE STEIN contributes what she pleases to *transition* and it pleases her and it pleases us.

transition first appeared early in 1927. The first three issues were monthly, then it was issued quarterly. Paul's association with it lasted little more than a year, after which he perhaps felt that he had extracted all the fun possible from modernism. Joyce never associated himself with the editorial statements, his interest being as usual completely confined to his own work. Stein appeared constantly in the early issues, not at all in the later ones. The contributor who appeared most often, apart from Joyce and Stein, was Kay Boyle, who was overwhelmed by Jolas's phrases like 'only the dream really matters', and wrote something in almost every number. Five translations of the almost unknown Kafka were printed, and three pieces by Samuel Beckett appeared, including his first printed story. One could make a list of occasional contributors whose work had little connection with Jolas's desire for the magical and irrational: Allen Tate and Yvor Winters among poets, Katherine Anne Porter, William Saroyan, Hemingway, Morley Callaghan among prose writers. They were very much in a minority, however, and unrepresentative like the pages of 'Slanguage' which explained such phrases as 'on the up-and-up', 'making whoopee' and 'having a yen', along with now arcane terms like 'Garbo-Gilberting', said to mean 'an ardently enamored couple minding their own business'. There was an American number which contained such tart verses as

> I'd rather live in Oregon and pack salmon
> Than live in Nice and write like Robert McAlmon

The names of Eliot and Pound were missing from the magazine. So was that of Lewis, who attacked this 'New Romanticism' as being the old diabolic romanticism of Wilde and Beardsley, Baudelaire and Huysmans, plus a New Nihilism that played with the idea of the total destruction of Western society and was in effect pro-communist, although Jolas and Paul would never admit as much. Lewis had some good heavyweight fun with Jolas/Paul, saying 'Give the Devil his due! ... let's set the Thames on fire with Adelphi brimstone, let's storm the Bastille and Kremlin not only at the same time, but *in the same place*.'[12] Certainly one is reminded of Marinetti when reading some of *transition*'s editorials, with the difference that the Futurists were in earnest, whereas Paul at least was concerned 'simply and purely to amuse [himself]', an unfortunate phrase used in one editorial. Futurism was concerned with romantic action, *transition* with romantic words. Lewis was mistaken, however, in linking the verbal revolution proposed by Jolas with any practical activity. When he was asked to comment on a collection of poems about the Sacco–Vanzetti case called *America Arraigned* Jolas said he thought the book utterly unimportant, adding that it was a waste of time for a poet's activities to be diverted into the dissemination of subversive ideas.[13] Jolas was looking for a 'pure' literature, Romantic and new. Dada and Surrealism did not quite fill the bill. They were linked with the subconscious, and Jolas thought the subconscious was not enough (although he was opposed also to those like Eugene O'Neill who 'worked from the exterior'[14]). He opposed Surrealism for the opposite reason, because in print it was so very literary and insisted on referring to the past, calling Swift surrealist in malice, Mallarmé in confidence, Heraclitus in dialectic, Carroll in nonsense, Mrs Radcliffe in landscape, and so on. Jolas wanted no such reference back, the verbal past irritated him as the physical past of museums angered Marinetti. It was the *new* he wanted, new words like anamyth, 'a fantastic narrative that reflects preconscious relationships', and psychograph, 'a prose text that expresses hallucinations and phantoms'. In *transition* 16/17 he announced the Revolution of the Word, which was followed two years later by the announcement, 'Poetry Is Vertical'.

The Revolution of the Word, which was accompanied by half a dozen fairly predictable quotations from Blake and one from Rimbaud, consisted of a prefatory note deploring 'the banal word, monotonous syntax, static psychology and descriptive naturalism', and a dozen precepts and injunctions, most of them extolling a hallucinatory approach to writing, the replacement of anecdotal narrative by a 'metamorphosis of reality', and the literary creator's right to 'disintegrate the primal matter of words imposed on him by textbooks and dictionaries', to disregard grammatical and syntactical laws, and to use words 'of his own fashioning'. Time was a tyranny to be abolished, and writing was not communication but expression. The final injunction said: 'The plain reader be damned'. Joyce and Stein were not asked to sign this manifesto, presumably because it was felt that in their work the revolution had already been achieved. The sixteen signatories included Jolas, Paul and Sage, and a number of others among whom the only names with a claim to remembrance are those of Hart Crane and Kay Boyle, for whom signature meant nothing at all, since it did not affect their own writing. Crane almost immediately regretted having signed the manifesto. For the rest it was part of the game they were playing, a game which for some involved the use of drugs, the consumption of much alcohol, and the infuriation of the bourgeois. Joyce never concerned himself much with the Revolution of the Word. Perhaps Jolas (who signed twice, once under a pseudonym) was the only person who took the dozen precepts seriously.

CHAPTER ELEVEN

The Genuine Phoneys

Joyce assented to *transition*, even though he may not have approved it. How could he fail to assent when the periodical was so eager to print his work? Stein was more overtly friendly, although she rebuked Jolas for paying so much attention to the dirty Irish publican James Joyce.[1] But they must both have realised that somebody like Jolas, disinclined to reject anything that seemed to contain even the smallest fingernail-size fleck of newness, was wide open to exploitation by the most fantastic freaks, not Spectrics playing jokes but what might be called genuine phoneys. Notable among them were Abraham Lincoln Gillespie, the Baroness Elsa von Freytag-Loringhoven, Emanuel Carnevali, Ernest Walsh, Harry Crosby. Walsh edited his own magazine, but the rest exemplify McAlmon's remark that *transition* was a constant example of how not to write.

Gillespie was teaching mathematics in a Philadelphia high school when he suffered a head injury in a car accident which left him with a marked squint and a sudden realisation that he was part of the modern movement. Was the idea to invent words? Then Gillespie, a signatory to the manifesto, could invent with the best of them. First Paul, and then Jolas, read and were impressed: impressed by pieces like 'ABSTRAKTIDS (Phrase Moments illustrating Grammar-conduced-to Horizont-Sequence)' which began:

infradigit-enunceColor Plastic
nowhere-within-Space   transcend   Command   Nirvaia
nowhere-within-handy-Space   Chinese   FloatInfinity
sweettrustmisery-Eyed   hurtbyher   Man-Woman

Pieces like these appeared in several numbers. Not only Paul and Jolas had a high opinion of Gillespie. When Boyle returned from a visit to Germany, she told Gillespie that it was his work, rather than

Joyce's, that interested the *avant-garde* writers there. Why had Gillespie left America? 'Because in Europe I find MeaningScurry in their Organise-Self-Divert'. And what future did he foresee for his country? He envisaged a time when 'the American Spirit will commence-sing as naive-Divert – hours loll here all simmer-rife-Expect-lush-stat, GET is less-necessary'. McAlmon said that when they first met Gillespie called him 'the only form-packing symbol-realisticator, tuckfunctioning moderncompactly'.[2] This literary deformity sired by Joyce faded from the scene with the end of *transition* in 1938.

Jolas cannot be held responsible for the Baroness, who first appeared as a writer in the *Little Review*, and physically in Greenwich Village. Her name is said to have been Ploetz, her father a German builder, her husband a wealthy German businessman. Her title's origin remains mysterious: perhaps it was assumed, like that of Baron Corvo. In the later years of World War I the Baroness walked the Village streets dressed sometimes in a Mexican blanket, sometimes in Scotch plaid with a kilt, sometimes still more eccentrically clothed. She appeared with shaven head, with postage stamps stuck on her cheeks and nickel tea balls hanging from her breasts, on her head a coal scuttle or a velvet tam-o-shanter adorned with spoons and feathers. She is said to have survived by working in a cigarette factory and by posing as a life-class model.

Williams, told by Anderson or Heap that the Baroness was crazy about his work, unwisely agreed to meet her. She had just been released from prison for stealing an umbrella, and he took her to breakfast. A little later she told him that he should contract syphilis from her and so free his mind for serious art. Perhaps in pursuit of this end she arranged for a friend to call out Williams in his medical capacity to attend a non-existent sick baby and then tried to force him to go home with her, opening proceedings with a brisk punch on the neck. After this Williams bought and used a punch bag, and the next time she accosted him flattened her with a blow in the mouth. She was arrested, but he refused to press charges and later gave her money to leave the country.[3] She went, inevitably, to Paris, and just as inevitably appeared in *transition*. A brief sample of her work, from the *Little Review*, will be enough. This is how 'Appalling Heart' began:

[207]

A Movement in Decline

City stir–wind on eardrum –
dancewind: herbstained –
flowerstained–silken–rustling –
tripping–swishing–frolicking –
courtesing–careening–brushing –
flowing–lying down–bending –
teasing–kissing: treearms–grass –
limbs–lips.
City stir on eardrum –
in night lonely
peers –:
moon–riding!

In Paris the Baroness caused less stir than she had done in Greenwich Village. In 1927 she turned on the gas in her tenement room, leaving a suicide letter for Djuna Barnes who befriended and apparently admired her. Barnes printed this letter, with some others, in *transition*. They show that, like the rest of these freaks of modernism, the Baroness had not mastered English. For such writers the example of Joyce, whether received at first or second hand, was disastrous.

The same is true of Emanuel Carnevali, an Italian born in Florence in 1897, who came as a youth to America together with his wife, looking for poetic fame. He made a little money as dishwasher in an Italian restaurant, she taught French to small girls. Williams met them and thought Carnevali intelligent, but an obviously lost soul. Carnevali's wife adored him, and continued to do so even when he went up to Chicago to work on an Italian-language magazine there, and told her she would be an obstacle to his literary career and that their relationship was now ended.[4] He quarrelled with the editor of the magazine and left after two weeks. Harriet Monroe, who had been impressed by a poem comparing the world to a hotel, rashly appointed him associate editor of *Poetry*. There he stayed for six months, dashing in and out of the office and skipping all the routine work. She was relieved when he resigned and returned to New York.

'Jesus, Jesus, save Carnevali for me,' Williams pleaded in print, saying that the young man was beginning to disintegrate at twenty-one.[5] He suffered from a mysterious illness, later diagnosed as encephalitis lethargica, a form of sleeping sickness. His family sent him money to return to Italy and he was there, in hospital, when McAlmon published Carnevali's book *A Hurried Man*. McAlmon also, without publicising the fact, supported him financially. From the early twenties until his presumed death during World War II, Carnevali remained ill and in Italy, writing an autobiography for which his friends tried unsuccessfully to find a publisher.

This sad story in no way justified the ludicrous claims made for him as a writer. 'The reason for our having been alive is here!' Williams wrote in 1919 of Carnevali's poetry and went on to say that the young Italian was wide open, out of doors, did not look at life through a window.[6] Kay Boyle called him the Rimbaud of the twenties, the stranger that other writers had been writing and waiting for. She paid him a visit in Italy, and found him 'the gayest person alive', although he shook with his illness. Boyle emerged feeling that she should be with him always, although in fact she never went to see him again. Perhaps her opinion was influenced by Ernest Walsh, founder and editor of *This Quarter*, who called Carnevali a Keats of the period, adding for good measure: 'He has more to say than Keats. He is more important than Keats. He has lived in a more important age and known a larger world ... You must think of Carnevali as Carnevali. You do not need to ask which Carnevali. There is but one man by that name who will live beyond this century.'[7]

What particularly impressed these admirers was Carnevali's primitive approach to the English language, something perfectly in tune with the anti-intellectualism of American modernism. He represented for them a child of nature, one whose lack of verbal sophistication confirmed his own fervent certainty of his genius. This limited vocabulary meant that Carnevali put things down jerkily, rather with the effect of an early silent film running imperfectly. The material of his poems was generally commonplaces put down in uneven lines, like the opening of 'The Doctor':

> Very elegant
> in spite of age
> finds enough warmth
> in his heart
> to embrace woman
> and whisper
> in her ears
> shocking and thrilling
> little mysteries of love.

A Movement in Decline

Much the same is true of what friends agreed to be his master work, *A Hurried Man*, which blends assertions of the necessity for violence, vague invocations of Blake and Rimbaud, and cries for 'a coalition of the artists, a new religion, a universal prohibition forbidding ... everything that is now being said', with little bits of poetry:

> I received from a friend
> a letter where
> was a portrait of yours
> cut from a paper;
> and was kinda nostalgic
> the way a man would be
> who'd left a barrel of rotting apples
> uneaten

As Lewis said: 'The daring of this takes your breath away, and the bitterness of the ending fair turns yer up: am I right?'[8] Pound, attacked by Carnevali in *A Hurried Man*, was not deterred from making attempts to get money for what he called, only half-ironically, this lily white soul. He expressed no opinion about Carnevali's work. McAlmon said: 'He thinks he's a troubadour, but he's just an organ grinder and the monkey too.'[9] That seems just about right.

What joined these genuine phoneys was a refusal to accept that the writing of poetry or prose involved a discipline to be learned. Their desire to write was genuine enough, but they insisted that their work must not be set against anything written in the past, its merit was total newness. It was a tenet of such figures that a Day One existed when Modern Literature, unconnected with the past, began. The nearer they got to that Day One of immaculate birth, the more incoherent their work became; the more the product owed to the past, the more its absurdity was obvious. They might be called the victims of modernism, those who had read the men of 1914 without at all understanding the implications or purposes of what they were trying to do.

Ernest Walsh, known to his friends as Michael, was among those most ardently pursuing Day One. He founded *This Quarter* in the spring of 1925 with the financial help of a mother figure – or at least a woman much his senior – named Ethel Moorhead. A Scot, tall, lean and angular, Moorhead had been an active suffragette before

World War I, smashing windows, tying herself to railings, suffering arrest and forcible feeding. After the war she took up literature and Ernest Walsh, whom she first met at Claridge's where she paid his unsettled bill. They jointly edited the magazine, the first number of which ran to more than three hundred pages, including extracts from *Work in Progress*, Hemingway's 'Big-Two Hearted River', a ten-page poem by Carnevali, and seventeen poems by Walsh. The number was dedicated to Pound, 'hero by his creative work, his editorship of several magazines, his helpful friendship for young and unknown artists'.

Pound, who was busy preparing a new paper of his own to be called the *Exile*, seems not to have been much impressed by the dedication. With his usual interfering good nature he suggested to Walsh a Lewis number of *This Quarter* and mentioned this to Lewis, adding unwisely that his work was now not well known to many people. Lewis, however, had already been approached by Moorhead, who asked why he had dropped out, as she put it ('Perhaps you have a big Canto or something in hand?'), and said they would like anything he sent, long or short: *'We want you!'* Lewis suggested sending something almost of book length, for which he asked £80, and Walsh replied offering £30 which he refused.[10] The upshot was a savage letter from Lewis to Pound which began, 'I do not want a "Lewis number" or anything of that sort in *This Quarter* or *anywhere* else at this moment,' and continued menacingly:

> Please note the following: because in the glorious days of Marinetti, Nevinson, machinery, Wadsworth, Wormwood Scrubs and Wyoming, we were associated to some extent in publicity campaigns, that does not give you a mandate to interfere when you think fit, with or without my consent, with my career. If you launch at me and try to force on me a scheme which I regard as malapropos and which is liable to embarrass me, you will not find me so docile as Eliot.[11]

Pound did not take offence at this, but could not resist writing again to say that Walsh had only £10 to spend per contributor, and perhaps Lewis should send him that amount of work. Lewis replied that Walsh was lying, but ended on a friendly note by calling down blessings on Pound's shaggy head, although he added: 'That Walsh has consumption interests Miss Woodpigeon but does not interest me.' Miss Woodpigeon, although still the periodical's financial prop, had by now parted from Walsh, moving out of their apartment to make way for Kay Boyle, who was pregnant by Walsh when he died in October 1926. It is hard to say whether Walsh's prose or his verse was more abysmal. His praise of Carnevali is typical of the girlish gush which he splashed also over McAlmon and Hemingway. Near the end of his life he had begun to write poems in an Olde Englisshe Tea Roome style:

> Iffe I cud have a sonne I wude want his mother to
> Be a beutiful happye ladye andde she to shayke her hed atte me
> Lyke a marygolde O the wynde has notte anye nose to mayke
> Its chekes thynne butte a brest itte has to crushe
> The flowers offe springe against inne yonge wulde wulde tormente[12]

Perhaps it should be set to Walsh's credit that he had turned away from free verse to the sonnet, and also that he wrote two good lines, the first of which Boyle used as title for a novel: 'Gentlemen I address you privately/And no woman is within hearing.' After Walsh's death Pound left unanswered a request to write a tribute, and the indignant Moorhead revoked what she called the too-generous dedication of the first number. A year or two later *This Quarter* passed into the hands of the wealthy patron of the arts Edward Titus, and became a different kind of magazine.

It has been said that Jolas was the only signatory who took the Revolution of the Word manifesto seriously, but perhaps there was one other: Harry Crosby, who with his wife Caresse signed it. Crosby was the most ludicrous and most dislikeable of the genuine phoneys. His lacquered fingernails, and the black cloth flower in his buttonhole, suggested a throwback to the nineties, but unlike the nineties poets Crosby was rich and thus able to tell his father, an investment banker, that he refused to take money seriously.[13] In 1928 he rented an old mill on the edge of the Forest of Ermenonville belonging to the Rochefoucauld family, added a swimming pool and a racing track (donkeys, not horses, were raced), turned a stable into a huge banqueting hall, converted the hayloft into bedrooms and there held large parties which sometimes became orgies. Visitors to the mill included Salvador Dali, Max Ernst, Douglas Fairbanks and Mary Pickford, Aldous Huxley, the Lawrences, and several of the writers connected with *transition*, although not Joyce or Stein. Caresse Crosby collected people with titles and claims to

titles, especially if they had a royal connection, and Hart Crane
found himself making 'violent love to nobility', presumably male.
Crane recorded polo played with golf clubs on donkeys, skating,
oysters, absinthe, opium, and 'five days out there working all by
myself, with just the gardener and his wife bringing me food and
wine beside a jolly hearth-fire'.[14] In fact Crane did no more than
tinker with 'The Bridge', but drank enormously, tattooed his face
with Indian ink, read *Tamburlaine* aloud, and proclaimed his own
poetic greatness. In a sober passage he wrote to Stein, introduced
himself as 'a friend of your friend, Laura Riding', and asked for the
privilege of calling on her.[15] When he did so he found her delightful
and, more surprisingly, beautiful. The Black Sun Press, which
Crosby ran with his wife, published from 1927 onwards minor
works by Joyce, Lawrence, Pound and Proust in handsome limited
editions.

The desire to become a savant, entertained by Crosby soon after
he came to Paris in the early twenties, was replaced by sun worship
practised from a Sun Tower in the mill. He wore a silk robe while
intoning prayers from the Sun Tower, and drank a ritual cup of wine
from an appropriately counterfeit Byzantine gold vessel.[16] Did
anybody take seriously the nine volumes of verse he published in six
years, all of course at his own expense? Yes, *transition* did so,
printing poems by him in several issues, as well as his articles
defending the Revolution of the Word. In December 1929 Crosby
paid a visit to New York, and shot himself and a girl friend in a
borrowed apartment. In his pocket were the Cunard Line tickets he
had bought to return to Paris with Caresse.[17]

Most of Crosby's poems are mere decorative rubbish, but a
minority are implicitly nihilistic or Fascist in sentiment. 'The
Assassin' invokes the Mad Queen, Goddess of the Sun, who
demands that the weak shall be destroyed and damage done to the
multitude, so that 'a new strong world shall rise to worship the Mad
Queen'. Such poems are too intelligible and literal to be surrealist,
too vigorous to be called decadent. They are savage reactionary
pieces, particularly disagreeable because Crosby did not understand
the implications of what he was writing but simply expressed the
angry misery of a poor little rich boy unable to come to terms with
the world. Perhaps it was not surprising that *transition* should have
published a 'Harry Crosby Memorial Issue' with praise from Boyle,

Crane, Philippe Soupault and Archibald MacLeish as well as from Jolas, but it seems even now surprising that Eliot and Pound should have joined the elegiac chorus, although neither committed himself to praise of Crosby's writing.

Eliot ended a more than usually muffled piece by saying that what he liked about Crosby was the fact that he was 'going his own way whether I like the way or not'. Pound said Crosby was not an artist, but his life had been a religious manifestation, his death a vote of confidence in the cosmos.[18] Almost equally nonsensical was Malcolm Cowley's much later attempt to establish Crosby (who like others had served in World War I and seen a good deal of death and horror) as one whose life cast 'a retrospective light on the literary history of the whole decade',[19] and who adopted the Sun as the symbol of worship because his life was empty. 'His death, which had seemed an act of isolated and crazy violence, began to symbolise the decay from within and the suicide of a whole order with which he had been identified.'[20] The life and death of Harry Crosby symbolised nothing and carried no moral, except perhaps that it emphasised the difficulties of being a rich young man and a good writer.

CHAPTER TWELVE

Pound's Progress: The *Cantos*

Pound's retirement from the social life of Paris to a fifth-floor flat on the sea front at Rapallo did not imply a lack of interest in the current literary scene. Hundreds of letters still came from his ancient typewriter, some pressing on the newly-established Guggenheim Foundation the merits of Lewis, Eliot and Antheil as recipients for awards, others urging Monroe to print new poets he had discovered. Some were jokey, like a letter telling William Bird that Hemingway had been killed by a bull, Antheil crushed by an auto-caterpillar while on his way to fight in the Riff War, and that McAlmon was standing as Conservative candidate in a British by-election. Some expressed admiration for Mussolini and Henry Ford. The well-laundered edition of his letters gives little indication of the variety of his correspondence, much of it still concerned with encouraging and advising those who sent him poems. A typical example is his letters from 1928 to 1931 to Helene Magaret, an example chosen because she remains unmentioned in biographies of Pound and apparently never had a volume published.

Pound told the girl who became in the course of the correspondence 'La Belle Helene' what she should read, how she should write. It seems that Magaret wrote in regular metres, and Pound deprecated this. English poetry, he said, was bad for writers and Helene was showing an unhappy tendency to subside into the Longfellow tradition, although he added that she had a better chance of writing something good than 'any other female in amurika'. By this time he had advanced to 'Dearest Helene' in letters, and while deploring her 'husky bolchevik friends' said he would recommend her work to T. C. Wilson, who was editing the magazine *Bozart-Westminster*.[1] But the special number of this magazine, edited in part by Wilson and Pound, contained no poems by Helene Magaret.

A Movement in Decline

She was one of many. Lewis exaggerated only a little when he said that he encountered many Pound protégés who produced a packet of letters 'typed in a violent-blue ink, and written in the most fantastic jargon'.[2] As the years passed, Pound's letters were indeed written in an ever more extraordinary blend of hectoring jocosity, mock or deliberate slang and misspellings and exclamatory anger, and were increasingly marked by unannounced shifts from one subject to another, so that many letters need an interpreter rather than a reader. They never lost the manic enthusiasm of the London years, but this enthusiasm was now wholly disordered, as if a never very reliable machine had gone completely out of control. The ability to spot new talent, to distinguish real from counterfeit, seemed to have left him. He was most easily excited by any verse that seemed to him technically revolutionary, but took up other poetic causes too, in particular that of Ralph Cheever Dunning, a dim Enoch Soames-like figure who was quietly coughing away his life in a Paris garret when proclaimed by Pound a writer of genius. A portrait of Dunning shows him long and languid, sitting miserably beside a kettle on an iron stove. Pound worked hard to publicise him, pushed Monroe into printing some poems, urged Mencken to use his influence in getting a volume published, and spurred Joyce into reading him when he acclaimed Dunning's talent in the course of advising against the republication of *Chamber Music*. Joyce read a few poems and pronounced them drivel. He may have seen some of those in the posthumously published *Windfalls*, with their mourning for lost loves:

> Where did you learn that smile? From what dead lips
> Of little children and a queen's disgrace
> Rose the immortal butterfly that sips
> Upon your mouth and flits about your face?

Pound printed some of Dunning's work in the *Exile*, along with that by other familiar names like McAlmon and Williams, Yeats's 'Sailing to Byzantium', and work by the young Jewish poet Louis Zukofsky, who became perhaps Pound's closest disciple. *Exile* lurched through four issues and then faded away, because as Pound said other publications were doing similar things, but really it was less literary than socio-political affairs that occupied him now. In *Exile 3* his editorial said: 'Quite simply: I want a new civilization.'

He never defined just what sort of civilisation it should be. His readers knew it was something to do with Social Credit and what Pound called Volitionist Economics, which expounded such ideas as that 'a country CAN have one currency for internal use and another good for both home and foreign use', and expressed outrage at the fact that exchange or barter of commodities was subject to taxation. An advertisement for Volitionist Economics, which invited letters from those interested, appeared in several little magazines. This civilisation also had something to do with politics, at first almost any kind of politics that promised change ('Pound Joins The Revolution' was the heading of a letter from him in the left-wing *New Masses* in 1926), but before long with Fascist ideas in general and Mussolini's practice in particular. Pound's single meeting with the dictator took place in 1933, and left him convinced that Mussolini was a great and extraordinarily perceptive man. (He was never so enthusiastic about Hitler.) Mussolini on his side was, not surprisingly, baffled by Pound's ideas.

This self-publicising, socio-political and literary activity was the foreground of a life to which the Cantos were the background. They had been conceived perhaps as early as 1904 and began to be published in 1917, although the early Cantos were much changed over the years. In the end there were over a hundred of them, and although only some thirty had appeared by the end of the twenties, their theme and nature had by then been settled. Dozens of books and hundreds of articles have been written about the Cantos in recent years, and those who call Pound a great poet do so on the basis of this long poem. Very often critics assume the Cantos' greatness and, the assumption made, go on happily to discuss the endless problems and intricacies of the work. The case, however, needs proving. In 1946, when Robert Graves refused to sign a petition for clemency to Pound organized by Eliot, he said he could never regard Pound as a poet.[3]

The Cantos were shaped, at first no doubt unconsciously, to fit Pound's erratic personality. Since his interests constantly shifted, and he was unable to concentrate on a single subject, the Cantos are constructed deliberately to avoid continuity. There would be no plot in them, Pound told Yeats, and no chronicle of events, but they would show the descent into Hades from Homer, and within this would be introduced modern or mediaeval characters. Into this

[217]

framework Pound inserted scenes and people from his own life, especially those known in an increasingly distant past, plus fragments of Italian history in the Middle Ages, plus all kinds of cross-references in a variety of languages. These scenes were designed to fit into each other like blocks in an infinitely complex jigsaw. To see the whole picture you had to understand that the way the blocks fitted into one Canto affected their presence in another, and with each new Canto the possible permutations became greater, the jigsaw more complex.

For Yeats's benefit Pound made scribbled notes representing archetypal events or emotions, 'ABCD and then JKLM, and then each set of letters repeated, and then ABCD inverted and this repeated and then a new element XYZ, then certain letters that never recur and then all sorts of combinations of XYZ and JKLM and ABCD and DCBZ and all set whirling together.'[4] Yeats's account makes the poem clearer only if the jigsaw blocks are understood, but Pound himself said many other contradictory things about the Cantos, calling the whole design a Divine Comedy, a fugue, or even – going back to *Blast* days – a vortex. He said the first eleven Cantos had been no more than a preparation of the palette, although that was not the way he thought of them at the time. And then in his last years he pronounced the Cantos a mess, a work in which he had picked out this and that thing of interest to him, then jumbled all the things into a bag. That was not the way, he said, to make a work of art.[5] We need not accept the more grandiose statements about the poem's design, nor take too seriously the total condemnation he pronounced near the end of his life. The point is that the Cantos do not show the steady progress towards a purposed end that marks Eliot's poetic career. They are, rather, the record of a lifetime's confusion.

Pound was, not least in the Cantos, often an extremely pretentious writer. The opening 67 lines of Canto 1 (that is, almost all of it) are a translation into Poundian language of what was itself a Latin translation of a fragment of the *Odyssey*. The practice of resetting Greek, through a Latin translation, into a Poundian version of Anglo-Saxon, seems odd to the point of absurdity. The reason (surely a most curious one) was, we are told by one of Pound's most reasonable expositors,[6] to introduce the *Odyssey* and also suggest the strata of languages and motifs that lie ahead. Sure enough we are soon being offered bits of Greek, Latin, French and Italian, dozens of references back to Greek mythology, slabs of Italian history relating to the Italian condottiere Sigismondo Malatesta regarded as a heroic figure, and a passing reference to a Provençal troubadour, Guillen da Cabestan, killed by a jealous husband who cooked and served Cabestan's heart to his wife. This last is the kind of story out of which Pound's early master Browning might have made a tale in verse, but in the Cantos it is merely an incident used to link twelfth-century France with a passage in Ovid about Procne, who served her son's flesh to her husband as an act of revenge. Does it matter that Pound explains nothing, so that we do not know who Cabestan was? Perhaps not, but the glancing nature of the link to Ovid, and of other similar links in this single Canto – these emphatically do matter. Did Pound mean to mystify? Whether he did or not, here as in the four Malatesta Cantos he made large, unjustified assumptions about his readers' knowledge, or of course felt no concern for them at all.

As the Cantos increased in number and widened in scope they introduced more and more incidents of Pound's life. The first half of Canto XII is about a lively little crook named Baldy Bacon whom Pound met in New York in 1911; the second half, a long and corny dirty joke about a sailor induced to believe that he is a mother. Canto XIII switches to Confucius and the advice he gave to his disciples, Cantos XIV and XV are a portrayal of Hell. In suggesting that Lewis might do a set of initials for these two Cantos Pound remarked that the artist would readily understand that Hell was a portrait of the England Pound had rejected. He had come to think of those years as ones in which his gifts had been generally unacknowledged, and his language about unidentified politicians 'addressing crowds through their arse-holes' and journalists called 'the betrayers of language' and crusaders against vice named as 'harpies dripping shit through the air' is savage, although Eliot observed that this was a Hell for other people, one that the elect could contemplate with equanimity.

Any attempt to be literal about the Cantos in this way – I have mentioned only some of the first fifteen – is likely to make them seem more coherent than they are in reading. It also ignores their effect as poetry. One attitude towards them (not the one, it need hardly be said, adopted by academic commentators) is that we should let the meaning go, and submit ourselves to the words on the page:

A Movement in Decline

'It is Cabestan's heart in the dish.'
'It is Cabestan's heart in the dish?'
'No other taste shall change this.'

That is very effective, and so are the following lines in which Cabestan's lover commits suicide. The poetry is most successful when Pound is giving rein to his romanticism, his love of the past, his obsessive idea that there was a distant civilisation which had equalled the new one he vaguely envisaged. The beautiful opening to Canto XVII is an evocation of a distant time and place, and whenever Pound's lyrical impulse is stirred it is by some aspect of the past, either through the physical embodiments of myths, or stories about them, or reference to figures out of Italian history that grow larger than lifesize as he writes about them. He is charmed by flowers, colours, strange names: it is typical that he calls frankincense olibanum and devotes whole Cantos to semi-factual accounts of the magnificence and decline of Venice, placing them next to chatty discussions of Jefferson's attempts to civilise America. His valued contemporaries, Eliot, Ford, Hulme, Lewis, become historical figures in the vast frieze of the poem, and also look more than lifesize as they are seen in the context of the past.

Pound did himself an injustice of a kind when he implied that the various things jumbled into the poem had got there by accident. They represent rather, for the most part, his passionate concern with history and romance. History was chiefly Italian history, with American and French some way behind – British history held little interest for Pound, the development of parliamentary rule being alien to him. It has been suggested that he was influenced by Joyce's example in his frequent casting back to themes from the *Odyssey*, but he had no need of Joyce as a spur to interest. What he hoped to do by mixing past and contemporary, classical and modern, chatty autobiography and lyrical desire, was to produce a work that combined history and autobiography so that it was finally a comment on the nature of civilisation.

The poem was composed in a variety of styles, the rhetorical, lyrical and factual predominating, and the verse patterns used are often said to be unmetred. It is true that they have no consistency and almost never use rhyme, but they have a general pattern. We hear a voice when we read them, more than in reading any other modern poetry, the voice of a chronicler and prophet, much given like prophets in the Bible to use of the emphatic connective 'And':

> And
> I came here in my young youth
>   and lay there under the crocodile
> By the column, looking East on the Friday,
> And I said: Tomorrow I will lie on the South side
> And the day after, south west,
> And at night they sang in the gondolas
> And in the barche with lanthorns (Canto XXVI)

The Cantos contain dozens of similar *and*-linked passages. There is a form to them, and stresses in the verse, best appreciated by listening to the poet's sing-song semi-chanting of the poem when he read it aloud. Such semi-chanting is the poem's predominant manner, impressive in brief passages, monotonous in longer ones. It is used for all sorts of purposes, even to accommodate the most vulgarly abusive jokes.

> The tale of the perfect schnorrer: a peautiful chewisch poy
> wit a vo-ice dot woult
> meldt dh heart offa schtone
> and wit a likeing for to make arht-voiks
> and ven dh oldt ladty wasn't dhere any more
> and dey didn't know why, tdhere ee woss in the
> oldt antique schop and nobodty knew how he got dhere
> and venn hiss brudder diet widout any bapers
> he vept all ofer dh garpet so much he
> had to have his clothes aftervards pressed
> and he orderet a magnificent funeral
> and tden sent dh pill to dh vife. (Canto XXXV)

Even those heretical about the existence of the Cantos as in any sense a coherent poem can make dips into these hundreds of pages and come up with memorable passages: but of course to look at the work in this way is to call the total poem a total failure.

CHAPTER THIRTEEN

Lewis and Eliot Separate Themselves from Modernism

Lewis's ambitions in the twenties, like those of Pound in the Cantos, ranged widely. *The Art of Being Ruled* was about politics and society, *Time and Western Man* dealt with the 'time philosophy' embodied in the ideas of Bergson, Whitehead and others, *The Lion and the Fox* looked at Shakespeare in political terms, attempting to replace the figure of 'divine impersonality' current in the decade by a man of his time who had social and political opinions. *Paleface* attacked the cult of Negro art and of the Negro himself as an embodiment of primitive wisdom (Carnevali being, as one might say, a white Negro in his primitiveness). *The Childermass*, part politico-literary satire and argument, was only in the most formal sense a work of fiction. These long books all appeared between 1926 and 1929, and to them should be added *The Apes of God*, on which Lewis worked through most of the twenties.

They provided a reply to those, like Eliot, who on occasion suggested that Lewis was dissipating his energies by working on several books at once, or that he spent too much time on petty squabbles and love affairs. They did not, however, give their author the position of philosopher-king – like, say, that of Sartre in Paris after World War II – that he had expected. All received high praise in Britain, were less warmly greeted in America, sold few copies. Five months after publication *The Art of Being Ruled* had sold only just over 500 copies, and the advance subscription for *Time and Western Man* was a derisory 225. Yet these books contained speculations and suggestions about the modern state, the individual's place within it, and the implications involved in sexual and political liberalism that even today astonish by their acuity and far-sightedness. They contain analyses looking forward to the spread of unisex clothing and behaviour and the increasing power of homosexuality, they suggest the likely development of giant trusts and cartels that in their internal pattern would resemble socialist states. Lewis saw the likelihood that the 'democratic' nature of the capitalist state would be a source of weakness rather than strength, linked the disintegration of the family (something hardly contemplated at the time) with the development of feminism, condemned the idea that Negro culture should be considered as at all equivalent to white. Why was the writer who advanced these disturbing, novel ideas not proclaimed as an important sociological philosopher, why was there not a cult of his work among the intelligentsia?

Some of the answer is to be found in the conventional philistinism of literary and political Britain during the period. The Conservative government that was firmly settled in the saddle during most of the years between the wars was far less receptive to any novel ideas than had been Asquith's Liberal administration before World War I. The outspokenly authoritarian nature of Lewis's thought and the daring quality of his speculations would have made Tory politicians frown, and his suggestion that it was necessary for mankind to 'hasten to its unification under one unique control' to avoid another European bloodbath would have left them thinking that there could never be much wrong with a Britain under *their* control. And if Lewis held little appeal for orthodox Tories, he was even less congenial to orthodox *New Statesman* and *New Republic*-reading liberals, who expected any modernist to support 'progressive' causes. To them Lewis was anathema, even though they were sometimes fascinated by his attacks on them. Edgell Rickword's homosexual aesthete Twittingpan conveyed the blend of fear and adoration they felt:

Don't you think Wyndham Lewis too divine?
That brute male strength he shows in every line!
I swear if he'd flogged me in his last book but one,
As some kind person informed me he has done,
I'd have forgiven him for the love of art . . .
I'd lived in Time and Motion and Sensation,
Then smashed my watch and burnt the Bloomsbury *Nation*.[1]

But his own shortcomings as a writer also limited Lewis's readership, chief among them his inability to make one point rather than a dozen, or stick to a central theme. It would be necessary, he said at the beginning of *The Art of Being Ruled*, for him to create an audience, since the book aimed 'at no audience already there with which I am acquainted'.[2] But any would have found it hard to follow the course of an argument which moved from analysis of the ideas of 'revolution' and 'progress' and the struggle between 'Liberalist democracy and authority' to a quotation from the *Daily Mail* about English visitors to Deauville playing with kites and model yachts as an indication of the 'child cult' among adults, thence to an attack on feminism and sexual inversion, comments on Proudhon, Rousseau and the social contract, and a glancing attack on Stein and Joyce, the whole ending with a spirited defence of the intellectual life. The main drift of Lewis's thought, the defence of 'intellect' against 'sensation' or 'primitivism', was easy enough to follow, but the interconnections between his various themes often remained obscure. Equally tenuous were the links, in *Time and Western Man*, between the literary analyses of Stein and Joyce and of Pound as the ideal 'revolutionary simpleton' in love with anything new, and the discussion of 'time philosophy' that followed it. One of Lewis's most intelligent admirers, the mathematician J. W. N. Sullivan, expressed his bafflement. 'You give Bergson, Einstein, Joyce, Stein, etc. as different people to have *succumbed* to it [time philosophy]. You seem to regard it as a sort of pestilence that has now, you hope, reached its maximum.' Sullivan went on to a technical criticism of Lewis's linking of Bergson with Einstein's theories in which he said that 'the non-Euclidean geometrics are matters of logic ... You cannot invalidate the logic of Einstein's equations by showing they have produced Miss Gertrude Stein.'[3] He added that he was still not sure about the nature of Lewis's own philosophy.

With 'The Revolutionary Simpleton' Lewis signed a declaration of divorce from some of the most notable experiments of literary modernism in his generation. His view of Stein as a *faux-naïf*, a sophisticated literary practitioner pretending to childishness; the lengthy examination which admired the achievement of *Ulysses* but called the characters walking clichés; the picture of Pound as a revolutionary simpleton prepared to applaud anything with a 'brand new' label on it: these, along with an attack on 'that literary wonder we will call Bud Macsalmon' (Robert McAlmon), the tearing to pieces of *This Quarter* under the name of the *Q Review*, and denunciation of Russian ballet as the perfect exemplification of the 'High Bohemia of the "revolutionary" rich', meant that he parted company from many previous friends and admirers. Joyce's reaction has been mentioned. Stein saw nothing more of Lewis, and later wrote of him with derision. McAlmon, who had made a vague arrangement to publish a long book by Lewis, broke off relations with him. Only Pound, with the indifference to personal matters that he often showed, seems to have ignored the attack on him, never referring to it in letters.

When Lewis said that mere technical exercises and verbal innovations were not enough to make a writer modern but must be accompanied by new ideas, he no doubt had himself in mind: and his attempt to demonstrate this in fiction was *The Apes of God*, published in 1930. This was a long book, made to seem longer by the hefty nature of its production. It weighed five pounds, was three inches thick, and Lewis published it himself in the guise of the Arthur Press, with the financial aid of his friend Sir Nicholas Waterhouse. If he wanted to produce a physically bigger book than *Ulysses* he succeeded, but it did not get a friendly reception. It is the general view among Lewis's friends, enemies and biographers that his reputation was hopelessly damaged by publication of his book about Hitler, the short study published in 1931. No doubt that did him a good deal of harm when Hitler came to power two years later, and Nazi designs and attitudes became clear: but among British and particularly American literati, *The Apes of God* damaged him even more.

It is not merely in a physical sense that *Apes* is a heavyweight work. Partly in accordance with his theories, partly to contrast his method with that of Joyce, Lewis's approach throughout is external. We see the characters, watch them, read lengthy descriptions of them, hear them utter the inanities of party and other conversation, but never know what they think. (If Lewis had been showing Bloom at stool he might have described his clothing in detail, remarked a strained expression on his face, the pattern of his skin, even his droppings – but not his randomly connected thoughts.) The external approach, thus strictly applied, meant that the narrative lumbered along at carthorse pace. The book's subject is literary London and the activities of a group of characters representing literary High Bohemia. They are described with much power and hostile wit, and all are recognisable: the most notable are the three Sitwells, Lytton Strachey and Dora Carrington, Edward and Fanny Wadsworth, McAlmon, Sidney and Violet Schiff. These figures are wound up, set in motion, made to demonstrate the insignificance of their ideas, the limits of their fashionable intelligences. Above or outside them, voicing what are at times Lewis's opinions, is Horace Zagreus, and directing Zagreus is the unseen master of the story, Pierpoint. The book is less a work of fiction than an examination of the condition of intellectual Britain. The characters are all in one way or another fakes, and to point up their hollowness the book ends with an event which in Lewis's terms was also a fake: the half-hearted General Strike of 1926. It is appropriate to the absurdity of this mock revolution that the semi-moronic Dan should interpret the offers of lifts from gentlemen strike-breakers as homosexual approaches.

The intention was to satirise society. Why, then, make the apes so easily identifiable? Pound said that in eighty years' time nobody would worry about the identities of Puffin, Guffin and Mungo, but the colossal masks would remain. The splendour of these Easter Island figures of the imagination would have been more easily perceived, however, if they had not shown so clearly the 'blond pencilled pap rising straight from his sloping forehead' and 'galb-like wings to his nostrils' of Osbert Sitwell, or the 'earnest mask of a beardless, but military-moustachioed, spectacled Dr Freud' presented by Sydney Schiff. The British press generally was unfriendly. How could it be otherwise when much of the reviewing was done by the apes' colleagues? In America the book waited two years for a publisher and aroused little interest. For publishers in both countries it marked Lewis as a man whose writing ran the risk of involving them in legal difficulties. This happened later, but not with *Apes*. The Sitwells were shocked and angered by the book but decided against suing Lewis, and the Schiffs were unmoved by the vicious portraits of them. Sydney, who had signed a letter written after reading *The Art of Being Ruled* 'with fervent admiration and unchangeable friendship', said that the picture of him was distressing, but 'our personal relations have not been based upon your approval of my work but on my admiration for yours'. Violet wrote of the loss to her that they no longer met. 'If you don't want to meet Sydney that is no reason why you should not meet me.'[4] There can be no greater proof of the magnetism Lewis exerted than the Schiffs' reactions to his caricatures. Three years after the book appeared, when Lewis was ill, Sydney again gave him financial support.

Lewis and Eliot Separate Themselves from Modernism

Eliot's movement away from modernism, like Lewis's, had something socio-political about it. In its origins European modernism had been based on the superior culture and intelligence of an elite, opposed to the optimistic lyricism about human beings and their place in society that marked the work of Williams, Crane, Hemingway, and many lesser Americans. Eliot may have admired some of these writers, but he had no sympathy with the attitudes from which their work sprang, any more than he had for those of the group round *transition*. Literary modernism for him could not be separated from the view that Western society, 'worm-eaten with liberalism',[5] was moving towards early destruction. In 1929, when he took the youthful Stephen Spender out to lunch, he spoke of Western civilisation's collapse, and when Spender asked what form the collapse would take, Eliot replied that it would be internecine warfare. He expanded the reply: 'People killing one another in the streets.'[6]

These are the ideas behind some of his essays, behind *Poems 1909–1925*, and behind the brilliant fragments of *Sweeney Agonistes* that try to show this decline 'visible in every department of human activity'[7] dramatically, in the jazz rhythms of the period. But Eliot's conversion to Christianity in 1927, publicly announced in the following year, precluded the continuation of *Sweeney Agonistes*, or the writing of any more Sweeney poems. His Christianity was undertaken seriously, like every other important action of his life. When asked directly, he would say that he believed in all the ritualistic details of the faith, invocations and sacraments, and – perhaps particularly – confession and communion. Such beliefs involved for him changes of attitude and of literary style. It was quite possible for a Christian to believe that civilisation was in decay and that blood would run in the streets, and possible for a Christian to make or condone anti-Semitic remarks of a kind common at the time. (Like Pound, who was accused with much more justice of being anti-Semitic, Eliot and Lewis had many Jewish friends.) It was not possible, however, for such a Christian as Eliot to write flippant or ironical verse about faith and the Christian religion. If serious subjects were to be considered – and for Eliot all subjects were potentially serious except cats – it must be from a specifically Christian point of view.

Adjustment to the new Christian Eliot was a problem for many

A Movement in Decline

British admirers. 'Ash Wednesday' (1930) was evidently a religious poem, full of borrowings from Christian texts and references to Dante, meditative, philosophic, at times sombre, and throughout distinctly and insistently Christian. Always inclined in verse to express his age and world-weariness, Eliot envisaged himself as an aged eagle reluctant to stretch his wings, aware that 'what is actual is actual only for one time/And only for one place' – aware, that is, of his own temporal weakness, and feeling able only to ask that 'the judgement not be too heavy on us'. The six parts of the poem contain more than this, but the more is mostly elaborations and metaphysical refinements on the theme stated in the opening section, and the whole is the apologia of a man with a taste for self-examination and self-condemnation. The latter quality held a great attraction for Eliot. It was undoubtedly one of the aspects of *Nightwood* that fascinated him and made him praise the work so highly. It was also perhaps the reason for his interest in Harry Crosby.

It was hard for readers in 1930 to accept this change of course. What had happened to Eliot's irony? The Authorised Version, one writer said, broke out on every hand in the poem. An English Plain Man reviewer, Thomas Moult in the *Bookman*, remarked that the poem was not for the plain man, although it is far easier to understand than *The Waste Land*, only the choice of symbols seeming at times private or arbitrary. Edmund Wilson praised the 'metrical mastery which catches so naturally . . . the faltering accents of the supplicant', but called the imagery literary and conventional. Most critics and readers who admired the earlier work regarded the poem as a wayside stopping place from which Eliot would soon move on to something nearer in spirit and style to the Sweeney poems. They were mistaken. Eliot had found his true poetic subject, the salvation of his soul, and the manner in which he wrote about it did not vary greatly from 'Ash Wednesday' to the *Four Quartets*. He lost a good deal of his youthful audience, although in the end he gained a much bigger one. Rickword's character Twittingpan said that 'Eliot's later works/are merely sanctimonious quips and quirks', and Aiken observed not without relish that Eliot in 1928 seemed a lost man, unsure of himself, wary, 'faced with a growing opposition and a shrinking following'.[8]

'Ash Wednesday' and the poems and plays that followed over the years amounted to an almost total break with modernism. As one of Eliot's biographers has said: 'He helped to create the idea of a modern movement with his own "difficult" poetry, and then assisted at its burial.'[9]

CHAPTER FOURTEEN

'The Good Days Are Finished': Americans Go Home

In 1931 Edmund Wilson published *Axel's Castle*, a collection of essays suggesting a literary progress from the Symbolist movement heralded by Arthur Symons into personal worlds of the writers' own – Yeats's astrological excursions, Proust's cork-lined room, Joyce's increasingly private language and Stein's reduction of language to an artificial simplicity. He found a neat opposition to such Parnassianism, represented for him by Villiers de Lisle Adam's Axel who regarded life as inferior to ideal dreaming and died in a suicide pact with his lover, in the career of Rimbaud who rejected literature utterly, became a trader in Africa carrying a belt of gold round his waist, and referred to his youthful poetry as absurd or disgusting. For writers who were artists rather than reformers or satirists there were from now onwards, Wilson suggested, only Axel's way or Rimbaud's (the latter was taken by Lawrence, Sherwood Anderson, and all those in love with the primitivism denounced by Lewis in *Paleface*). He concluded that 'the time is at hand when these writers, who have largely dominated the literary world of the decade 1920–1930, though we shall continue to admire them as masters, will no longer serve us as guides.[1]' Without calling in so many words for a return to realism, Wilson suggested that within a few years the writers then so highly praised might be treated just as intolerantly as those they had displaced in favour, among whom he named Wells, Shaw and Anatole France.

He spoke for an American literary generation rather than for any sizeable part of what could be called a general public when he called the writers he had in mind 'our guides'. Even the best-known among them, Valéry, Proust and Eliot, were not guides for Mr and Mrs Average Intelligent Reader, who were devoted to Somerset Maugham or Louis Bromfield. But it was true that the American literary generation of the twenties was in a state of shock, caused by the Stock Market collapse of 1929 and the Depression which followed it. The desire of those connected with *transition* and others to create a literature as fully sealed off from the pressures of 'society' as Axel in his Black Forest castle could not survive when society so urgently threatened their lives and incomes. Many of them felt, to put it crudely, that it was time to pay more attention to society, less to art.

There had been signs before 1929 of opposition to that romanticism of the dream which aimed at producing pure art uncontaminated by social ideas. Although Jolas thought it a waste of time for artists to concern themselves about Sacco and Vanzetti, he rashly agreed that *transition* 13 should be a wholly American issue, and invited Josephson to organise it. Josephson, a persuasive talker, assured Jolas that an American literary resurgence was in being, and Jolas expected contributions which would show a movement inspired by his own neo-romanticism. What he got was a variety of pieces by known and unknown Americans and a 'Group Manifestation, New York 1928' which must have disconcerted him. Josephson had recently produced his biography of Zola and was now devoted to social realism. He and four friends (Malcolm Cowley and Kenneth Burke among them) had shut themselves up in a New York hotel for a day and produced a mixture of squibs and serious articles, the tenor of the latter being that Europe was finished in a literary sense, and a good American should go back home. Some of the squibs were genuine crackers, like 'We See Them Every Three Years':

> Exiles often return to the lands of their mother
> With their hats in one hand and their palms in the other.

Another commented on Pound's retreat to Rapallo, and the central statement, an 'Open Letter to Mr Ezra Pound and the Other "Exiles"' stressed the need to realise that man is an economic animal and urged artists to play their part in mass society. The game of 'making words play with each other' was dismissed in almost Lewisian terms as 'a genteel bourgeois sport'. Add to this manifesto, no doubt chiefly the work of Josephson, an article from another pen which called on *transition* to abandon its damp ineffectual dreams and nourish the incipient social revolution in America, and it is easy to understand why Jolas was taken aback. Pound asked Williams what Josephson and his friends had against him. Williams told

[231]

Pound he was being attacked for his conservatism.

In the next issue Jolas tried to redress the balance with an enquiry: 'Why Do Americans Live in Europe?' The replies varied from the ludicrous, like that of Gillespie already quoted, through those who objected to Prohibition or said they were bowled over by Europe's romantic charm, to Stein's 'America is now early Victorian very early Victorian, she is a rich and well nourished home but not a place to work.' McAlmon, in one of the longest and best answers, said he found in Europe 'a fanciful freedom and grace not obtainable elsewhere', called Americans sentimental, and said he saw no revolutionary spirit in the age, all the artistic revolutions having taken place before World War I. 'My vision of myself in relation to 20th century reality is one of remaining myself, or hoping to. If that is impossible, what bad luck.' On the last night of 1928 McAlmon told Kay Boyle that the good days were finished, and his own behaviour grew wilder as the decade neared its end. In fashionable Bricktops he made a speech saying that he hated everybody and the rats had taken over, and on another occasion said he would sing an aria from his Chinese opera and then howled constantly like a mad dog. Extracts from his vast unfinished prose work appeared here and there, and an occasional short story was published, but everything he wrote now had an evidently tentative air. Most of the 'crowd' of artists and non-artists he had been pleased to lead from one café to another had left Paris: 'All of the old crowd gone and the Quarter impossible.'[2] He heard rumours that a vital art movement was going on in Mexico City. 'Why not go and see?'[3]

In 1929 the *Little Review* ended, its great days only a memory. Seven years earlier Anderson and Heap had made the trek to Paris, and from 1924 to 1927 the magazine had been run by Heap alone, appearing irregularly, and paying more attention to German Expressionism, French Surrealism and Russian Constructivism than to literature. A final, and very typical, Heap editorial said they had given space to twenty-three new systems of art, all now dead. The magazine had been a trial track for racers, and they had hoped to find 'artists who could run with the great artists of the past or men who could make new records', but had been disappointed. Joyce, with *Ulysses*, had been the only runner to breast the tape in record-breaking time, and Heap signed off with a few remarks about the state and nature of art which was, she said, 'not the highest aim of man', and in any case had lost connection with its original function. The last number contained, besides this editorial, answers to a questionnaire containing such women's magazinish questions as: 'What has been the happiest moment of your life? The unhappiest? . . . What do you look forward to? What do you fear most from the future?' Joyce asked the ladies to tea, said he would give them his views later, then telephoned with the news that he had nothing to say. Lewis replied: 'The examination paper is too difficult for me I am afraid.' The reactions of Eliot and Pound remain unknown.

The flight from Paris was general. Hemingway left the city for good in the late twenties, his first novel published, his first marriage ended, the years of the moveable feast over. Shakespeare and Company felt the pinch, as both Beach and Monnier made clear to Joyce when he made one of his requests or appeals for money. No longer did one member of the Crowd suggest to another that they should grab a towel and go down to Sylvia Beach. Beautiful red-haired Mary Butts had left Paris for a house in Cornwall and a serious attempt to use her talent, Djuna Barnes had gone to New York, partly in an attempt to escape the sexual entanglements of her life. With Crosby's death the group attracted by his money or his personality disintegrated. It was no longer true that, as Josephson had once said, cafés like the Dôme and the Select were thick with Americans clinging closely to each other.

Most of these young Americans had done their share of drinking, talking, theorising, sleeping around, and had gone back home to take up their literary, political or journalistic careers in earnest. New little magazines were appearing in America, 'most of them full of class-conscious "proletarian" writing: that was the new mode'.[4] A minority of those who returned understood and heeded the call to social realism, but most simply felt like McAlmon that the good days were finished. In the end few were much influenced by the experience of Paris. Josephson, Cowley, Archibald MacLeish and others who had felt that Paris, rather than New York, London or Berlin was the place to be, brought their own Americanism to the city rather than returning infused with French culture. 'It was to America that we came back,'[5] one of them said, but spiritually they had never been away.

[233]

EPILOGUE

CHAPTER FIFTEEN

The Fates of the Founding Fathers

I. JOYCE GLORIFIED

By 1930 the founding fathers had produced everything in their work that was truly modern, in the sense of refusing allegiance to the standards or language of the nineteenth century. Thereafter they elaborated, revised, reshaped, but made no substantial additions to the innovations of *Ulysses*, *Work in Progress*, *Tarr*, *The Waste Land*. It is true, however, that for Joyce 1933 was a year of supreme importance, for it was then that Judge John M. Woolsey, sitting in the court of the Southern District of New York, decided that *Ulysses* 'did not tend to excite sexual impulses or lustful thoughts but that its net effect . . . was only that of a somewhat tragic and very powerful commentary on the inner lives of men and women', and that the book might be sold freely in the United States. An appeal against this verdict failed, and in 1934 Random House sold 35,000 copies of the book in the first three months of publication. Several of the journalists who commented on the decision stressed the difficulty of reading *Ulysses*, but few were opposed to its free circulation. Joyce said triumphantly that half of the English-speaking world had surrendered, and the other half would follow.[1] It did so, but not at once. Although plans for British publication were made, the printers found some passages unacceptable, and Joyce had already rejected Eliot's suggestion that Faber might bring out an expurgated edition. He had to wait until 1936, when John Lane ventured on an edition of no more than a thousand copies, for the book's British appearance. No prosecution followed, and Lane produced an ordinary trade edition, although the sales never approached those in America.

For Joyce the years between the first Paris edition and the free publication of his book in America and Britain were marked by worsening sight, and by family problems. In 1924 he had his fifth eye operation, a second iridectomy on his left eye, and this was quickly followed by two minor operations, conjunctivitis of a peculiarly painful kind involving the need for leeches, and little recovery of sight. He was in the hands of a Paris specialist, Dr Borsch, who told Joyce, one of whose eyes was sightless and the other inflamed, that he should walk five or six miles a day. Borsch also put him on a strict diet. Two more operations followed, and then there was a long period of remission. The ingenious Dr Borsch gave his patient injections of arsenic and phosphorus followed by pilocarpine and then, perhaps fortunately for Joyce, died. The author passed into the hands of a Swiss eye surgeon named Professor Vogt, who performed further operations with only moderate success. It may, however, be a tribute to Joyce's eye surgeons that he never became completely blind.[2]

The emotional strain of this eye trouble was exacerbated by the problems of Joyce's daughter Lucia. Joyce gave his children all the freedom they could have wished, except freedom to interfere in any way with his own life and work. Lucia's variety of schools and the slapdash nature of her home background were felt by friends to be reason enough for her seeming a little odd. She was much attached to her father, and perhaps it was as a reaction to his eye trouble that she became concerned about her own slight squint and insisted on what proved an unsuccessful operation. She took piano, singing, drawing and dancing lessons, and pursued a dancing career seriously over a period of four years. In December 1931 Joyce's father died, something that brought on one of his bursts of penitential self-reproach, even though he had rarely seen his father in the past quarter of a century. A short, touching poem he wrote to celebrate the birth of a child to his son George ended: 'O, Father forsaken,/ Forgive your son.' It now became impossible to ignore Lucia's mental condition. She became obsessed by her father's young disciple Samuel Beckett who passed long, almost silent sessions with the master, the stillness interrupted only by some Joycean observation like: 'For me there is only one alternative to scholasticism, scepticism.'[3] Of scepticism Joyce could never be accused. He believed in astrology, the importance of coincidence, all kinds of signs and portents, and although he expressed constant doubts about Catholic doctrine his desire to believe much of it is evident.

Beckett, Oblomovically idle, oppressed by the problem of having to exist at all, was an unfortunate object of love. When Lucia declared her passion, Beckett told her that he came to the Joyces' flat only to see her father. He was banned from the apartment for a year, and Lucia became unwillingly engaged to a young Pole. At the end of a party held to celebrate the engagement she lay down on a sofa and remained there in a catatonic fit. With the serious nature of her condition now unavoidably apparent, a variety of treatments were attempted without success. During the course of them she set fire to her room, attacked her mother, was alternately apathetic and violent. Jung was a consultant at one of the various clinics she entered, but proved no more successful in treating her than nineteen other doctors. Lucia went back into her parents' care, then agreed to accompany Joyce's sister Eileen on a visit to Harriet Weaver.

For several days she behaved reasonably in Weaver's company, apart from talking about buying a pistol, and then embarked on a series of adventures which began with her disappearance one night and return next morning after having slept in the open. She paid a visit to Ireland, and on return stayed again with the heroic Harriet. Joyce had decided that a glandular treatment involving a series of twenty-five injections offered hope, and these were given by a Harley Street specialist. During them Lucia remained under Weaver's care, and by the specialist's instructions in bed. She threw books out of the window, one hitting an indignant passer-by. For several months she stayed in England and when, early in 1936, she returned to Paris, she was no better. Three weeks after her return she had to be taken to a sanatorium in a straitjacket.[4]

There is no doubt of Joyce's deep emotional attachment to Lucia. At one time he claimed that schizoid features of poems she wrote were anticipations of a new literature, and Jung believed that 'his Anima, i.e. unconscious psyche, was so solidly identified with her, that to have her certified would have been as much as an admission that he himself had a latent psychosis'. Lucia, Jung added, was not a genius like her father, but only a victim.[5] Joyce's attitude to his daughter's illness was a compound of self-reproach, unjustified optimism, and an inverted pride which took Lucia's insanity as proof of a superior sensibility. Any spark of a gift he possessed, he said, had been transmitted to her and kindled a fire in her brain. He discovered hundreds of incidents showing that she was clairvoyant, and fiercely attacked anybody less than sympathetic about her behaviour. He even, for a time, distrusted Weaver when she expressed sympathy with his sister Eileen. Did Harriet like Lucia or not, he asked? Lucia was not to be mentioned in comparison with his sister or anybody else. 'If she should be so mentioned it is I who am mad.'[6] He expressed no regret about his behaviour as a father, or Nora's as a mother, beyond what may be implied in saying that freedom and isolation were essential to him. During the latter thirties he visited Lucia weekly in Ivry sanatorium.

The cost of caring for Lucia was between £1000 and £1500 a year, and Joyce's own expenditure did not lessen. He was abstemious by day as he had been for years, but his evening drinking increased, so that Nora several times threatened to leave him, and even briefly did so. Yet although she said occasionally that she wished she had never heard the name of James Joyce, it does not seem that she ever seriously contemplated permanent separation. Weaver's benefactions had continued through the twenties, and in 1932 she cancelled all outstanding debts as Joyce's fiftieth birthday present. Later, as has been mentioned, she consented to the sale of most of the stock meant to provide a permanent income for him, so that by 1936 three-quarters of it had gone.

By this time the relations between them had cooled. Her lack of enthusiasm for *Work in Progress*, and his unfounded suspicion that she had behaved badly to Lucia were partly responsible, but the basic cause was that the tenor of her life had changed. In 1935 she was bowled over by reading Marx, impressed by the lucidity of the social analysis, and emotionally overwhelmed by that vision of the final communist condition of mankind in which each would give according to his ability and receive according to his need. From committee membership of St Marylebone Labour Party she moved, via reading of the Webbs and John Strachey, to joining the Communist Party. She remained a devoted Party member during the war years in which the Party flourished, and the increasingly lean ones that followed. The Hungarian Revolution of 1956 and its suppression disturbed her, but did not affect her allegiance. She remained a Party member until her death in 1961.

Yet she did not lose interest in Joyce. Did she ever, as a communist, feel a need to justify the gap that yawned between Marxist theory and her admiration of work that any Marxist who did not simply condemn it as decadent must have thought at best a bourgeois game with words? It does not seem so, although in her last months she brooded sometimes on decisions and problems of the past, the break with Dora Marsden caused by her refusal to type Dora's last 'cosmo-historical' book (the great work launched in the *Egoist*, eventually called *Definition of the Godhead*, received only two reviews when it appeared in 1928), the cooling of relations with Joyce because of her failure to appreciate his later work ... But generally she was content, and had reason to be. She lived to become a legend consulted by all Joyce scholars, and to receive the dedication of Eliot's collected essays as a mark of gratitude for her services to literature. Indeed, they had been great. She had financed the *Egoist*, financed and encouraged Joyce and, without ever abandoning the decorum implied in those grey gloves laid straight beside her plate – without, even, being much aware of anything called a 'modern movement' – had supported and encouraged and tolerated writers of genius.

The publication of *Ulysses* in America was carefully planned. The obstacles were not only legal. One was the fact that Joyce had given Sylvia Beach world rights in the book. She had published eleven editions, the great majority bought by Americans, and feared – rightly – that her sales would vanish if the book was issued by a large American publishing house. Joyce said once that Beach had given him ten years of her life, and her activities had been no less essential to him than Weaver's support, but tensions arose between them when she positively refused to consider an offer from Huebsch. When, eventually, she agreed to waive her claim, Bennett Cerf of Random House drew up an agreement which gave Joyce an immediate $1000 (cash in hand being always a vital consideration for him) and a further $1500 when and if the book was published. Then the legal battle began.

It was conducted by Morris Ernst, well-known for his success in handling civil rights and censorship cases. Ernst gambled by taking a comparatively small retainer, plus a five per cent royalty on a trade edition and two and a half per cent on a reprint. Alexander Lindey, Ernst's assistant, thought it would be 'the grandest obscenity case in the history of law and literature',[7] and longed to get it going. There was reason for optimism. The literary climate in America was far more liberal than that of Britain, and Radclyffe Hall's *The Well of Loneliness* had recently been found acceptable. *Ulysses* was one of the very few contemporary works still banned that had any claim to literary importance. It was two years, however, before Ernst could get to grips with the authorities. A suggestion to Oliver Wendell Holmes that a copy of the work should be mailed to him from Paris in order to provide a test case was rejected by the famous Supreme Court judge on the ground that 'regardless of his opinion of the book' he had retired from public affairs.[8] A draft letter was then sent to five hundred selected authors, critics, sociologists and clergymen, asking their opinions of the volume, and another to nearly a thousand librarians asking if *Ulysses* was on their shelves and enclosing a questionnaire for completion. The response from authors was predictably friendly. ('Time has crept up on *Ulysses* and many people are under the daisies who were horrified ten years ago,' Scott Fitzgerald replied.) Many librarians wrote to say that they regarded the book as a work of genius and had it on their shelves. A copy was sent from Paris, the Collector of Customs was notified, and invited to approve it. It was seized, however, as being obscene under Section 305 of the Tariff Act, thus setting the wheels of prosecution in motion as Ernst had wished. But the Attorney's office took its time about reading the book, and then started proceedings only reluctantly.

It was agreed by both sides that the case should be tried by a liberal judge, and it was with dismay that Lindey heard in June 1933 that Judge Coleman, who had been listed to hear the case, was 'a strait-laced Catholic . . . about the worst man on the bench for us'.[9] Ernst hastily moved to adjourn the motion until it could be heard by Judge Woolsey, and after some awkward manoeuvring this was done. The judge also took his time, and several more weeks passed before he had finished reading the book, a key to it, and a critical study of Joyce. Ernst's immensely long argument, prepared in collaboration with Lindey, was based principally on the work's classic quality and the changes in social behaviour that now made the coarsest realism acceptable in literature. When the case finally came to court the genial, balding Woolsey enjoyed himself. Talking freely from the bench while smoking a cigarette in a long holder he said that his own feeling was against censorship, and recalled the recently repealed Volstead Act prohibiting hard liquor. 'The people see about as much of the prohibited article as they otherwise would, and the profits get into illegal channels.'[10] Still and all, there *was* the

The Fates of the Founding Fathers

Molly Bloom soliloquy. 'Parts of it are pretty rough, really, but other parts are swell,' the judge said in his role as literary critic. So, on 6 December, Judge Woolsey proceeded to his judgement, which ended with the remark that although the effect of *Ulysses* might occasionally be emetic, it was nowhere aphrodisiac.

The decision made little difference to Joyce's literary standing. Many thousands of copies had been brought into America, the book was in dozens of libraries, thus breaking a law that librarians and readers had almost ceased to worry about, and any young author who approached his art seriously had read it. Morris Ernst did not exaggerate when he said *Ulysses* was already an accepted modern classic in America. In Britain the case was different, and although the John Lane publication brought appreciative reviews, it did not ensure a wide readership, nor was the book openly displayed on many library shelves. It was customary in Britain at that time to make available only on request books with a sexual content that might disturb some readers, and *Ulysses* went under the counter along with such books as sex manuals and the expurgated *Lady Chatterley's Lover*. A strong current of opinion among the ageing, fading Squirearchy found the book obscene, unintelligible, or both.

Nor did the good American sales, and the French, Swedish, Polish and Japanese editions greatly change Joyce's financial position. Much of the money was used in paying for Lucia's illness and his own eye trouble, and he lived as he had always done, spending without stinting himself and appealing to friends and patrons when money ran out. He continued to work on the book that would eventually be *Finnegans Wake*, not unmoved but still not much disturbed by the remarks of Pound, who said that the goodman must have his relaxations but he preferred *The Apes of God* to anything Joyce had done since the Mollylogue, or by Eliot's cautious rather than enthusiastic acceptance of the new work in his role as publisher. Aware as much as Pound of the virtues of publicity, Joyce keenly supported the publication by Beach in 1929 of a collection of essays about his work in general and the new book in particular, called *Our Exagmination round His Factification for Incamination of Work in Progress*. The title, suggested by Joyce himself, was of some significance. Its mock pomposity suggested that portentous scholars had been building barriers round something really quite straight-forward, but in truth the Factification, the solemnity and pretentiousness, was Joyce's own. The contributors included Beckett, Joyce's old friend Frank Budgen on '*Work in Progress* and Old Norse Poetry', Williams and McAlmon. *Work in Progress*, Beckett said, contained pages and pages of direct expression. If readers were unable to understand it, the fault lay in their own decadence. 'You are not satisfied unless form is so strictly divorced from content that you can comprehend the one almost without bothering to read the other. This rapid skimming and absorption of the scant cream of sense is made possible by what I call a continuous process of copious intellectual salivation ... Here form *is* content, content *is* form.'[11] Most of the articles proceeded by a similar hectoring assertiveness. One or two essays attempted explanation, in particular Stuart Gilbert's and McAlmon's, but nobody questioned the validity of Joyce's intentions. Nobody, at least, except Vladomir Dixon, who in a letter to 'Mister Germ's Choice' confessed himself 'disturd by my inhumility to onthorstand most of the impalocations constrained in your work' and so felt compelled to address himself to 'mystere Shame's Voice'. Dixon's name, it is said, was James Joyce.

In November 1938 *Finnegans Wake* was finished, the last words written and rewritten. After finishing it, Joyce told Jolas, he had felt so utterly exhausted that he sat for a long while on a street bench, unable to move. The work took to an extreme the ideas about the flexibility of language implicit in *Ulysses*. Since, as that book had shown, almost any word could be regarded as reminding one of any other, since any phrase a man or woman used had its origins in or its connections with hundreds of other phrases, why should all these phrases not blend with one another down the vast arcades of memory and melt into a series of phrases, recollections, dreams, that would mean just what the writer's ingenuity in making verbal and visual connections cared to make it mean? *Ulysses* had ended with a sixty-page unpunctuated sentence that conveyed the essence of Molly Bloom. Perhaps it would be possible to roll *everything* up into one ball of language, not only everything but everybody, and not just everything and everybody here and now, but all past history as well. Such a book would expand continually, the title would refer not to one but all Finnegans, thence to Irish scenes and heroes, thence to Humphrey Chimpden Earwicker who would be in one aspect a pub keeper but in another the universal human, Here Comes Everybody, and Anna Livia would be not only the physical heroine but that liquid, flowing, dissolving heroine of Joyce's whole life, the Liffey. Interpenetrating dreams would be a means of destroying the fixity of personality, and language also would lose its roots and become part of an immense flux of words and phrases. *In dreams begin irresponsibilities* – so Joyce might have inverted Yeats's phrase, but so far as Joyce's imagination was under control in *Finnegans Wake*, the control was that of language. It could have been said of the book that the meaning was the language, in the sense that unless the reader or listener caught the drift of most of the neologisms and intricate verbal compounds he would merely float along on a sea of pleasant sound. The friend who said he liked the book when Joyce recited it had the heart of the matter. *Finnegans Wake* was a book to be heard rather than read.

By the end of the thirties James Joyce was the most influential, although not the most popular, novelist writing in English. Dozens of articles discussed his technique, a circle of disciples waited on his words, the sales of *Ulysses* continued and its influence grew. There were always people ready to help him, and when he again said that a copy of his new book must be ready in time for his birthday Mrs Jolas, Stuart Gilbert and Joyce's devoted admirer Paul Leon spent days in frantic proof-reading. The copy was ready in time for his fifty-seventh birthday on 2 February 1939, and there was a celebratory party. Yet Joyce always found something lacking in appreciation of his work, and this feeling was reinforced by the reviews of *Finnegans Wake*, several of them (especially in Britain) cavalierly dismissive, some treating the book as a fraud on the public. Only a few seemed to him at all perceptive.

The book's publication was in effect the end of James Joyce's life, for he wrote nothing more, and his life had been the making of literature. When the war came, he and Nora left Paris, and eventually France, for Zurich. There, in January 1941, he died after an operation for a perforated duodenal ulcer. It is not easy to set a precise date when the glorification of James Joyce began. A year or two after the war ended, Weaver, his literary executor, found she was giving more and more time to Joyce's affairs. *Stephen Hero*, the early version of *A Portrait*, was published, and there were requests for translations of this and other books from half a dozen countries. Two of Joyce's English publishers, Cape and Bodley Head, now found the demand for *Ulysses* and the early books such that, because of paper shortages, they had to reprint in Holland. (The demand for *Finnegans Wake* was much more limited.) In 1947 Weaver began to receive enquiries from Joyce scholars, the first trickle of what became a flood. By the fifties scholars were asking for information in connection with Joyce theses; Richard Ellmann, Joyce's most notable biographer, had appeared armed with a dictaphone; the flood of enquiries turned into an unending Liffey of books.

At first these were reasonable enough: Ellmann's and other biographies, a selection from the letters, a bibliography. The publication in three volumes of a finally corrected edition of *Ulysses*, amending the hundreds of mistakes made by the various typists and the French printers, clarified many previously obscure or even unintelligible passages, and made the book much less baffling, although not less allusive. It is the allusiveness that has particularly attracted analysts and commentators. Volumes have been published on Joyce and philosophy, Joyce and medicine, Joyce and Shakespeare, Dante and Mallarmé, Joyce and feminism, Joyce's Dublin and Dublin's Joyce. There is a volume on Joyce's sexuality and there is *Joysprick* which is not, as one might think, an addition to *James Joyce and Sexuality*, but an introduction to Joyce's use of language. There is, of course, *James Joyce and the Revolution of the Word*, there are Reader's Guides to *Ulysses* and *Finnegans Wake*, and much more, including a shortened version of the latter book. Stanislaus published his own view of his brother in their Irish days, *My Brother's Keeper*. Joyce scholarship has had alarming effects on otherwise intelligent men. Ellmann launched *Ulysses on the Liffey*, an examination of links between Homer, *Ulysses* and Dublin, containing conjectures and suggestions of a wildly eccentric kind. Since Joyce's works are endless mines for theorists, and every dug-up nugget can be claimed as pure gold with no final assayer around, the writing of theses does not diminish. There are of course Joyce Societies, and with the yearly celebration of Bloomsday Jhayzus Aloysius Chrysostum, as Pound once called him, truly achieved the glory he had always known to be his due.

2. ELIOT SANCTIFIED

As early as 1926 Archibald MacLeish, in a letter attempting to arrange a meeting with Eliot, said he was becoming legendary,[12] and in the thirties the legend grew. Eliot was so evidently a serious man that it was not easy to know when he was joking. When he remarked of *My Fair Lady* that Shaw had been greatly improved by music, was that a genuine criticism of Shaw or a joke? When a woman at a party said she could hardly believe she was meeting T. S. Eliot in person, and he replied that he had always wanted to meet Joe Louis but had never managed it, was he just brushing off a bore or did he mean it? His pleasure in practical jokes was carried even into Faber board meetings, and he enjoyed also the schoolboyish fun of giving comic names to friends. All this was both a real expression of part of his personality and a means of concealing inner grief about his relations with Vivien, whose behaviour became more eccentric and embarrassing with the years. In 1938 she was committed to a mental hospital by her husband and her brother Maurice, and there she died nine years later. Those who did not know this background invented more or less ingenious stories to account for the feeling of guilt that lay behind Eliot's fascination with crime and its detection. One typical theory was that he had at one time committed a murder and still feared the discovery of the body.

Such fancies lost little of their savour with the production in 1935 of *Murder in the Cathedral*. A couple of years earlier Eliot had been persuaded by E. Martin Browne, an actor turned theatrical director, to write some dialogue and verse choruses for a pageant play to be performed by amateur actors in aid of the Forty-five Churches Fund, the purpose of which was to build and endow new churches in London's growing northern suburbs. It was necessary to adhere to an existing framework of plot, so that the task was a fairly thankless one, something which may itself have attracted Eliot. Choruses and poems were written, and *The Rock* successfully performed, although the verse often seemed uneasy when it was colloquial, and prosy when it attempted gravity. ('Though you forget the way to the Temple/There is one who remembers the way to your door.') But the play was liked by the church authorities, and the Bishop of Chichester suggested that Eliot should write a play for the yearly Canterbury Festival. The theme, of course, had to be in some way religious, but the murder of Thomas Becket was Eliot's own choice.

Was poetic drama possible? he had asked in an essay some years earlier, at the time when Abercrombie's and Bottomley's dramatic verse was exciting Eddie Marsh. He had answered that the modern view of it began at the wrong end, with the poetry, ignoring the fact that few people consciously wanted to hear poetry on the stage. The Elizabethans had had the right idea: their drama was 'aimed at a public which wanted *entertainment* of a crude sort, but would *stand* a good deal of poetry'.[13] Drama that failed to be dramatic would also fail to be poetic, and following up this line of thought he suggested that a play might be written on two levels, one offering 'entertainment' for the groundlings, the other written for the elite that could stand a good deal of poetry – plus, in his own case, theology. The speakers in 'A Dialogue on Dramatic Poetry' (1928) put the case clearly. There is no such thing as pure amusement, one of them says, and those who pretend to it are merely flattering mob prejudice. Yet we need amusement on the stage, and need also religious faith. Another speaker (Eliot is not identified with any one of them) says that the only perfect dramatic satisfaction is a High Mass well performed.

Murder in the Cathedral, even more strongly than Eliot's later plays, bears very much in mind this division between entertainment and poetry. The high language of Thomas and the Choruses is alleviated by the chattiness of the Tempters, a phrase or two is deliberately borrowed from a Sherlock Holmes story, the Tempters themselves are variously lively. Eliot agreed to Browne's suggestion that the four Tempters should double in the roles of the four Knights who murder Becket, although later he came to think such doubling of parts confusing. Canterbury Cathedral was not, of course, suited to the presentation of a play. There was no curtain, and Robert Speaight, who played Becket, called the acoustics difficult and the lighting rudimentary. No impresario came down from London to see the play, but it attracted much attention and praise, and when, six months later, Ashley Dukes presented the piece at his little Mercury Theatre, it was acclaimed as the only great play to be seen in London. It played at the Mercury for more than a year, then was taken on tour, and in 1938 was presented in Boston and New York.[14]

The play was a turning point in Eliot's literary life. If, as is said, he regarded it as no more than a *tour de force*, the play's success persuaded him that it showed the way forward in the theatre. One problem for him as poet had always been how to express his own guilts, hopes, desires and memories while retaining the impersonality of never saying 'I'. Perhaps he was Prufrock, no doubt he was at the centre of *The Waste Land*, but everything personal in the poems was wrapped up in irony or scholarship. Although we may, if we wish, find echoes of Eliot's youthful exploits with Lewis, Pound and Aiken in the First Tempter's pleas to 'old Tom, gay Tom, Becket of London' not to forget his days of 'singing at nightfall, whispering in chambers', a long space is set between unregenerate past and holy present. And on the technical level the play's success meant that Eliot turned his back finally on the idea of constructing a verse play in terms of music hall comedy and songs adumbrated in *Sweeney Agonistes*. The verse of *Murder in the Cathedral* is sometimes solemnly and explicitly Christian, more often low-toned, colloquial, deliberately prosy. The prose self-justification of the Knights is clownish low comedy, '*entertainment* of a crude sort', although Eliot thought the actors played them too obviously for laughs. And after the play's success he rejected also the Group Theatre of Rupert Doone, which was much concerned with masks and dancing, and attempted to link verse drama with ballet. (Doone had produced *Sweeney Agonistes* effectively, with figures holding masks before their faces.) He ignored also the conventions of Auden's and Isherwood's verse plays *The Dog Beneath the Skin* and *The Ascent of F.6* produced by Doone, which blended Doone's balletic and ritualistic approach with Auden's view that modern poetic drama should have links with pantomime and tumbling. For Eliot poetic drama became instead more and more like drawing room comedy in verse, with symbolic attachments. A conflict between temporal and spiritual forces, sometimes relating to a climactic event in the past carrying a burden of guilt, was outlined, analysed, seen from several points of view, in a manner solved. The verse itself became more and more relaxed, conversational to the point of being deliberately undramatic:

> I hear that Harry has arrived already
> And he was the only one that was uncertain.
> Arthur or John may be late, of course.
> We may have to keep the dinner back.[15]

This is a parody of contemporary drawing room comedy which itself manages to be pretty dull, and there is a great deal of such verse in *The Family Reunion* (1939), *The Cocktail Party* (1949), *The Confidential Clerk* (1953) and *The Elder Statesman* (1958). It fulfilled Eliot's later requirements of poetic drama, however. Verse on stage, he said now, could be as natural as prose, so that even those who said they disliked poetry might be affected by it. The important thing was that it must be dramatically effective. *Murder in the Cathedral* now seemed to him a dead end. What the verse dramatist had to do was to bring poetry into the world in which the audience lived, and to which it returned after leaving the theatre[16] – which seems very much like adhering to the poetic standards of the audience in just the way he had condemned almost a quarter of a century earlier.

With *Murder in the Cathedral* Eliot became a popular playwright as well as a famous poet. To a certain extent the popularity of the plays was based on the fame, and for many people the obscurity, of the poems. If Lord Monchensey's guilt in *The Family Reunion* seemed hard to understand, it was encouraging to know that the play was really about Original Sin, and if, as one wit complained about *The Cocktail Party*, very little cock and rather less tail made a dull party, it was consoling to believe that there was some much deeper although undefined meaning about the guardians and devils and secret voices, underlying the chatter of the conversation. *Murder in the Cathedral* began a process of the sanctification of its author that gathered strength after World War II. There seemed to be something inevitable about the award to him in 1948 of the Nobel Prize for Literature, and his receipt of the Order of Merit. Edmund Wilson, when he saw *The Confidential Clerk* in 1953, was surprised to find that although others agreed with him in finding the play rudimentary, nobody liked to say so in print.[17] Eliot had become no longer a person but a myth, about whom heretical opinions were not to be voiced. The chorus of praise for the poems that make up *Four Quartets* was almost complete, although George Orwell caused some indignation by saying when reviewing 'The Dry Salvages' that Eliot might have been a more powerful poet if he had become consciously the last apologist of aristocracy. What Orwell objected to was the tone of resignation running through Eliot's last important poem, the elegiac acceptance of everything that could possibly happen, the hands so obviously joined in prayer.

Four Quartets are certainly a long way from the irreverence and the desire to upset the established patterns of poetic language with which he had begun. Yet there were ways in which his half-wondering remark after receiving the Nobel Prize that although 'one seems to become a myth, a fabulous creature that doesn't exist', really 'you remain exactly the same',[18] was true. He remained the same in his astonishing impersonality, the ability to appreciate the merit in writers whose attitudes he disliked. So when he printed Auden's 'Paid On Both Sides' in the *Criterion* he wrote, 'This fellow is about the best poet that I have discovered in several years,'[19] although the attitude from which the poem was written, and some of its language, must have been very uncongenial to him. His generous practical support of George Barker, his friendliness to Stephen Spender, his support of other writers whose approach to literature must have seemed to him naive or deplorable, all this had a unique kind of realism about it, an acknowledgement that although his own beliefs were firmly held, other beliefs demanded respect.

A similar realism was apparent in his acknowledgement, with the end of the *Criterion* in 1939, that the European cultural movement he originally envisaged had never really come to birth. The end of the magazine marked other things too. In January 1939, when the last issue appeared, it was hardly possible to avoid the conclusion that there would soon be a general war in Europe, between the countries he had called worm-eaten by liberalism and the states that expressed the reality of the authoritarianism he had advocated. He must have recognised that Nazism was a terrible caricature of his desire for authority, the culmination of the 'tendency' he had tried to develop. He did not retract the belief that a right political philosophy implied a right moral theology, but in the struggle that found Hitler and Mussolini on one side and worm-eaten liberal Europe on the other, he was bound to support the liberalism he disapproved. Indeed, during the war he did not flinch from the implication of accepting Stalin's Russia as an ally when he rejected *Animal Farm* with the comment that this was not 'the right point of view from which to criticise the political situation at the present time'.[20]

Christianity to some extent fulfilled the desire for some kind of external authority that marked Eliot's adult life, but he never altogether gave up the hope of an undefined European culture that would link the ideas and art of an elite, although he no longer looked for it with the expectant enthusiasm he had shown during and just after World War I, nor did he any longer use the high tone in which he had suggested to Lewis that a separation between them would be harmful to the public good. He did not falter in his attachment to Lewis and Pound, nor in his high regard for their work. His old friends, on the other hand, viewed his development both technical and religious with dismay. Pound, listening to *Murder in the Cathedral* on the radio, commented: 'My Krissz, them cawkney woices. Mzzr Shakspeer *still* retains his position.'[21] His new names for Eliot were the very reverend episcopal ELYot, his somnolence and his eminence. When Eliot received the OM, Lewis envisaged him groomed and disinfected for his dubbing ('"Rise, Sir Thomas"'),[22] reported that Eliot and Valéry were running neck and neck for the Nobel Prize, and in a response to Pound's suggestion that he too might be looking for a knighthood replied with dignity:

> As to your implying that my remarks were motivated by envy of the dangling crosses and those letters you stick after your name, oh sir, has my life been that of one prizing the values of the career-man or directing his gaze ahead to covet the dignity of knighthood? You know it has not. Every day I have lived is my witness to the contrary.[23]

Neither Pound nor Lewis commented on the plays, but when in 1950 Eliot sent Lewis a copy of *The Cocktail Party* he acknowledged it with a facetious letter suggesting that the psychoanalyst Sir Henry Harcourt-Reilly was Eliot himself 'disguised as a psychopathic quack'. Eliot replied in the same vein, saying that nobody else had remarked on Reilly's mother being a Sweeney.[24] (Neither Lewis nor other commentators spotted the sly King Bolo humour that gave Sir Henry a couple of verses derived from the obscene song 'The One-Eyed Reilly'.) When in 1938 Eliot's portrait by Lewis was rejected by the Royal Academy, he wrote to the painter of his relief that a portrait of him should not appear in the show, adding that he thought it a very fine painting, by which he would be content that posterity should know him. The portrait, showing the handsome, enigmatic, slightly melancholy and remote figure seen across the studio, is Lewis's finest tribute to his friend.

As Eliot grew older he became more benign, less cautious and captious. His second marriage in 1957 to his secretary Valerie Fletcher, who was thirty-eight years his junior, was extremely happy. It is likely that the eight years left to him were the most serene of his life. Shortly after the marriage he completed his last play, but he wrote no more poems, nothing else of consequence. Honours were loaded on him, an award in Germany, the Dante Gold Medal. It was a world and a life away from that of the young man who had written so tartly in the *Egoist*, the bank official who had made *The Waste Land* out of his frustrations. In 1952 Edward Marsh was given a party on his eightieth birthday. There were no more than a dozen guests, all but one familiar faces. The exception was Eliot, whose presence brought tears to Marsh's eyes. In a short speech Eliot said they had been regarded as opponents, but both had worked to the same end. Schools and fashions gave rise to heated argument, but after all they came and went. Poetry, however, remained.[25]

3. LEWIS OSTRACISED

For Lewis the decade that began badly with the failure of *The Apes of God* to win the acclaim he expected, continued with a series of hammer blows that would have crushed a man less resilient. His quickly written book on Hitler, which sprang from a series of articles commissioned by the weekly *Time and Tide*, received considerable attention, most of it unfriendly. Today it seems slight and in places trivial, although an awareness in 1930 of Hitler's potential importance was unusual. In 1932 *The Doom of Youth*, which offered background material for Lewis's theories about the cult of childishness in the West already examined in other books, led to libel actions from the columnist Godfrey Winn who had been called a hack and a salaried revolutionary agent, and from Alec Waugh who was said quite untruly to be crazy about small boys. In the end the cases petered out, but by that time the publishers Chatto & Windus had withdrawn the book. They also rejected as potentially libellous *The Roaring Queen*, a rumbustious satirical novel introducing recognisable caricatures of Arnold Bennett in his capacity of puffing book reviewer, Virginia Woolf, Nancy Cunard who had briefly been Lewis's mistress, and a number of other characters less easily identifiable. Lewis then parted from Chatto, and Jonathan Cape agreed to publish the book, only to flinch after it had reached proof stage. Nancy Cunard, who ran the Hours Press in Paris, told Lewis she was closing it down and so was 'bitterly sorry that we could not

[253]

do the Roaring Queen together', and later in the thirties Jack Kahane, who ran the Obelisk Press and made his living chiefly but not entirely by publishing pornography, contemplated issuing it.[26] In the event the book remained unpublished until 1973.

More trouble was to come. In *Filibusters in Barbary*, a travel book written after a trip to Morocco, Lewis was charged with libelling a retired British officer living in Agadir. He refused to apologise, but the publishers withdrew the book and paid damages, which they deducted from his royalties. Add to this the fact that in 1932 Lewis suffered from diseases of the bladder springing from past venereal infections which necessitated four operations in a period of five years, and it may seem surprising that he produced any new work at all. Yet this was a furiously productive period of his life, one in which some of his finest work was done, along with a good deal of slapdash book-length journalism. *One-Way Song* (1933) is a vigorous, always good-humoured and often finely comic and witty poem written mostly in the rarely used measure the fourteener, its chief targets the thirties poets with their verbal passion for machinery, and in 'The Song of the Militant Romance' the Stein–Joyce insistence on the value of letting language run free without bothering about the results:

> Break out word-storms! – a proper tongue-burst! Split
> Our palate down the middle – shatter it!
> Give us hare-lip and cross us with a seal
> That we may emit the most ear-splitting squeal!
> Let words forsake their syntax and ambit –
> The dam of all the lexicons gone west! –
> Chaos restored, why then by such storms hit
> The brain can mint its imagery best.
> Whoever heard of perfect sense or perfect rhythm
> Matching the magic of extreme verbal schism?

The poem conveys, more than any other single work, the overwhelming humour of Lewis's personality, the laughter that could within the space of a few minutes be aimed at himself and then turned derisively on other people. When he wrote

> The man I am to live and to let live.
> The man I am to forget and to forgive . . .
> I am the perfect guest, the perfect host.

The Fates of the Founding Fathers

The man I am (don't take this for a boast)
To tread too softly, maybe, if I see
A dream's upon my neighbour's harsh tapis

he partly meant what he said. In any personal assessment of Lewis it is important to remember that, even for some who found his social and artistic attitudes unsympathetic, he *was* a perfect guest and host. Sir Nicholas Waterhouse wrote angrily when Lewis suggested that temporary withdrawal of financial support was prompted by dislike of his work, to say that he was simply short of money. 'The fact that I am "uneducated" and have always hated your pictures and utterly failed to understand or appreciate your writings has nothing to do with the matter.' It was Lewis in person he liked, 'such a genuine, human and kind fellow, with such a lovely sense of humour',[27] he wrote to Froanna, who became Lewis's wife in 1930 after having lived with him for some years.

Lewis's often desperate need for money was temporarily assuaged when through his friend A. J. A. Symons he signed a contract with Cassell for publication of three books. The terms were good, and the first book *Snooty Baronet* appeared in 1932. Here and in *The Revenge for Love* Lewis used some techniques of modernism in the service of novels that he hoped would sell in large numbers. His style remained distinctive, his handling of dialogue unlike that of any contemporary and the slow-motion cinematic device he had developed in the twenties was given effective play. Both Lewis and Eliot were keen readers of detective fiction, and in terms of plot these books are thrillers. The action in *Snooty Baronet* hinges on the attempt of a writer's agent to get publicity for him by staging a fake kidnap arranged with an amiable local chieftain on a trip to Persia. The more complex and ingenious plot of *The Revenge for Love*, written before the Spanish Civil War but published after it had been in progress for almost twelve months, involves the running of a load of guns (which turn out to be bricks) into Spain.

This sounds a long way from modernism, yet the author of *Tarr* is plainly present in these novels. *Snooty Baronet* contains perhaps the funniest scenes Lewis wrote, but is consistent only in manner. It veers about in all directions, from a parody of D. H. Lawrence to an attack on the fashionable doctrine of Behaviourism. In *The Revenge for Love*, the fictional masterpiece of Lewis's maturity as *Tarr* was of

[255]

Epilogue

his early manhood, the book's political theme is kept under perfect control, and its ultimate 'meaning' – like that of *Snooty Baronet* and *The Vulgar Streak* (1941) – is to show the violence of the period, the way in which it was manipulated by power-lovers for their own purposes, and the pretences by which most people live. Almost all of the characters are living lies: they paint fake van Goghs, put out counterfeit money, devise a fake kidnapping. The reality of violence, when it enters almost casually, is truly shocking. Lewis's purposes were basically political: but where the anti-left propagandist non-fiction he wrote in the thirties is either absurdly over-stated or simply wrong (as in his picture of Hitler as a man who sacrificed himself to the principle of national freedom), the fiction is subtle, perceptive and humane.

These books too ran into trouble. Lewis's agreement with Cassell had been made through the youthful Desmond Flower, but it was his father Newman who ruled the roost, and Newman Flower was shaken when Boots and Smith's libraries, which normally took several hundred copies of their novels, objected to the coarseness of *Snooty Baronet* and in effect banned it by taking only twenty-five copies. Lewis, summoned to a conference, was told his advance would be cut, and any further fiction 'must be of such a character as to pass the Library censors of Messrs Boot and Smith'.[28] He protested that Desmond Flower had told him outspokenness was positively expected of him, comparisons had been made with D. H. Lawrence, and now what did he find? Either he would be expected to emasculate his work, or his agreed advance would be reduced. Was this fulfilling the promise made by Newman Flower himself: 'We intend to put *Snooty* over big'?[29]

The only concession he got was in relation to the advance. *The Revenge for Love* was submitted to the Library censors, and the reader for Boot, in a report no more than semi-literate, demanded considerable changes if they were to stock the book. He called the original title, *False Bottoms*, unacceptably vulgar, requested the alteration or deletion of words like 'bastard' and 'bugger', and of references to excretion. The objections were very similar to those made to *Dubliners*, and show that in a quarter of a century British censorship, exercised by printers and circulating libraries, had changed very little. Lewis made many of the changes asked for, and Cassell altered his idiosyncratic punctuation to conform with their standard house style. In spite of an appeal he made to Desmond Flower to 'forget its politics – if you find them displeasing',[30] *The Revenge for Love* received little critical attention, the ubiquitous Boots and Smith's readers remained unsatisfied, and the result was poorer sales than those of *Snooty Baronet*.

One reason for the book's failure was the prevailing literary-political climate. It appeared when sympathy for the Spanish Republican cause was at its peak in Britain, and was taken as an attack on the Republic rather than on Communist Party double-dealing, and exploitation of liberal gulls within and outside Spain. At a meeting of the popular and influential Left Book Club, a prominent poet suggested that members should visit bookshops and demand that the works of this pro-Fascist writer be removed from the shelves. No organised campaign was carried out, but in effect Lewis was ostracised by publishers and booksellers. Eliot was forgiven for his sympathy with Fascism, Pound for his active support of it, but the dislike and even hatred roused by Lewis was lasting. His recantation, *The Hitler Cult*, was regarded as a piece of time-serving because it had been published after World War II began, although in fact the book was written after Munich, and he was permanently stamped pro-Fascist even though many of his friends were on the left. Sympathy with left-wing causes can be found in many of his remarks and actions. In 1938 the painter Julian Trevelyan was sent to ask Lewis for a picture to be auctioned in aid of the Spanish Republic. Trevelyan was nervous, but Lewis gave him a picture, with no more than a few grumbles about Bloomsbury.[31]

Just before World War II began, Lewis sailed with his wife for Canada, feeling that he would be unable to earn a living in wartime Britain, and believing wrongly that things would be better for him in Canada and the United States. But if he had been ostracised in Britain he was almost forgotten in America, and unknown in the cultural desert of Canada. He endured six years of misery and poverty, doing commissioned portraits that were mostly hackwork, and paintings for his own pleasure, which he found it hard to sell. In August 1945 he returned to England and his semi-derelict flat in Notting Hill, a chastened man, anxious to make his peace with the world.

In 1946 he began to write art reviews for the *Listener*, which gave

Epilogue

him for the first time in his life a regular earned income. He found a British publisher, J. Alan White of Methuen, who was prepared to publish his new books and reissue some old ones. A novel based on his Canadian experiences, *Self Condemned*, went into three editions within a year. In 1956 the Tate Gallery put on what was in effect a Lewis retrospective, 'Wyndham Lewis and Vorticism'. The BBC broadcast on radio *The Childermass* and its successor *The Human Age*, following them by *Tarr* and *The Revenge for Love*. He received a small Civil List pension.

It may seem that these last years before his death in March 1957 saw a full acknowledgement of his genius, but that was not the case. In 1949 his sight began to fail, and from 1951 onwards he was almost wholly blind. Naturally enough, his principal fiction in this last period, *Self Condemned* and *The Human Age*, lacks altogether the extraordinary power in external description that makes the grotesques of *The Apes of God* memorable, and has fixed irrevocably the meeting between Joyce, Eliot and Lewis, so that it is used by every biographer. The visual quality was one of Lewis's chief contributions to literary modernism, and with the loss of sight that had gone. Along with it went a distrust of recent developments in art. In *The Demon of Progress in the Arts* (1954) Lewis praised again the flowering of British art after the war which he had extolled in *Listener* articles, and said this was 'the finest group of painters and sculptors England has ever known', but went on to add that there were limits beyond which experiment could not usefully go, or a point would be reached 'in which only zero is tolerated – in which nothing is preferred to something'. Minimal art, André's bricks, collections of odds and ends labelled art, would no doubt have been targets for Lewis if he had lived to see them. How did such views comport with Vorticism? But Lewis no longer thought much of any movement towards complete abstraction. 'No one but an idiot – or a Dutchman, like Mondrian – would pass his life in that vacuum, any more than he would voluntarily live in an iron lung,' he said in one of his last *Listener* reviews.[32]

He made some new friends in these last years, particularly among young artists, and Eliot visited the blind man in his Notting Hill studio, offered to write an introduction to a paperback edition of *Self Condemned* (although this in fact never appeared), greatly admired the last two parts of *The Human Age*, and introduced the radio adaptations of them. He discerned a Christian tendency in the work, and was naturally attracted by it. In an obituary tribute he said these last works had a seriousness absent from *Tarr*, and went on: 'We have no critic of the contemporary world at once so fearless, so honest, so intelligent, and possessed of so brilliant a prose style.'[33]

4. POUND IN A CAGE

Pound's multifold artistic ambitions had always included music, which he regarded as a medium nearer than painting to poetry. In Rapallo he organised concerts with as chief performers his mistress Olga Rudge and a German pianist named Gerhart Munch. The programmes included sonatas by Mozart, Debussy, Purcell, Bach and others, the whole devised (he said) to illustrate the ideo-grammatic methods of criticism originated by Ernest Fenollosa, an instructor in rhetoric at the Imperial University of Tokyo, whose views on the Chinese written character as a poetic medium had much impressed Pound when he became aware of them in 1913, five years after Fenollosa's death. Whatever their ideogrammatic basis, the concerts were very successful and continued until 1940, but it was important to Pound that one form of art should cohere in his imagination with another. The concerts fitted in somehow with poetry, with Volitionist Economics, the need for monetary reform, the fact that nobody but himself, Mussolini and a few others understood the nature of a proper, civilised future. He did his best to increase this number by correspondence, urging Dorothy L. Sayers to abandon writing mystery stories in favour of detective work into the activities of the 'secret and dangerous REAL govt' that ruled most of Europe, a suggestion Sayers ignored.[34]

These activities left time for letters about literature, not only to the man he sometimes called 'my fine ole Marse Supial' which arrived in such quantity and written at such length that Eliot began to acknowledge them through his secretary, nor merely to ole SawBUKK Williams or vynDHAMN as he called Lewis, but to the hundreds of literary aspirants like Helene Magaret. He had re-mained on good terms with Harriet Monroe, and if she was irritated by the pedagogical manner he sometimes adopted, and his sugges-tions that she should 'come abroad an git eddercated',[35] she did not

Epilogue

show it. When she died in 1936, he wrote an obituary altogether sensible, appreciative and moving. Three years earlier he had entered his candidates in the Modern Poetry Stakes, in the collection *Active Anthology* which he edited. Auden had been praised by Eliot and admired by Lewis as 'all ice and woodenfaced acrobatics',[36] but Pound thought he loomed so large in the British landscape because there was little of interest around him. The ten poets represented in *Active Anthology* were those 'in whose verse a development appears or in some cases we may say "still appears" to be taking place'.[37] They included Pound himself, Eliot (represented by the first part of *Sweeney Agonistes*), and Louis Aragon, translated by Cummings. The other names were Hemingway (included surely as a friendly gesture), Geoffrey Bridson (who soon abandoned poetry for radio production), Williams, the little-known Basil Bunting, Louis Zukofsky, leader of the Objectivists, George Oppen and Marianne Moore. Bunting, Williams and Zukofsky are the poets most prominently represented, and what links them is a rejection of any rhythm operating continuously throughout a poem. For Pound they were, thus, 'modern' and 'revolutionary', continuing the breaking-up of speech rhythms that had begun with Imagism. It was probably Auden and his followers, as well as such users of standard poetic rhythms as Wallace Stevens, whom Pound had in mind when he said: 'If I was in any sense the revolution, I have been followed by the counter-revolution.'[38] Eliot, as Pound told an acolyte, thought nothing of the work in *Active Anthology* apart from his own contribution, and those of Pound and Moore.

The admiration felt by the disciples for Pound as master was unfaltering. Bunting, who wrote a short poem on the fly-leaf of his copy of the Cantos beginning, 'These are the Alps', came eventually to be regarded by a sizeable minority of readers as a great poet, chiefly on the strength of his long, autobiographical 'Briggflatts'. Zukofsky has also been much praised. It is hard to tell one Objectivist poet or poem from another, but 'Wire' is fairly typical Zukofsky:

> Wire cage flues
> on
> the roofs:

The Fates of the Founding Fathers

Paper ash-whole
        sheets
in gusts –

Flawed by winds
        fly
like doves.[39]

Oppen also was an Objectivist, one who took 'word and thing as forces in motion, and the poetic act as a play of mind-and-breath over the field of objects', so that 'a given word lives on in the action-context of the poem after its physical existence under the eye [has] ceased', as the gobbledygook of one admiring critic put it.[40] Williams was the kingpin of the Objectivist movement, his poems being an almost perfect exemplification of Objectivist principles, but Pound beamed on it approvingly from Rapallo.

Throughout the thirties Pound moved further from Eliot, and from the kinds of social poetry most praised during the decade. He remained undisturbed, remarking disdainfully that Bunting and Zukofsky were more thoughtful than toffee-lickers required. His artistic, political and economic stances became more defiant, his statements more desperate, his anti-Semitism totally obsessive. He said after the invasion of Abyssinia that nobody had done as much to preserve European peace as Mussolini, called the French Prime Minister Léon Blum a kike, labelled the Governor of the Bank of England Montague/Sheeny/Norman, and so on. Joyce, who had no sympathy with Fascism, told Weaver that Hitler would soon have few admirers in Europe except 'Masters W. Lewis and E. Pound'. Lewis, to whom Pound wrote some of his most frantic letters of this period, replied to them with some reserve.

Reading Pound's always rambling, often ranting, sometimes almost unintelligible prose writing of this time, is to feel oneself in the presence of a mind unhinged, shifting from one subject to another without notice or explanation, and less concerned to explain than to dictate. *How to Read* was a lexicon useful only to those who already shared Pound's belief that a literary education must include all of Confucius but not necessarily Shakespeare, Stendhal and Flaubert but not Dickens or George Eliot, a Provençal song book but not Campion or Herrick. *Guide to Kulchur*, dedicated to Bunting and Zukofsky, was a collection of almost random notes and jottings

Epilogue

in which literature, Poundian economics, pro-Fascist comments and abuse of anti-Fascists slither around together with little attempt made to order them. To the complaint that anybody who seriously wished to make converts would write less elliptically, Pound would probably have replied that those who failed to understand his message were beyond hope.

What did he hope to achieve by the visit he paid to America in April 1939, his first trip home in nearly thirty years? Something immense, certainly. He told Lewis that he had been advised to travel first class if he wanted to achieve anything. Lewis in reply said he should not go wearing a Fascist cockade and suggested he might make some money by lecturing to women's clubs.[41] Pound had grander intentions. He took a first class suite on the Italian liner *Rex*, gave a press interview when he landed, raised the Social Credit banner, and praised Mussolini without exactly sporting a Fascist cockade. In Washington he talked to right-wing Congressmen and had an interview with the Secretary of Agriculture Henry Wallace, who could not understand his ideas. The visit lasted several weeks, and on a literary level was pleasant enough. He saw some old friends, to whom he aired his views about Joyce's retrogression, Hemingway's political mistake in backing the Spanish Republic, the 'pseudo-pink blah' of young British poets. He was given an honorary degree as Doctor of Letters by Hamilton College and interrupted the principal speaker on the occasion, H. V. Kaltenborn, who said that dictatorships didn't last. A lengthy verbal row ensued when Pound praised Mussolini and Fascism, and there were arguments about politics with some friends. Considerable offence was caused by Pound's attitude to Jews. On his return to Italy, angry and frustrated, he wrote an article for an Italian paper entitled 'The Jew, Disease Incarnate'.

His attitude led, perhaps inevitably, to the broadcasts on Rome radio that began in January 1941. They were from the beginning the rantings of a psychologically unbalanced personality about a world run, as he saw it, by Jews and usurers. The British Empire was called a syphilitic organisation, the Australians were said to deserve a Sino-Japanese invasion, their contribution to civilisation not deserving even a Jewish medal. ('Criminals were their grandads.') With America's entry into the war after the bombing of Pearl Harbor, Pound's frantic voice became a shriek. Any Jew remotely connected with banking or with the Roosevelt administration was attacked again and again, Roosevelt himself said to be a puppet of the Jews and to be out of his mind. Twice or three times a week Pound broadcast, his voice being, he said, that of a patriotic American. Every broadcast he made after Pearl Harbor was preceded by a brief preamble to that effect and when, in July 1943, he was indicted in the United States for acts designed to give aid and comfort to the enemies of his country, he wrote indignantly to the US Attorney-General that he had said nothing contrary to his duties as an American citizen. After the fall of the Italian government and the establishment by Mussolini of his ghost republic at Salo on Lake Garda, Pound remained in touch with his officials and continued to write articles and pamphlets. In April 1945 he was arrested by partisans and in May handed over to the American military authorities.

For six months he was held in Pisa at the Disciplinary Training Centre, the only civilian in a camp designed for tough military criminals. He was put into a cage very much resembling those housing dangerous animals in a zoo, and lived in it for several weeks until he became so weak that the prison doctor thought he might die and had him moved to a tent in the medical compound. Even there the conditions were wretched, but they had little visible effect on Pound. His health recovered, he took brisk daily walks in the compound, played imaginary games of tennis and baseball, lectured the medical orderlies about the evils of usury and the virtues of the American constitution. He was allowed to use the dispensary typewriter and wrote to Eliot asking whether Faber would publish his new versions of Confucius, 'the only basis on which a world order can work'.[42] He wrote Cantos LXXIV to LXXXIV, the Pisan Cantos, the most touching and memorable – or containing the most memorable passages – of the whole work. Often confused and obscure, they are also in places a record and recollection of the poet's life and beliefs more poignant than anything to be found elsewhere in his writing. From the first of these Cantos the memories crowd in, of Fordie (about whom Pound wrote eloquently when he died in 1939), Yeats and Joyce ('Jim the comedian singing:/"Blarrney castle me darlin"'), and such distant figures as Victor Plarr, Edgar Jepson, Maurice Hewlett, Henry Newbolt. These memories were mixed up with incidents at the camp, bits of

[263]

Epilogue

Chinese history and Pound philosophy, a Canto offering Chinese characters translated as 'explication', recollections of paintings and painters. The mixture as before, it might seem, but less marked by the usual obsessions, the history less tedious than elsewhere, the clownish jokes less objectionable, the sense of a life misspent or a life's mission failed coming through painfully. The poet's past seems a magical time, the people who inhabit it are transformed into characters mythical as those in Homer.

It was the Pisan Cantos, and the picture of the poet confined in what he called the gorilla cage, that moved literary opinion in favour of Pound. He was flown out of Italy to Washington, found unfit to plead to a charge of treason, and transferred to St Elizabeths Hospital, where he remained for thirteen years. The hospital's superintendent then testified that he had been suffering from a paranoid condition during his whole time at the hospital, the charge of treason was dismissed, and he was released. 'Paranoid' hardly seems an adequate term for the condition Pound had suffered, or enjoyed, for many years. The four doctors who said he was unfit for trial were surely more accurate in saying he could not reason properly or rationally and had delusions about his own relationship with the world. At the time of his release in 1958 this had been true for at least thirty years.

He had suffered, he was an American, he was forgiven. One is bound to feel, when one reads some of the Rome broadcasts, that he was extremely lucky. In 1949 the Pisan Cantos received the first annual award of the Bollingen poetry prize for the best new volume of the year. Aiken, Auden, Eliot, Robert Lowell, Katherine Anne Porter, Allen Tate and Robert Penn Warren were among the judges. A storm of controversy followed, which left the prizewinner indifferent or amused. In the following years Eliot worked actively for his release. Lewis did what he could but had the problems and troubles already mentioned, and was not very sympathetic to Pound's increasing concern with the past. 'I am told you believe yourself to be Napoleon – or is it Mussolini?' he wrote. 'What a pity you did not choose Buddha while you were about it.'[43]

The later years at St Elizabeths were comfortable, perhaps almost pleasant. He was allowed many privileges; a steady stream of friends, admirers, disciples came to see him, some of them liberals, rather more neo-Fascists like the bookseller who became a propagandist concerned to preserve the United States from black and Jewish domination. The imprisoned poet was an increasing embarrassment to the government, and in the end a deal was done. A statement by Robert Frost, approved by Eliot, Hemingway and MacLeish, acknowledging that Pound had done wrong but saying he was not sane enough ever to be tried, was the key that opened the doors. The indictment was dismissed, the martyr (as some thought him by now) freed. Asked what he thought of Frost's efforts on his behalf Pound said: 'He ain't been in much of a hurry.'[44] He returned to Italy, and on his arrival was photographed giving the Fascist salute. He told reporters that America was an insane asylum.

In Italy and free, the hyper-activity he had shown at St Elizabeths faded. From 1960 onwards his physical condition deteriorated, his memory began to fail. In 1961 he became mostly silent, talking neither to reporters nor to friends, cared for now almost entirely by Olga Rudge, although Dorothy Pound had been his standby in the years of incarceration. When occasionally he did speak to visitors, it was to express regret for much of the past, say he had done everything wrong and had understood things too late. Occasionally he suggested that his political activities had been mistaken.[45] He went to Zurich to see the grave of Joyce, came to England to attend the memorial service for Eliot, wrote an introduction, never used, to Lewis's letters in which he said: 'It is a nuisance to have outlived one's intelligence.'[46] In his last years he walked alone in Venice, feeding the cats, a man preoccupied with the past and especially his own past, its romance, its shape, the people he had known. In Venice, on 1 November 1972, the last of the founding fathers died.

CHAPTER SIXTEEN

Some Other Endings

Gertrude Stein longed as much as any writer for popular fame, particularly in her native country. She achieved it in 1933 with the publication of *The Autobiography of Alice B. Toklas*. The ingenious device she adopted here of writing a book about her own life in the voice of her live-in cook and lover enabled her to say things about herself, her present and former friends, and the slights she had received from American publications like the *Atlantic Monthly* and *Who's Who in America* ('Gertrude Stein's name was never in *Who's Who in America*') without doing so in the first person. The voice was obviously Stein's in its mock or real simplicity, but the consciously childish archness was amusing, the narrative straightforward, the portraits of writers and Cubist painters done sometimes with sugar, but occasionally with acid. The *Atlantic Monthly* serialised the book, its success was both critical and commercial, the American public took this grey-haired iron-featured lesbian lady to its heart. In France too the book was extremely successful, and as she said a few years later in *Everybody's Autobiography*, 'it was pleasant being a lion, and meeting the people who make it pleasant for you to be a lion.'

A lion or lioness she remained. Her name appeared in lights on Broadway when her opera *Four Saints in Three Acts*, with music by Virgil Thomson, was performed. An immensely successful lecture tour followed. The six lectures made no concessions to those who wanted to know more of her life story, but she was now a cultural object, and what she said was of less importance than what she was. And she could turn a stylish, not necessarily accurate phrase. She did so when, replying to a question about her line 'a rose is a rose is a rose', she said that in this line the rose was red in English poetry for the first time in a hundred years. In England she lectured to Oxford undergraduates who gave her a generous welcome, although the *Autobiography* created much less stir than in her homeland.

Some Other Endings

The book contained slighting or patronising references to Matisse and Picasso, called Braque Picasso's imitator, said that Hemingway had been formed by Stein and Sherwood Anderson. She deeply offended the Jolases by saying inaccurately that Elliot Paul had been responsible for the publication of her work in *transition*. 'Testimony Against Gertrude Stein', issued as a supplement to *transition 24*, contained protests by Matisse, Braque, Tzara and others about her inaccuracies, and an attack by Jolas on the 'hollow, tinsel bohemianism' of the *Autobiography*, and a telling comment from Maria Jolas about Stein's Barnumesque publicity and rejection of any relationship that did not accept her own view of herself as a great writer.

It is likely that the Jolases' enthusiasm for Stein would have diminished even if the *Autobiography* had not been published, for by the early thirties they had moved on from the Revolution of the Word to the 'Laboratory of the Mystic Logos' and the view that 'at the limit of the creator's spirit there is always the pre-logical'.[1] The periodical now supported what Jolas called pan-romanticism, a term concerned particularly with Verticalism. The manifesto announcing that 'Poetry Is Vertical' was signed by Hans Arp, Beckett, and a few lesser names, including that of Jolas under his own name and that of Theo Rutra. How was poetry vertical? The ten commandments do not tell us, but they are opposed to the 'factitious sense of harmony' induced by the 'classical ideal', and in favour of work produced under the influence of 'the dream, the daydream, the mystic-gnostic trance, and even the psychiatric condition'.[2] Jolas must have been disconcerted when he gave space to 'Cambridge Experiment, a Manifesto of Young England', to find the young English editors saying that the main need of contemporary literature was not a pan-romantic approach but formal discipline. The last issues of *transition* contained a great variety of texts and reproductions, most of them properly pan-romantic, but including reproductions of work by Mondrian and Moholy-Nagy which, if not exactly classical, were without doubt the reverse of romantic. The tenth anniversary issue was the last. In 1935 Jolas had returned to newspaper work, and in 1941 he joined the US Office of Information. He stayed for nearly ten years in government service, and in 1952 the man from Babel died.[3]

Robert McAlmon found no vital art movement in Mexico. In 1932 a collection of his stories was published by the Black Sun

Press, now run by Crosby's widow. Thereafter life became for McAlmon a series of intervals between some expected but non-existent great event, as he moved around from country to country. Friends, not only members of the Crowd, were concerned about him. Was he just playing the fool, Pound wondered, or had he gone plumb to hell?[4] He kept up a correspondence with Williams who, as he later said, felt towards McAlmon as to a son, appeared in an Objectivist anthology edited by Zukofsky, and in 1937 published a book of poems, in part through Williams's influence. And that was all. McAlmon's last years were spent in the American Southwest, where he died of tuberculosis in 1956, his unquestionable talent not in any way fulfilled. Williams himself died in 1963, by then established as a grand old man, perhaps even the Grand Old Man, of American modern poetry. The sign on his house in Rutherford reading William C. Williams, MD seemed to many of the young an emblem of his fine homespun Americanism, and they were delighted by his readiness to become enthusiastic about any poetic experiment providing he could discern in it a truly national flavour. He had moved from Objectivism to Projectivism, a movement of which he thought so highly that he reproduced several pages of Charles Olson's Projectivist Manifesto in his autobiography. The so-called Black Mountain group of poets, who flourished in the late fifties, did so under Williams's auspices. In Britain he had few admirers, fewer followers, and the poetic division between two countries sharing a language could not be expressed more clearly than by reactions to Williams. English, he told a correspondent in 1948, denoted a historical background that could never be real for Americans, who had a language – and hence a prosody – that was distinct and separate.[5] In another letter he said Eliot should be branded as the worst possible influence on American letters. On the other side of the Atlantic there were and remain many who would reserve that position for Williams himself.

Among other writers discussed here, only Djuna Barnes calls for particular mention. In 1940 she settled into a small apartment in New York, which remained her home until she died in 1981. There she worked on *The Antiphon*, gave up drink, told Eliot when he visited her that she had wasted too much time in her life. For years she suffered from emphysema and arthritis, but still survived. Young admirers lingered in the courtyard of Patchin Place where she lived, hoping for a glimpse of her, and she was assailed by what she called idiot children writing theses for their Ph.Ds. She told Edmund Wilson that she was doing her best to be a sweet old lady, but there is no sign that she wished to succeed. One of the quatrains in a poem of her old age expresses something of her humour, her oddity, and her uncompromising spirit:

> Somewhat sullen, many days,
> The Walrus is a cow that neighs.
> Tusked, ungainly, and windblown,
> It sits on ice, and alone.[6]

CHAPTER SEVENTEEN

The Achievement

There is a view, an offshoot of Marxist determinism about society and the individual, that literary changes are no more than reflections of social and technical development. Once Freudian and other psychoanalytic theories had become widely known, it is said, in reference particularly to *Ulysses*, somebody was bound to write a work of fiction based on them and likely to try to express the operations of the unconscious by using something like a stream of consciousness technique.[1] With the loosening of social restrictions it was inevitable also that somebody would write a book containing words previously denied entry even into reputable dictionaries (for instance the *Shorter Oxford* before World War II). It is said also, in explanation of the colloquial tone in passages like the pub conversation in *The Waste Land*, that the steady increase in the use of demotic language after World War I was bound to affect poetry. By this view social, psychological and philological developments created a gap between things done and things written that was bound to be filled in literature, the names of those who filled it being of minor importance.

This is true only to a very limited degree. The ideas of writers, like those of everybody else, are partly shaped by the society they live in; but literary creations are individual and unique and may affect the very nature of society. The poetry of Shelley, Tennyson, Whitman, Eliot, Auden, played a part in forming and shaping the attitudes of whole literary generations. No doubt it is right to say that new ideas about the human psyche were bound to find literary expression, but it made a great deal of difference that Joyce was one of their chief expositors: and while British and American 'poetic' language was ready for the junk heap in 1914, it might have been changed by writers quite different from Eliot and Pound. Some kind of modernist movement must have replaced the Victorian novel,

Georgian poetry, the American literary vacuum, but it is not irrelevant to ask whether this particular revolution succeeded or failed.

The answer is not simple. That the twentieth-century novel has been changed utterly by the example of Joyce is beyond question. It is through Joyce's example that many writers have abandoned the narrative structure that, with a very few exceptions like *Tristram Shandy*, had ruled the novel since the seventeenth century. For Americans particularly his practice showed a way of escape from the novel's formal restrictions, as dramatists found Ionesco, Brecht, Beckett and others offering ways of escape from the three-act play. In Britain the effect of Joyce has been much less, most of the notable novelists of the past half-century owing little or nothing to him; yet even in Britain there are many younger writers who have explored and used Joyce, in particular the elements of dream and fantasy strongly present in both *Ulysses* and *Finnegans Wake*. Often the writers influenced may have had no thought of Joyce when writing, perhaps may not have read him. He has become a climate of opinion, a way of looking at fiction for anybody who contemplates writing it. Joycean wordplay has had less effect, although there are novels that have used it, and some of Tom Stoppard's plays are verbal fantasies of a Joycean kind. His use of forbidden words has shown the way to a situation in which any words may be used, any actions described in print. Lawrence's sexual descriptions in *Lady Chatterley's Lover* also played a part here, although sexuality in modern fiction owes much more to the genial obscenity of Joyce than to the sacramental approach of Lawrence.

Eliot's role in the ruthless rejection of archaic diction through his own verse and criticism had an equally profound effect on poetry, and along with it went Pound's tireless advocacy of work avoiding the accepted forms of English verse. Eliot was too markedly individual a writer to have many poetic disciples, but during the twenties and thirties almost every new poet in Britain took him as a starting point, however great the later divergence from the model. This applied even, or especially, to the poets of the thirties who reflected Eliot's poetic practice while often violently dissenting from his view of society. The 'narrow strictness' Auden eulogised as a poetic stance was wholly Eliotian, and the precision of the Sweeney quatrains affected poets as diverse as Norman Cameron, Geoffrey

Grigson and Cecil Day Lewis. Other influences worked on Auden in his early poems: Gertrude Stein (at Oxford he briefly thought Stein marvellous), Laura Riding, and more particularly Robert Graves. If one does not regard Auden, or Graves for that matter, as a modernist, it is chiefly because they originated nothing in language or manner, but adapted the work of others. In spite of Malcolm Cowley's statement that until 1925 Eliot's influence was omni-present, it is much less apparent in American poets than in British. If one excludes Crane, Allen Tate and John Crowe Ransom, most Americans found Eliot's narrow strictness temperamentally uncon-genial, since they equated modernity increasingly with freedom to write just the way they pleased about anything they wished. Pound's emphasis on making it new, plus Williams's exhortations that they should make it new in an American way, marked their necessary divergence from Eliot.

So modernism succeeded? But three of the founding fathers (Joyce excluded) envisaged it as part of a changed society that never came into being. Only Pound explicitly welcomed Fascism, but Eliot's insistence on a 'right theology' which remained undefined, implied support of a right-wing political regime, and Lewis in 1926 saw 'a world state and a recognised central world-control' as both inevitable and desirable. This central world-control, authoritarian in nature, would find 'more profitable occupations for everybody', and the 'soft and peaceable' generality of human beings would 'be left alone and allowed to lead a peaceful, industrious and pleasant life'. Their artistic demolition work was done with such a society in mind, and its failure to materialise inevitably affected their art and their attitude. Yet there was from the beginning a gap between demands like Lewis's early 'Kill John Bull With Art', Hulme's insistence on classicism and Original Sin, Eliot's right theology, and the actual art works they produced. The ideas were reactionary, the art works revolutionary. How far, given their social views, could the call for freedom of subject and treatment be carried? Were there limits to the usefulness of experiment?

By the very early twenties Eliot and Lewis had realised that the end of complete freedom was the gibberings of Gillespie and the incoherence of the Baroness in literature, and in visual art the pure white or pure black canvas. (Pound's ideas were never coherent enough for him to recognise such a contradiction between social theory and artistic practice.) Lewis did not live to see Warhol's soup cans or minimalist art, but he anticipated them in *The Demon of Progress in the Arts* when condemning the artistic extremism 'in which only zero is tolerated – in which nothing is preferred to something'. He was writing about pictures, but a similar logic applied to literature. If one was intent to destroy *all* existing standards, sever *all* links with rhyme and metre, replace the logic of narrative form by the haphazardness of dream – why then, a Carnevali might easily be found the equal of Keats. Pushed beyond a certain point, the purpose of experiment in the arts became simply the perpetuation of experiment, with nothing more in mind than endless novelty, Heap's twenty-three systems of art, Jolas's Vertical Poetry. The stage work of Beckett, Joyce's most famous disciple, has been given more and more to the reduction of action, language, meaning, conveying the least possible information in the fewest possible words, pointing up the pupil's distinction from the master by a concern to extinguish language where Joyce was eager constantly to expand it. Beckett is concerned, indeed, not only to extinguish words but to blot out human existence, so that in *Not I* all that remains of the protagonist is a mouth.

The truth understood by Eliot and Lewis, not by Joyce or Pound, was that the usefulness of technical experiment has limits, and beyond them brings no returns. Hence Lewis's call for the abandonment of totally abstract painting and Eliot's realisation that *The Waste Land* was the end of something and not the beginning. Hence also Eliot's sympathy for young poets like Auden and George Barker who were taking what they needed from the preceding generation and adapting it to their own ends, and his distrust of those pursuing revolutionary romanticism, Jolas-style, or looking to a modernism that rejected all connection with English verse. By the mid-twenties modernism held many potentialities for those prepared to adapt its creators' original intentions, as Hemingway adapted Stein and Barnes used Joyce, but further progress towards either extreme simplification or extreme complication of language was no longer profitable. It was Joyce's refusal to recognise this that made *Finnegans Wake* a signpost to nowhere, Pound's yearning for new -isms that made his later activities as artistic mentor useless or ridiculous.

A change, almost a reversal, of cultural attitudes in the last two decades, has much affected literary modernism. It was conceived as an assertion of the values of Highbrow Culture, its enemy the Middlebrow creator or reader, about whom Eliot and Pound were so often contemptuous, although for Lowbrow Culture (Marie Lloyd and George Robey) they had an affectionate regard. But since the sixties Lowbrow, or Popular, Culture has been in the ascendant, with highbrows falling over one another to acclaim the genius of the Beatles or elevate John le Carré and Dick Francis to the status of master novelists. There has followed a revulsion against all modernism's attitudes and most of its works. This has been mainly British, its most outspoken proponents being Philip Larkin and Kingsley Amis. Larkin looked back quite consciously to Britain before World War I as a very good time and place and praised the Georgian poets in words almost echoing those of Edmund Gosse, as representing 'a robust zestful upsurge of realism'.[2] Amis attacked the idea that experiment was 'the life-blood of the British novel'. (In America there has been no similar swell of anti-modernist feeling.)

To the extreme anti-modernists the founding fathers are figures to be execrated or disregarded. For Larkin, Picasso (and presumably other Cubists, Futurists, Vorticists, etc.) is to be regarded as a painter who has carried out a successful fraud on the public. Elsewhere he expressed in lyrical terms his admiration for some jazz musicians. To adapt Groucho Marx, one shouldn't be deceived about Larkin. He may have sounded like a philistine and expressed philistine views, but in much that concerned literature he really was a philistine. To say that is not to express an opinion about the worth of his poetry. Yet, however much Larkin, Amis and others yearned for past simplicities, they had been influenced by modernism and particularly by Eliot, as any poet of their time unswayed by the heresies of Williams must have been. Larkin's mostly colloquial language, casual rhythms and rhymes, urban settings, deliberate avoidance of poeticisms in favour of lines like 'the fobbed/ Impendent belly of Time' and 'What does it prove? Sod all', are proof that he used the poetic currency of his period, a currency first circulated through modernism. The Georgianism he momentarily approved of happily found no place in his work.

Modernism as Highbrow Culture is now out of fashion, its founding fathers providing much food for academics but suffering temporary public disregard. Yet the achievements of the men of

1914 were great. If one were looking to convey them in a sentence, it would say that they changed permanently the language in which poetry is written, and enlarged beyond measure what could be said and the way of saying it in fiction. A revolution determined to discard so much of the past inevitably contained the seeds of absurdities, excesses, perversions of the original ideas. Like other revolutions this one has not developed in the ways its founding fathers expected. Their fame has endured unevenly, and for what they might well think wrong reasons. In that sense this revolution like others has devoured its children, other than the unpolitical Joyce, and even Joyce would be disappointed by the almost universal agreement that *Finnegans Wake* is not a book to be read twice, or for most people even once. Yet the great works remain. Nothing written in recent years has the scope and universality of *Ulysses*, the moral and artistic intensity of *Tarr*, the virtuosity and daring of 'Mauberley' and *The Waste Land*. All poems and fictions look back to ancestors, yet these works made such dramatic breaks with the past that they truly justify the word new. Their creators deserve honour.

NOTES

PART ONE, *Chapter 1*

1. Christopher Hassall, *Edward Marsh*, London 1959. p. 120.
2. Edward Marsh, *A Number of People*, London 1939, p. 321.
3. Quoted in Robert Ross, *The Georgian Literary Revolt*, London 1967 p. 125.
4. John Drinkwater, *Autobiography 1897–1913*, London 1932, p. 229.
5. Ross, *op. cit.*, p. 140.
6. *Rhythm*, March 1913.
7. Quoted Hassall, *op cit.*, pp. 681–7.
8. John Cournos, *Autobiography*, New York 1935, p. 234.
   Richard Aldington, *Life for Life's Sake*, London 1968, p. 135.
9. *Egoist*, March 1918.
10. Hassall, *op. cit.*, p. 281.
11. *ibid*, p. 674.
12. Harriet Monroe, *A Poet's Life*, New York 1938, pp. 120–2.
13. Ezra Pound, *Letters, 1907–1941*, ed D. D. Paige, London 1951, p. 41.
14. *Poetry* (Chicago), November 1912.
15. Pound, *Letters*, p. 45.

Chapter 2

1. William Carlos Williams, *Selected Letters*, ed. John C. Thirlwall, New York 1957, p. 8.
2. H.D., *An End to Torment*, Manchester 1980, p. 3.
3. *ibid.*, p. 22–3.
4. Douglas Goldring, *South Lodge*, London 1943, pp. 47–9.
5. Ezra Pound and Dorothy Shakespear, *Their Letters, 1909–1914*, ed. Omar Pound and A. Walton Litz, London 1984, p. 3.
6. Violet Hunt, *The Flurried Years*, London 1926, p. 108.
7. Ford Madox Ford, *Return to Yesterday*, London 1937, p. 388.
8. Quoted in Alun R. Jones, *The Life and Opinions of T. E. Hulme*, London 1960, p. 187.
9. T. E. Hulme, *Further Speculations*, ed. Samuel Hynes, Minneapolis 1955, p. 106.
10. *ibid.*, p. 67.
11. *ibid.*, p. 98.
12. *ibid.*, p. 82.
13. Wyndham Lewis, *Blasting and Bombardiering*, London 1937, p. 39.

Notes

14. Quoted in E. Fuller Torrey, *The Roots of Treason*, London 1984, p. 78.
15. T. E. Hulme, *Speculations*, ed. Herbert Read, London 1924, p. 256.
16. William Carlos Williams, *Autobiography*, London 1968, p. 113.
17. F. S. Flint, 'The History of Imagism', *Egoist*, May 1915.
18. Christopher Hassall, *Edward Marsh*, London 1959, p. 229.
19. S. Foster Damon, *Amy Lowell*, Boston 1935, p. 49.
20. *ibid.*, p. 196.
21. Amy Lowell, *Tendencies in Modern American Poetry*, Cambridge (Mass.) 1917, p. 244.
22. Richard Aldington, *Life for Life's Sake*, London 1968, p. 124.
23. Quoted in Alister Kershaw, *Richard Aldington, An Intimate Portrait*, Carbondale, (Ill.) 1965, p. 125.
24. Damon, *op. cit.*, p. 336.
25. Wyndham Lewis, *Letters*, ed. W. K. Rose, London 1963, p. 47.
26. Lewis Collection, Cornell University.
27. Wyndham Lewis, *Rude Assignment*, London 1949, p. 111.
28. Lewis Collection, Cornell University.
29. *ibid.*
30. Wyndham Lewis, *Mrs Dukes' Million*, Toronto 1977, pp. 364–5.
31. Wyndham Lewis, *Tarr*, London 1951 (Methuen edition), pp. 326–7.
32. Ezra Pound, *Pisan Cantos*, New York 1948, p. 85.
33. *Blasting and Bombardiering*, p. 277.
34. Lewis Collection, Cornell University.
35. *ibid.*, Lechmere to Lewis, 1914 and 1951.
36. *ibid.*
37. Jeffrey Meyers, *The Enemy*, London 1980, p. 38.
38. Stanislaus Joyce, *Dublin Diary*, ed. George Harris Healey, London 1962, p. 15.
39. Richard Ellmann, *James Joyce*, London 1982, pp. 300–311.
40. Quoted *ibid.*, p. 79.
41. *ibid.*, Chapters 13, 20, 21.
42. *Pound/Joyce, Letters*, ed. Forrest Read, London 1968, p. 18.
43. *ibid.*, p. 18.
44. Conrad Aiken, *Selected Letters*, ed. Joseph Killorin, New Haven & London 1978, p. 8.
45. *ibid.*, p. 77.
46. *ibid.*, p. 72.
47. Quoted in *Ezra Pound, A Collection of Essays*, ed. Peter Russell, London 1950
48. T.S. Eliot, *New Criterion*, January 1930; Conrad Aiken, *Ushant*, London 1962, p. 134.
49. Peter Ackroyd, *T. S. Eliot*, London 1984, p. 26.
50. *ibid.*, pp. 48, 54.
51. Aiken Collection, Huntington Library, July 1914.
52. *ibid.*, 19 July 1914.
53. T. S. Eliot, *Poems Written in Early Youth*, London 1957.

Notes

Chapter 3

1. John Davidson, *Collected Poems*, vol. 2, Edinburgh 1973, p. 428.
2. *Blast* 1.
3. *Futurist Manifesto*, trans. Umbro Apollonio, London 1973.
4. *ibid.*, p. 71.
5. See Richard Cork, *Vorticism and Abstract Art in the First Machine Age*, vol. 1, London 1976, p. 27.
6. *Futurist Manifesto*, p. 27.
7. *ibid.*, p. 219.
8. *Wyndham Lewis and Vorticism*, London 1956, p. 3.
9. Timothy Materer, *Vortex*, Cornell 1979, p. 16.
10. Quinn Manuscripts, Berg Collection, New York Public Library.
11. H. G. Wells, *Satire and Fiction*, London 1931.
12. *Blast* 1.
13. Wyndham Lewis, *Tarr*, London 1951 (Methuen edition), p. 295.
14. T. E. Hulme, *Speculations*, ed. Herbert Read, London 1924, p. 84.
15. *ibid.*, pp. 76–7.
16. *Criterion*, April 1924.
17. Pound to Monroe, Ezra Pound, *Letters 1907–1941*, ed. D. D. Paige, London 1951, p. 58.
18. Thomas Carylyle, *Letters to J.S. Mill, John Sterling and Robert Browning*, London 1923, pp. 191–2.
19. *Quarterly Review*, October 1916.
20. Ezra Pound and Dorothy Shakespear, *Their Letters, 1909–1914*, ed. Omar Pound and A. Walton Litz, London 1984, p. 87.
21. Lewis Collection, Cornell University.

Chapter 4

1. Quoted in Jane Lidderdale and Mary Nicholson, *Dear Miss Weaver*, London 1970, p. 68.
2. Weaver to Joyce, 28 November 1920, Cornell.
3. *Dear Miss Weaver*, Chapters 1 and 2.
4. Richard Ellmann, *James Joyce*, London 1982, p. 179.
5. *Egoist*, 1 July 1914.
6. *Egoist*, 15 March 1914.
7. Weaver to Joyce, 28 July 1915, Cornell.
8. *Pound/Joyce Letters*, ed. Forrest Read, London 1968, p. 93.
9. Ellmann, *op. cit.*, pp. 390–2.
10. *Dear Miss Weaver*, pp. 105–7.
11. Weaver to Joyce, 28 January 1916, Cornell.
12. D. H. Lawrence, *Letters*, ed. Harry T. Moore, London 1962: letter to Waldo Frank, 27 July 1917, p. 518.
13. *D. H. Lawrence, The Cultural Heritage*, ed R. P. Draper, London 1970, pp. 91–103.

[278]

Notes

14. Weaver to Joyce, Cornell.
15. *Dear Miss Weaver*, p. 137.
16. Ezra Pound, *Letters 1907–1941*, ed. D. D. Paige, London 1951, p. 80.
17. *ibid.*, p. 104.
18. Wyndham Lewis, *Blasting and Bombardiering*, London 1937, p. 283.
19. John Gould Fletcher, *Life Is My Song*, New York 1937, p. 70.
20. *Pound/Lewis*, ed. Timothy Materer, London 1985, p. 8.
21. Lewis Collection, Cornell University.
22. *Pound/Lewis*, p. 8.
23. *ibid.*, p. 21.
24. Weaver to Lewis, 11 January 1916, Cornell.
25. B. L. Reid, *The Man from New York*, London 1968, pp. 198–9.
26. Quinn to Lewis, 15 March 1917, Berg Collection, New York Public Library.
27. Lewis to Quinn, 23 May 1917, Berg Collection.
28. Reid, *op. cit.*, p. 276.
29. Conrad Aiken, *Ushant*, London 1962, p. 215.
30. Fletcher, *op. cit.*, pp. 58–9.
31. Flint to Pound, 1915, British Library.
32. Quoted in Reid, *op. cit.*, p. 340.
33. Iris Barry, 'The Ezra Pound Period', *Bookman*, October 1931.
34. *ibid.*
35. Pound, *Letters*, pp. 137–8.
36. Barry, *op. cit.*
37. Barry to Lewis, 14 April 1921, Cornell.
38. Pound to Margaret Anderson, *Letters*, p. 160.
39. Berg Collection.
40. Margaret Anderson, *My Thirty Years' War*, London 1930, p. 35.
41. *Little Review*, November 1914.
42. *My Thirty Years' War*, p. 124.
43. *ibid.*, pp. 68–9.
44. Reid, *op. cit.*, p. 287.
45. *Little Review*, August 1916.
46. *My Thirty Years' War*, p. 124.
47. Quoted in *ibid.*, p. 165.
48. *Egoist*, November 1917.
49. *ibid.*, December 1917.
50. *ibid.*, March 1918.
51. Pound, *Canto LXXVIII*.
52. *Pound/Lewis*, p. 244.
53. *ibid.*, p. 234.
54. Ellmann, *op. cit.*, pp. 230, 265.
55. *ibid.*, pp. 422, 466.
56. Quoted in *ibid.*, p. 425.
57. *ibid.*, p. 716.
58. Stuart Gilbert, *James Joyce's Ulysses*, London 1931, preface.

Notes

59. *Pound/Joyce*, p. 129.
60. Barbara Guest, *Herself Defined, The Poet H.D. and Her World*, New York 1984, p. 121.
61. Reid, *op. cit.*, p. 345.
62. Pound, *Letters*, p. 188.
63. Weaver to Joyce, Cornell.
64. *ibid.*, 2 November 1919, Cornell.
65. *Dear Miss Weaver*, p. 147.
66. Virginia Woolf, *Diaries*, London,   , vol. 1, p. 140.
67. *ibid.*, p. 218.
68. *ibid.*, vol. 2, pp. 69, 199.
69. Eliot to Quinn, Berg Collection.
70. *ibid.*, 30 June 1919.

Chapter 5

1. Noel Stock, *Ezra Pound*, London 1985 (Penguin edition), p. 281.
2. Ezra Pound, *Letters 1907–1941*, ed. D. D. Page, London 1951, p. 207.
3. Quoted Stock, *op. cit.*, p. 295.
4. Lewis to Quinn, 3 September 1919, Berg Collection, New York Public Library.
5. Richard Cork, *Vorticism and Abstract Art in the First Machine Age*, vol. 1, London 1976, p. 545.
6. Lewis to Julian Symons, November 1937, *Twentieth Century Verse*.
7. Eliot to Lewis, 1921, Lewis Collection, Cornell University.
8. Quinn to Lewis, 25 May 1921, Berg Collection.
9. B. L. Reid, *The Man from New York*, London 1968, p. 491.
10. *New Statesman*, 8 January 1921.
11. Eliot to Sydney Schiff, British Library.
12. Eliot to Quinn, 25 January 1920, Berg Collection.
13. *ibid.*
14. *Blasting and Bombardiering*, London, 1937, pp. 272–5, in which the scene is described with wonderful comic effect.
15. Eliot to Aiken, Aiken Collection, Huntington Library.
16. *Egoist*, September 1918.
17. *Egoist*, June–July 1918.

PART TWO, *Chapter 6*

1. *Ushant*, London 1962, p. 218.
2. Alfred Kreymborg, *Troubadour*, New York 1925.
3. Amy Lowell, *Tendencies in Modern American Poetry*, Cambridge (Mass.) 1917, p. 183.
4. *Winesburg, Ohio*, introduction to 1922 edition.

5. Quoted in Irving Howe, *Sherwood Anderson*, London 1951, pp. 115–6.
6. For a full account of the hoax, and the poems, see William Jay Smith's *The Spectric Hoax*, Wesleyan University Press, 1961.
7. *Paris Review* interview, 1962.
8. William Carlos Williams, *Selected Letters*, ed. John C. Thirlwall, New York 1957, p. 48.

Chapter 7

1. Malcolm Cowley, *Exiles' Return*, London 1961 (revised edition), p. 46.
2. Quoted in Robert E. Knoll, *Robert McAlmon, Expatriate Writer and Publisher*, Nebraska 1957.
3. Robert McAlmon and Kay Boyle, *Being Geniuses Together*, London 1970, p. 45.
4. William Carlos Williams, *Autobiography*, London 1968, p. 175.
5. *Transatlantic Review*, January 1924.
6. The stories appear in Robert E. Knoll, *McAlmon and the Lost Generation*, Nebraska 1962.
7. *ibid.*
8. James Joyce, *Letters*, ed. Stuart Gilbert, London 1957, vol. 1, p. 169.
9. Sylvia Beach, *Shakespeare & Company*, London 1960, pp. 45–6. Written many years after the meeting, and perhaps not wholly accurate.
10. *ibid.*, p. 57.
11. Quoted Richard Ellmann, *James Joyce*, London 1982, pp. 506–7.
12. B. L. Reid, *The Man from New York*, London 1968, pp. 477–8.
13. The letter is quoted in full in Ellmann, *op. cit.*, pp. 511–2.
14. Gertrude Stein, *The Autobiography of Alice B. Toklas*, London 1933, p. 231.
15. *ibid.*, p. 7.
16. Janet Hobhouse, *Everybody Who Was Anybody*, London 1975, p. 3.
17. B. F. Skinner, 'Has Gertrude Stein a Secret?', *Atlantic Monthly*, January 1934.
18. Gertrude Stein, *Fernhurst, Q.E.D. and Other Early Writings*, London 1972.
19. Gertrude Stein, 'Composition As Explanation', London 1926.

Chapter 8

1. Richard Ellmann, *James Joyce*, London 1982, p. 528, gives the letter in full.
2. James Joyce, *Letters*, ed. Stuart Gilbert, London 1957, vol. 1, p. 194.
3. Jane Lidderdale and Mary Nicholson, *Dear Miss Weaver*, London 1970, p. 192.
4. *ibid.*, pp. 204–7.
5. Robert McAlmon and Kay Boyle, *Being Geniuses Together*, London 1970, p. 278.
6. *ibid.*, pp. 278–9.

Notes

7. Wyndham Lewis, *The Diabolical Principle*, London 1931, pp. 3–9.
8. Laura Riding, *Contemporaries and Snobs*, London 1928, pp. 183, 189.
9. Eugene Jolas, *transition* 1928.
10. Introduction to *Three Lives*, Modern Library edition, New York 1933.
11. Michael Reynolds, *The Young Hemingway*, Oxford 1986, pp. 180–5.
12. Ernest Hemingway, 'Summer People', in *The Nick Adams Stories*, New York 1972.
13. Quoted in Meyers, *Ernest Hemingway*, London 1986, p. 77.
14. *Quarterly Review of Literature*, December 1949.
15. Edmund Wilson, *The Shores of Light*, London 1952, pp. 119–120.
16. Alyse Gregory, quoted in N. T. Joost, *Scofield Thayer and the Dial*, Illinois 1964, p. 78.
17. Ezra Pound, *Letters 1907–1941*, ed. D. D. Paige, London 1951, p. 215.
18. *Dial*, April 1921.
19. Eliot to Aldington, quoted in *The Waste Land* facsimile edition, London,
20. Pound, *Letters*, p. 236.
21. Valerie Eliot to Sydney Schiff, British Library.
22. *The Waste Land*, facsimile edition.
23. It was not until after Eliot's death in 1965 that the manuscript was discovered among the John Quinn papers of the Berg Collection.
24. Quoted in Peter Ackroyd, *T. S. Eliot*, London 1984, p. 1984.
25. William Wasserstrom, *The Time of the Dial*, Syracuse 1963, p. 1
26. *ibid.*, p. 29.
27. Eliot to Aiken, 19 May 1924, Aiken Collection, Huntington Library.
28. Quinn to Eliot, 28 July 1922, Berg Collection.
29. B. L. Reid, *The Man from New York*, London 1968, p. 538.
30. Conrad Aiken, *Selected Letters*, ed. Joseph Killorin, New Haven & London 1978, p. 72.
31. Malcolm Cowley, *Exiles' Return* New York 1961, p. 112.
32. Hart Crane, *Letters*, ed. Brom Weber, California 1965, pp. 215, 220.
33. Wasserstrom, *op. cit.*, pp. 120–122.
34. Richard S. Kennedy, *Dreams in the Mirror*, New York 1980, pp. 190–1.
35. Bonamy Dobrée, in *T. S. Eliot, The Man and His Work*, London 1967, p. 87.
36. Conrad Aiken, *Ushant*, London 1962, pp. 232–3.
37. Pound, *Letters*, pp. 238–9.
38. Berg Collection.
39. Pound, *Letters*, p. 370.
40. Lewis Collection, Cornell University.
41. *ibid.*
42. Wyndham Lewis, *Letters*, ed. W. K. Rose, London 1963, p. 149.
43. *ibid.*, p. 152.
44. Eliot to Lewis, 5 September 1925, Cornell.
45. *English Review*, April 1919.
46. Quoted in Noel Stock, *Ezra Pound*, London 1985 (Penguin edition), p. 302.

Notes

47. *ibid.*, p. 323.
48. *ibid.*, p. 320.
49. *Enemy News* 21, Summer 1985.
50. Reid, *op. cit.*, p. 629.
51. Lewis to Sydney Schiff, *Enemy News* 21, Summer 1985.

Chapter 9

1. William Carlos Williams, *Autobiography*, London 1968, pp. 174–5.
2. W. C. Williams, *In the American Grain*, Norfolk (Conn.) 1925, p. 177.
3. Yvor Winters, *Uncollected Essays and Reviews*, London 1974, p.160.
4. W. C. Williams, *Selected Essays*, New York 1954, p. 17.
5. W. C. Williams, *Selected Letters*, ed. John C. Thirlwall, New York 1957, p. 264.
6. *ibid.*, p. 297.
7. Gertrude Stein, *Fernhurst, Q.E.D. and Other Early Writings*, London 1972 p. 137.
8. Williams, *Selected Letters*, pp. 129–34.
9. *Paris Review* interview, 1962.
10. *Hudson Review*, Winter 1961–1962.
11. David E. Shi, *Matthew Josephson*, Yale 1981, p. 56.
12. Wallace Stevens, *Letters*, London 1967, p. 251.
13. Hart Crane, *Letters*, ed. Brom Weber, California 1965, p. 90.
14. *ibid.*, p. 68.
15. Edmund Wilson, *The Shores of Light*, London 1952, p. 200.
16. Philip Horton, *Hart Crane*, New York 1937, p. 337.
17. *Criterion*, December 1927, p. 565.
18. John Glassco, *Memoirs of Montparnasse*, Toronto 1970, p. 52.
19. Ernest Hemingway, *Death in the Afternoon*, p. 233.
20. *The Fourteenth Chronicle, Letters and Diaries of John dos Passos*, ed. Townsend Ludington, London 1974, p. 225.
21. John dos Passos, *USA*, London 1938, *The Forty-second Parallel*, p. 224.
22. Andrew Field, *The Formidable Miss Barnes*, London 1983, p. 107.
23. Djuna Barnes, *Interviews*, ed. Alyce Barry, Washington DC 1985, p. 286.
24. *ibid.*, pp. 293–4.
25. *The Formidable Miss Barnes*, p. 17.
26. Glassco, *op. cit.*, p. 24.
27. Sharon Spencer, *Tone and Structure in the Modern Novel*, New York 1971.
28. Djuna Barnes, *Nightwood*, London 1937, with introduction by T. S. Eliot.
29. *Criterion*, October 1938, p. 85.
30. *Criterion*, July 1930, p. 724.

PART THREE *Chapter 10*

1. James Joyce, *Letters*, ed. Stuart Gilbert, London 1957, vol. 1, p. 246.
2. Ezra Pound, *Letters 1907–1941*, ed. D. D. Paige, London 1951, p. 276.

Notes

3. Richard Ellmann, *James Joyce*, London 1982, p. 587.
4. Wyndham Lewis, *The Art of Being Ruled*, London 1926, p. 401.
5. Wyndham Lewis, *Time and Western Man*, London 1927, p. 92.
6. *ibid.*, p. 109.
7. Ellmann, *op. cit.*, p. 590.
8. Robert McAlmon and Kay Boyle, *Being Geniuses Together*, London 1970, p. 268.
9. Bravig Imbs, *Confessions of Another Young Man*, New York 1936, p. 235.
10. *transition* 9.
11. *transition* 7.
12. Wyndham Lewis, *The Diabolical Principle*, London 1931, p. 59.
13. *transition* 18.
14. Quoted Dougald McMillan, *transition 1927–1938*, London 1975, pp. 43–4.

Chapter 11

1. Noel Riley Fitch, *Sylvia Beach and the Lost Generation*, London 1964, p. 296.
2. Robert McAlmon and Kay Boyle, *Being Geniuses Together*, London, 1970, p. 275.
3. William Carlos Williams, *Autobiography*, London 1968, pp. 164–5, 168–9.
4. *ibid.*, p. 268.
5. *Others*, 1919.
6. Quoted in *Being Geniuses Together*, p. 142.
7. *This Quarter*, Autumn–Winter 1925–6.
8. Wyndham Lewis, *Time and Western Man*, London 1927, p. 63.
9. John Glassco, *Memoirs of Montparnasse*, Toronto 1970, p. 131.
10. Lewis Collection, Cornell University.
11. *Pound/Lewis*, ed. Timothy Materer, London 1985, p. 150.
12. Quoted in *Being Geniuses Together*, p. 188.
13. Geoffrey Wolff, *Black Sun*, London 1977, p. 5.
14. Hart Crane, *Letters*, ed. Brom Weber, California 1965, p. 335.
15. *ibid.*, p. 339.
16. Wolff, *op. cit.*, p. 228.
17. *ibid.*, p. 9.
18. Eliot's introduction, Pound's notes, to volumes of Crosby's poems.
19. Malcolm Cowley, *Exiles' Return*, New York 1961, p. 245.
20. *ibid.*, p. 284.

Chapter 12

1. Pound-Magaret, Berg Collection, New York Public Library.
2. Wyndham Lewis, *Blasting and Bombardiering*, London 1937, p. 285.

Notes

3. *In Broken Images, Selected Letters of Robert Graves 1914–1946*, ed. Paul O'Prey, London 1982, p. 342.
4. W. B. Yeats, *A Packet for Ezra Pound*, Dublin 1934.
5. In late interviews, especially with Allen Ginsberg, *Evergreen Review*, June 1968.
6. Peter Brooker, *A Students' Guide to the Selected Poems of Ezra Pound*, London 1979, p. 237.

Chapter 13

1. Edgell Rickword, *Twittingpan*, London 1931, p. 13.
2. Wyndham Lewis, *The Art of Being Ruled*, London 1926, p. xii.
3. J. W. N. Sullivan to Lewis, 23 February 1927, Lewis Collection, Cornell University.
4. Sydney and Violet Schiff to Lewis, *ibid.*
5. T. S. Eliot, *After Strange Gods*, London 1934, p. 13.
6. Stephen Spender, *T. S. Eliot*, London 1975, p. 117
7. T. S. Eliot, *Notes Towards the Definition of Culture*, London 1948, p. 19.
8. Conrad Aiken, *Selected Letters*, ed. Joseph Killorin, New Haven & London 1978, p. 149.
9. Peter Ackroyd, *T. S. Eliot*, London 1984, p. 239.

Chapter 14

1. Edmund Wilson, *Axel's Castle*, New York 1931, p. 292.
2. Robert McAlmon and Kay Boyle, *Being Geniuses Together*, London 1970, p. 305.
3. *ibid.*, p. 309.
4. Malcolm Cowley, *Exiles' Return*, New York 1961, p. 284.
5. Samuel Putnam, *Paris Was Our Mistress*, New York 1947, p. 254.

EPILOGUE, Chapter 15

1. Quoted in Richard Ellmann, *James Joyce*, London 1982, p. 667.
2. *ibid.*, pp. 566–74, 657–9.
3. Quoted *ibid.*, p. 648.
4. Jane Lidderdale and Mary Nicholson, *Dear Miss Weaver*, London 1970, pp. 336–355.
5. Ellmann *op. cit.*, p. 679n.
6. Joyce to Weaver, 1 May 1935, quoted in *Dear Miss Weaver*, p. 346.
7. *The U.S. of America* v. *One Book entitled Ulysses*, New York 1984, p. 77.
8. *ibid.*, p. 115.
9. *ibid.*, p. 202.
10. *ibid.*, p. 285.

Notes

11. *Our Exagmination* . . ., etc, Paris 1929, p. 13.
12. Archibald MacLeish, *Letters*, New York 1983, p. 177.
13. 'The Possibility of a Poetic Drama', in *The Sacred Wood*, London 1920.
14. Bonamy Dobrée, *T. S. Eliot, The Man and His Work*, London 1967, pp. 185–6.
15. *The Family Reunion*, Part 2, Scene 2.
16. 'Poetry and Drama' (1951) in *On Poetry and Poets*, London 1957.
17. Edmund Wilson, *The Fifties*, London 1986, p. 121.
18. Peter Ackroyd, *T. S. Eliot*, London 1984, p. 289.
19. W. H. Auden, *A Bibliography 1924–1969*, ed B. C. Bloomfield and Edward Mendelson, Virginia 1972, p. 3.
20. Eliot to Orwell, 13 July 1944, quoted Bernard Crick, *George Orwell*, London 1980, p. 315.
21. Ezra Pound, *Letters 1907–1941*, ed. D. D. Paige, London 1951, p. 367.
22. *Pound/Lewis*, ed. Timothy Materer, London 1985, p. 249.
23. *ibid.*, p. 249.
24. Wyndham Lewis, *Letters*, ed. W. K. Rose, London 1963, pp. 518–9.
25. Christopher Hassall, *Edward Marsh*, London 1959, pp. 672–3.
26. Lewis Collection, Cornell University.
27. *ibid.*
28. Lewis to Newman Flower, *ibid.*
29. *ibid.*
30. Lewis, *Letters*, p. 242.
31. Quoted in Jeffrey Meyers, *The Enemy*, 1980 p. 228.
32. *Wyndham Lewis on Art*, ed. Walter Michel and C. J. Fox, New York 1969, p. 418.
33. *Hudson Review*, Summer 1957.
34. Quoted in Noel Stock, *Ezra Pound*, London 1985 (Penguin edition), p. 405.
35. Pound, *Letters*, p. 218.
36. Wyndham Lewis, *Blasting and Bombardiering*, London 1937, p. 304.
37. Introduction to *Active Anthology*, ed. Ezra Pound, London 1933.
38. *ibid.*
39. Louis Zukofsky, *All*, London 1967, p. 67.
40. Thomas Clark, *The Review* 10, p. 56.
41. *Pound/Lewis*, pp. 206–7.
42. Quoted Stock, *op. cit.*, p. 525.
43. *Pound/Lewis*, July 1946, p. 246.
44. Quoted Stock, *op. cit.*, p. 573.
45. *Pound/Lewis*, p. 305.

Chapter 16

1. *transition* 18.
2. *transition* 21.

Notes

3. Dougald McMillan, *transition 1927–1938*, London 1975, p. 74.
4. Pound, *Letters 1907–1941*, ed. D. D. Paige, London 1951, p. 354.
5. William Carlos Williams, *Selected Letters*, ed. John C. Thirlwall, New York 1957, p. 268.
6. Quoted in Andrew Field, *The Formidable Miss Barnes*, London 1983, p. 244.

Chapter 17

1. A point made by Francis Russell, *Three Studies in Twentieth Century Obscurity*, London 1954.
2. Review in *Spectator*, 18 December 1959, quoted Blake Morrison, *The Movement*, London 1980, p. 215.

Index

Index

Index

McAlmon, Robert 10, 109, 128-32, 135-6, 147-8, 151, 166-7, 181-2, 190, 201, 206-7, 209, 212, 216, 225, 232-3, 244, 267-8
MacCarthy, Desmond 112
Mackenzie, Compton 67-8
MacLeish, Archibald 214, 233, 246-7
Maeterlinck, Maurice 200
Mahoney, Dan 194
Mansfield, Katherine 20
Magaret, Helene 215, 259
Marinetti, F.T. 45, 60-4, 175, 204-5
Marquis, Don 116
Marsden, Dora 72-3, 75, 79, 85, 95, 103, 106, 145, 241
Marsh, Edward 15-20, 21, 23, 32, 35-6, 114, 253
Masefield, John 17, 69, 200
Masters, Edgar Lee 121, 122-5, 126
Mencken, H.L. 121, 129
Mew, Charlotte 20
modernism
    achievements of 114-17, 168, 270-5
    use of term 9-10
    victims of 210
Monnier, Adrienne 133, 233
Monro, Harold 16, 19, 35, 38, 57, 90, 96, 152, 157
Monroe, Harriet 20-5, 38, 82-3, 92-3, 121, 126-7, 156, 176, 208
    and Pound 23-5, 72, 259-60
Moore, George 50, 144
Moore, Marianne 109, 158-9, 176-7, 260
Moore, T. Sturge 17
Moorhead, Ethel 210-12
Muir, Edwin 193
Murry, J. Middleton 20, 113, 143

Neihardt, John G. 25
Nevinson, C.R.W. 32, 45, 62
New Freewoman 47-8, 72-4
Newman, Frances 189
New Nihilism 203-4

Objectivism 173, 260-1, 258
O'Donovan, Gerald 68
Olson, Charles 268
Oppen, George 260-1
Orage, A.R. 31, 108
Orwell, George 250-1

Paul, Elliot, 203-5, 206
Poetry (Chicago) 11, 22-5, 38, 66-7, 85, 121, 123, 158, 199
Porter, Eleanor H. 68
Porter, Katherine Anne 204, 264
Pound, Dorothy 30, 82, 91, 108, 167, 265
Pound, Ezra Loomis 26-34, 69, 71, 83, 91, 107-8, 214, 268
    anti-semitism 66, 104, 227, 261-3
    Cantos 38, 88, 110, 131, 164, 217-21, 263-5
    early/other poems 22-3, 28-9, 46, 115
    and *Egoist* 72-5, 77, 85, 95-6
    and Eliot 82-3, 85, 88-9, 91, 97, 152, 162-4, 168, 252, 259-61, 263, 265
    fascism 217, 257, 259, 262-3, 265, 272
    and Hemingway 150-1, 182
    'Hugh Selwyn Mauberley (Life and Contacts)' 109-10, 275
    and Imagisme 34-8, 53, 77
    imprisonment of 263-4
    insanity 261, 264
    and Joyce 53, 75-6, 79, 81-2, 89, 91, 97, 108, 113, 136, 200, 243-6, 262, 265
    and Lewis 44-5, 48, 77, 84, 87-9, 91, 97, 111, 167-8, 211, 225, 261-2, 265
    and *Little Review* 91, 94-5
    and Lowell 39-41, 72, 74-5, 94
    and modernist movement 9, 27, 66-7, 71, 83, 85, 89, 91, 115, 168-9, 271-5
    and Monroe 23-5, 29, 36, 82-3, 259-60

[293]

Index

Index

Tate, Allen 179-80, 204, 264, 272
Thayer, Scofield 151-2, 154-6, 158-9, 167
This Quarter 209-12
Thomas, Dylan 161
Thomas, Edward 17, 20
Tietjens, Eunice 93
Toklas, Alice B. 139
transition 10, 203-8, 212-14, 231-2, 267
Trevelyan, Julian 257
Trilling, Lionel 124
Turner, Mary Borden 83-4

Untermeyer, Louis 83, 112, 114, 156-7

van Vechten, Carl 149, 189
von Freytag-Loringhoven, Baroness Elsa 10, 206-8, 272
Vorticism 45-7, 63-6, 87, 108-9, 175

Wadsworth, Edward 32, 45, 65, 107, 165
Waley, Arthur 95
Walpole, Hugh 68, 180
Walsh, Ernest 206, 209, 210-12
Warren, Robert Penn 264
Waterhouse, Sir Nicholas 255
Watson, James Sibley Jr 151-2, 155-6
Waugh, Arthur 70
Weaver, Harriet Shaw 72-80, 84-5, 109, 191-2, 240-1
  and *Finnegans Wake* 201, 240-1

and Joyce 73, 76-82, 89, 99, 132, 135-6, 144, 191-2, 239-41, 245
and *Ulysses* 95, 102-3, 117, 134, 144-6
Wells, H.G. 64, 68, 70, 81, 161, 230
West, Nathanael 131
West, Rebecca 46-7, 72, 115
Wharton, Edith 68
Whitman, Walt 58
Williams, William Carlos 10, 36, 77, 93-4, 122, 126-9, 152, 170-4, 176, 178, 181, 207-9, 216, 227, 244, 260-1, 268, 274
  In the American Grain 170-1
  and Pound 26-7, 34, 72, 231-2
Wilson, Edmund 143, 151, 175, 179, 190, 230
  and Eliot 156, 228, 250
Winchell, Walter 190
Winters, Yvor 176-7, 204
Wood, Thelma 190-2, 194
Woods, Margaret L. 69
Woolf, Virginia 103-4, 117, 190
Woolsey, Judge 242-3
Wordsworth, William 58-9
Wylie, Elinor 189
Wyndham, Richard 165

Yeats, W.B. 23, 25, 34, 59-60, 94, 134, 216, 230
  and Joyce 50, 53, 79
  and Pound 29, 90, 218

Zukofsky, Louis 216, 260-1, 268

About the Author

Julian Symons is well known as the biographer of Carlyle, Poe and Dashiell Hammett, a critic and a novelist. He is both a master of the detective story and one of its leading critics.